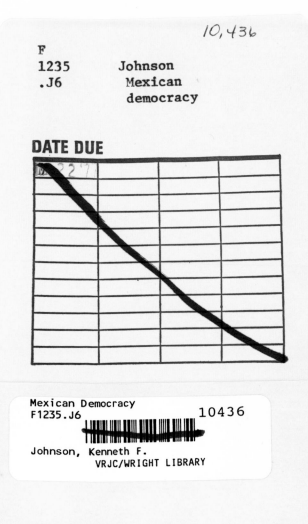

Mexican Democracy: A Critical View

The Allyn and Bacon Series
in Latin American Politics

FEDERICO G. GIL, EDITOR
THE UNIVERSITY OF NORTH CAROLINA

ARPAD VON LAZAR, ASSOCIATE EDITOR
THE FLETCHER SCHOOL OF LAW AND DIPLOMACY
TUFTS UNIVERSITY

ALLYN AND BACON, INC.   BOSTON

Mexican Democracy: A Critical View

KENNETH F. JOHNSON

University of Missouri at St. Louis

LIBRARY OF CONGRESS CATALOG CARD NUMBER: 70-143696

Second printing . . . August, 1972

for Maria Mercedes

who inspires my hope that the throes of Latin American political life will yet bring an era of change, one that yields much more than a mere harvest of paper triumphs.

Contents

Preface and Acknowledgments

My critical view of Mexican democracy must not prejudice the reader into a jaundiced conclusion about the future of Mexican political practices. There is no doubt that the Mexican picture is one of the brightest in all of Latin America. Mexican democracy functions through a strange entanglement of rituals whose complexity, and denouement, will fascinate the political psychologist. Voting is a constitutional obligation for all those over eighteen years of age, and public money is spent generously every six years to encourage participation at the polls. The people are told to vote, as the cartoon shows, for the Mexican flag and for the single party that it represents. *Yo para diputado* means "me for deputy"; the candidate knows that if he has the endorsement of the PRI—any other endorsement would be unpatriotic—his name does not matter to the voters.

Following the most recent presidential election (July 5, 1970), the government's press secretary Lic. Humberto Lugo Gil told the newspaper *El Día* (on July 14) that the official party PRI had won all contested seats in the nation and that the opposition party PAN had lost everywhere. This, he said, was evidence of Mexico's political maturity and democratic advancement. This is also what I have chosen to term *esoteric* democracy in this book. But Mexico's political system has its dilemmas. While PRI spokesmen celebrated their triumph, a defeated opposition candidate (who still had hopes of becoming a deputy-at-large) wrote me this letter which I translate, with his permission, as a succinct glimpse of the other side of the coin.

I am pleased to honor your request for a written narrative of several events that occurred during our recent presidential campaign which reveal the permanent contradiction between the verbal declarations of social justice made by our political leaders and the human wretchedness in which millions of Mexicans must live.

Three weeks prior to the elections the official candidate (Luis Echeverría) visited a poor rural village known as Anenecuilco, the place where over half a century ago the famed agrarian leader Emiliano Zapata was born. A sizeable group of starving peasants, in whose faces one could see the scourge of hunger and misery and who had been brought like animals in cattle trucks to the village, listened to the words of the candidate (Echeverría). He offered them *now*, at last, justice, land, schools, loans, etc. etc. While he spoke an old worker commented that he had been hearing such promises for the past fifty years while he grew old with suffering and humiliation. Later, a young peasant remarked wryly that according to that which the official candidate had just said the first stage of Mexico's agrarian reform would come to fruition during his regime, or exactly fifty years after the "agrarian reform" had been officially proclaimed; he added that the government would probably need one hundred additional years to reach the final stage of the oft heralded but enigmatic agrarian reform.

Surprisingly, among the miserable peasants who were taken by force to this meeting so as to create the facade of popular support for the government's candidate was the son of Emiliano Zapata who, sometime earlier, had disclosed publicly that for the past twenty years he had been applying to the Department of Agrarian Affairs and Colonization (DAAC) for four parcels of land which his family needed to subsist. At that moment, he had still not succeeded.

This true anecdote shows the PRI to be a regime of pantomime, hypocrisy, and antidemocratic fraud that exists in Mexico for the benefit of an official oligarchy which, across the years, has converted the Mexican Revolution into the most immoral and profitable of businesses.

Lic. Raúl González Schmal
Mexico, D.F.

There are two faces to every coin, and this book is, in part, intended to show "the other face of Mexico," an expression that I owe to the writer Carlos Chavira Becerra, whose works are cited herein. Also, I am grateful to his son, Carlos Chavira Rodríguez, whose international career as a cartoonist begins with this book. Throughout the years, other Mexicans of opposition political groups have assisted me generously. These include Manuel de la Isla, José León Toscano, Mario Menéndez Rodríguez, Raúl Ugalde, and the late Carlos A. Madrazo. In the United States, I am principally indebted to my former professor, L. Vincent Padgett, whose brilliant teaching stimulated my interest in Mexico and in all of Latin America. It is no secret that he and I have not viewed Mexico in quite the same way in our respective works. Nor can I resist telling this anecdote: on one occasion when I experienced difficulty securing biographical information on high ranking members of the PRI, I asked a Mexican colleague to go in my place; my colleague was told that if any North American social scientist wanted information about the PRI, he should contact Professor Padgett in San Diego, who was considered informally to be their US representative. For this reason, the interested scholar could profitably read Padgett's work along with mine to get a totally balanced and relatively unduplicated view of Mexican politics. In addition I am grateful to Arpad von Lazar, Federico Gil, and Kenneth M. Coleman whose criticisms are reflected herein, but who are exempt from liability for the errors for which I alone must bear the responsibility. I would like to acknowledge also the excellent assistance of my editor, Elydia P. Siegel, who saw the manuscript through production. This book could not have been written in and about Mexico except for the courage of some of that nation's political paladins who dared, and some who deigned, to open their ideological coffers to this academic sleuth.

KFJ

Introduction

Pacification has been the traditional lifeblood of Mexico's single-party democracy. When the people are tranquil and willing to acquiesce in the rule of a heterogeneous but self-proliferating elite they are considered to be satisfied, and the governmental process is said to have been "good." The Mexican government has been labeled authoritarian; it has also been called the needed catalyst whereby competitive democracy might be spawned on a sort of loose yet esoteric basis. Mexico's dominant party, the PRI (*Partido Revolucionario Institucional*), is an experienced dispenser of human satisfactions. Since President Lázaro Cárdenas' socioeconomic reform programs of the 1930's, and the Lopez Mateos welfare expansion of the early sixties, the federal government located in Mexico City has been viewed increasingly as a giant cornucopia of reliefs and rewards for both enterprising and simply deserving Mexican citizens. Popular folklore had it during the 1960's that citizens who attacked (with words) the government were against the Revolution, spelled with a giant patriotic R. Indeed, that is one of the things that this book is about: the meaning of *revolucionario* spelled according to your own preference. It is a charismatic term that in today's Mexico appears to be losing the magic of its earlier vogue.

As the decade of the 1970's begins, the task of saying something new about Mexican politics that will be at once creative, and yet serve a heuristic purpose, appears as a severe challenge. In this book I will speak of political change, rather than of development, for the

1

latter term tends to imply a directional thrust of "improvement" or "betterment" which is often understood to be moving toward various components of the Anglo-American pattern. The concept of change, it seems to me, does not commit one to assuming "betterment" in any normative or substantive sense. I understand Mexico to be now in the throes of a difficult and uncertain era of political change. As both a humanitarian and a social scientist, I hope that Mexico can look forward to a bright future of political stability and economic progress, accompanied by an increasingly equitable distribution of her national wealth. Most scholars would locate this hope under the rubric of "betterment." But there is a strong and ominous chance that Mexico will not be so fortunate. In this book, therefore, I have felt it necessary to become the devil's advocate and to paint a rather grim picture, one that has seldom emerged from the writings of North American social scientists.

Students of Mexican politics will know the names of a series of scholars who have become classic figures in the study of this genre: names such as Frank Brandenburg, Howard Cline, Charles C. Cumberland, William Weber Johnson, Robert Scott, William Tucker, and L. Vincent Padgett. Most of these scholars have taken a position that is substantially in support of, or at least normatively sympathetic toward, Mexico's unique and dominant ruling institution. This is understandable. The PRI has stewarded what has been Latin America's most lasting social revolution. For this reason PRI is often seen as a model, tacitly or openly imitated by political (group) hopefuls in a handful of other nations about the hemisphere. Most North American social scientists have been preoccupied with the PRI as an agent of political stability in Mexico. I will be concerned in this book with many of the PRI's more negative features.

What is needed is a presentation that will serve the necessary pedagogical requisites of academia (i.e., do justice to the single-party political system), but which can still tell more of the story of Mexican political life than is found only in abbreviated fashion, if at all, in most other works. Thus, I have sought to write not what is a better book than those studies of the Mexican political system that are now available, but a different one. From the beginnings of my interest in Mexico I felt that too much laudatory attention was heaped upon the PRI, and that surely not all Mexicans could seriously be expected to blend so easily into such a "harmonious," yet heterogeneous, melting pot of political ideologies. It occurred to me that something bordering on magic was being attributed to the PRI, ascriptively and gratuitously. Could any single political mystique be so effectively inculcated as to command the unchallenged allegiance of nearly an entire nation composed of some fifty million people?

Mexico is one of the most difficult Latin American countries in which a North American academic sleuth can try to study the political process. This is especially true of Mexico's "official" politics. In the introduction of his book, L. Vincent Padgett stressed this point: "the Mexican politician must know the observer very well before the silence is broken. Most scholarly observers have neither the time nor the inclination to invest in such enterprises. Much about Mexican politics goes unknown for these reasons." He has a point to be sure, but there is a reverse corollary to his dictum that I would put as follows: Much about Mexican politics goes unknown simply because scholars *did invest* in *such enterprises*, namely by taking the safe route of a "sweetheart contract" with the PRI. The Mexican political system has a curious anomaly. It is that once the researcher is welcomed into the official family, he is not likely to be free to mingle openly with the unofficial congeries of "out-groups" that do not enjoy the PRI's favor. The "out-groups" may welcome him, but if friends of the official family find him on enemy soil, his usefulness as a researcher within the PRI may very well be ended. This is a serious constraint that one must understand in evaluating the writings of North Americans who have undertaken field research in Mexico. That nation's ideological structure has certain properties of a "zero-sum game." The interests of one group of political contenders are likely to be seen as inversely correlated to those of the opposition. A partial win for one is taken to be an equivalent loss for the other. One cannot have an easy and open *entrada* into both *esoteric* and *exoteric* politics at the same time, for the loyalty and confidence requirements of the opposing groups tend to be mutually exclusive and incompatible. Some Mexicans find it possible to switch loyalties, but it is difficult to maintain a duality of involvement. North American scholars, thus, often find themselves typed as researchers with a commitment in favor of the "ins" or the "outs," that is the PRI or its opposition satellites.

Mexico now faces a severe crisis of political legitimacy. The legions who belong to its dominant political institution, the PRI, have been socialized into "professing" their own sanctity and "revealed" truth. There is only one legitimate road to power. Anyone who opts for another is a heretic.

In Mexico today there is an official traffic in what might be termed "indulgences." These are programs designed to show Mexicans and all the world that Mexico is "modernizing," that is, building subways while doing little about one of the world's most critical problems of industrially caused air pollution in the capital city; promoting international Olympic Games when hundreds of thousands of children have no basketball courts, football fields, or playgrounds; making loans to other nations, a prestigious international activity, but ironic when, for lack of capital to create new jobs, thousands of women work in each of the major cities as prostitutes (the author and his associates counted upwards of 1500 in Cuernavaca's Colonia Acapazingo alone), and thousands of people go begging to live on mere subsistence incomes.

It is a common practice to purchase administrative and judicial favors, as well as public office itself. Legitimacy is a saleable attribute. It appears that nearly everything is for sale in Mexico including the honor of men and the virtue of women. But not *everyone* is for sale, and here we approach the crux of the matter. Vice, administrative corruption, dishonor are no more intrinsic to the Mexican people, to their nature, than to any other nationality. Ironically, however, Mexicans seem to have a great complacency toward the many abuses of their public officials. I truly believe that most Mexicans are cynical about their government's performance and the politics that sustain it. I also know many who are ashamed and profoundly wish to change the status quo, by violence if that is the only way.

El que tiene la sartén por el mango (loosely translated as the man who is "on top of things") is a winning ticket in Mexican political life. It matters little how he seized advantage or at whose expense, except that honor among family and intimate friends was maintained. The public honor and trust may be sacrificed freely. As a result, a variety of groups have emerged in protest against PRI dominated governments. They rebel at the self-perpetuation of a single regime or political family through what are often seen as authoritarian methods. This author refers to these formations as "out-groups" or as participants in the *exoteric* political system. PRI and its subunits may be said to constitute the *esoteric* political system. The former are in quest of legitimacy for their desired status as bona fide contenders for political power. The latter have a monopoly on legitimacy. Their unwillingness to relinquish it is the cornerstone of the conflict on whose threshold the Mexican body politic currently stands.

In 1968 thousands of university and high school students poured down the fashionably shaded sidewalks of Mexico City's principal boulevard the *Paseo de la Reforma*, marched past the Palace of Fine Arts and on to the Zócalo, or main square, screaming for the blood of governing officials in the Federal District, carrying signs that demanded the death of their President. That was a serious breach of tradition. Since the single-party system started its drive toward institutionalization around 1929, it has seldom been acceptable in Mexican politics to attack publicly the presidency or the incumbent, although the man himself could be attacked after leaving office. This relatively sacred maxim now seems to have been discarded. Mexicans today, especially the nation's youth, are tired of waiting for a promised but never-arriving change.

In searching my archives and travelling to renew old Mexican friendships, in preparing this book, I have been singularly impressed with one inescapable fact: the out-groups are not fading away as PRI stalwarts always have said they would; indeed such groups are multiplying, and they are much more dedicated than was the case when I first studied this phenomenon in 1962. While more militant in their dedication, the out-groups have shown also increased confidence in their capacity to challenge the government (the PRI) via peaceful elections or by violence in the streets. The principal out-group, PAN, *Partido Acción Nacional*, was considered a party of the reactionary, indeed "theocratic," right in 1962. Today it must be considered, by and large, a centrist party that edges the PRI wherever it can. The second rated out-group of 1962, PPS, *Partido Popular Socialista*, has moved so close to the center that many consider it to be an adjunct of the PRI; PPS lost cohesion when its titular leader, Vicente Lombardo Toledano, died in 1968. Radical militants of the old PPS have either ceased to be radical or have joined the growing number of guerrilla and conflict groups that function throughout the country. The opposition to PRI, though fragmented, is clearly on the increase. Many observers had thought that the gifted PRI renegade, Carlos A. Madrazo, would consolidate the opposition left and either oppose the PRI openly or force its top leadership into a deal. I interviewed Madrazo during 1968, and he hinted that such were indeed his plans. But a tragic airplane crash in 1969 deprived Mexico of the hope that Madrazo represented; Mexicans follow men, not ideas.

In this book I will draw heavily upon a type of literature that is not well-represented in the annals of North American academia, namely, the clandestine literature of protest. This I will supplement with the extensive interview material I have gathered over a period of years, interviews with persons of the far right and far left who are not generally viewed as "respectable" in the official parlance of Mexico's revolutionary family or coalition. The danger of this is, of course, the same one that curses the scholar who has made a "sweetheart contract" with officialdom: I may become *comprometido* or obligated ideologically to those who have helped me and with whom I have become friends. Fortunately, over the years I have maintained a few confidants within the PRI who have served to restrain my occasionally excessive zeal. Also, I have invited a Mexican scholar who represents what I consider to be a definitely bourgeois, well-informed, and moderate centerist position to write an epilogue which I have translated and which conveys a message that only a Mexican has a right to express in any language. This contributor, Lic. Manuel de la Isla, has himself known intimately the rewards of officialdom and the privations of satellite group politics.

In evaluating this book, I ask the reader not to forget one cardinal dictum: to suggest that a regime may be improved upon is not *ipso facto* to urge that it be terminated. Thus at the onset I feel obliged to apologize for the regrettably perjorative, but sincerely meant, words I have chosen to introduce the political system of a magnificent country for whose people I hold deep affection. The book's first chapter sketches the historical development of the Mexican political system. The second reflects a range of views of natives and observers about the style and character of political life. Chapter 3 treats the PRI as a power organism and explains how it is organized and how a system of cliques makes it work. Chapter 4 deals with what the PRI dominated government does for the people in the areas of labor policy, agrarian reform, and economic development policy, with emphasis on the alienation potential of selected programs. Chapter 5 is a study of the political dilemmas faced by satellite and out-groups. Chapter 6 is a case documentary of the Mexico City student riots of 1968, as an example of the PRI's liability to internal systemic breakdown. The remaining chapters contain an analysis of some of the socioeconomic factors that generate demands for political reform and sharpen the crisis of legitimacy for all of Mexico.

Sourcewise, this is a book of contrasts: deliberately so. Some will be accepted, some may be scorned, but in that case the reader will have lost much that is real in the minds of Mexicans. I choose to believe that niceties and crudities can be joined in effective pedagogy.

Witness the following sample contrast as a preview of this book: a respected contemporary North American scholar writes "all intellectuals active in the Mexican Revolution tended to fight among themselves rather than to unite behind a single revolutionary group or leader. In part, this pattern of division among its intellectuals caused the Mexican Revolution's worker and peasant followers to end up fighting one another, instead of uniting behind antibourgeois goals. . . ." (from James D. Cockcroft, *Intellectual Precursors of the Mexican Revolution*, University of Texas Press, 1968, pp 232–233). This same writer calls the Mexican Revolution's only lasting victory an ideological one, a "paper triumph," which is to say the Constitution of 1917 that is *formally* the basis for Mexican government and politics today. Let us now skip to the same year in which the above words were published, but the scene is real-life Mexico according to a clandestine publication that treats the student riots of 1968. This work, rumored to have been secretly commissioned by President Diaz Ordaz himself in order to shed his blame for the student riots at the doorsteps of others, shows that the various student groups associated with the National Strike Committee often fought among themselves, at least verbally. Again, half a century following the carnage of the Mexican Revolution of 1910–17, the victory won was ideological and could be said to be a paper one . . . the government issued a long list of student prisoners who had been freed. The clandestine publication said that agents of the CIA, posing as cultural officers from the United States Embassy in Mexico City, gave money to Communist groups in order to sabotage the Olympic Games and divert them to Detroit (from *El móndrigo*, México, Editorial Alba Roja, 1968, p. 47).

Does Mexican political behavior repeat itself over a long time span, despite the socioeconomic thrust toward modernity? Are all of Mexico's political victories paper ones? Must the people's ideological disunity render them forever helpless before a dominant elite class? Let us see!

1
How the Revolutionary Axis Grew

The Rise of an Independent Mexico

Cloaked beneath tapestries boasting the great seal of the Spanish crown, an era of broken dreams was born in 1808; it was an era forged by men with visions of wealth, greatness, and the good life in their quest for enigmatic wonders of an independent New Spain. The Napoleonic incursions into Spain and Portugal left many creoles (Spaniards born in the New World) desirous of balancing out the structure of power between themselves and the *gachupines* (colonists from Spain). As news spread of the fall of the Bourbon crown in the mother country, young generations of New World Spaniards increasingly saw in this an opportunity to separate politically and to create locally managed sovereign states. In Mexico, the governing council of the capital city cajoled the vain José de Iturrigaray, the viceroy of Mexico City, into convening a special junta whose purpose would be to create a provisional government and ultimately declare independence from Spain. The creole ambition to displace the colonists was thinly veiled as was the ingenuous sympathy of Iturrigaray for the idea of establishing himself as the ruler of an independent Mexico. The Spanish loyalists responded with a coup that unseated the junta and replaced the viceroy with an infirm old man, Pedro de Garibay, who proved ineffective in suppressing the creole unrest; it did little to bridge the widening abyss between Mexico City and the artificial regime of the French-imposed Joseph Bonaparte in Madrid. The beginning of an indigenous Mexico, was at hand. All it needed was a catalyst and a spark of life.

The catalyst was found in the Querétaro Club of 1810, a social and literary circle whose membership included Ignacio Allende, a creole officer of the local militia, and Father Miguel Hidalgo, a creole priest who shared visions of an indigenous Mexicanism while resenting all the while his diminished ecclesiastical status because he lacked true Spanish birth. Padre Hidalgo undertook to recruit clerics to the cause of independence while Ignacio Allende and his companion, Juan Aldama, organized military support for an eventual uprising. But the activities of the Querétaro Club became too overt for the Spanish loyalists to continue to ignore. On the evening of September 13, 1810, the Army seized a number of secret arms caches and arrested a small group of followers of Hidalgo. Aldama, learning of the arrests, carried word to the small village of Dolores where Padre Hidalgo's parish was located. Before dawn on September 16, Padre Hidalgo had assembled at his church what would become the nucleus of revolutionary anarchy. Instead of offering sacraments he called upon his parishioners to support him in a march for independence that would be directed against Querétaro. The gullible and downtrodden peasants responded, believing that God had sanctioned the displacement of their foreign oppressors. They marched on Querétaro voicing the famous cry of Dolores which in essence meant death to the colonists.

Hidalgo, Allende, and Aldama had unleashed a massive wave of human violence which they were helpless to control. Disaster followed upon disaster, the first and perhaps most poignant of which occurred in late September in Guanajuato where Spanish loyalist bullets slaughtered some two thousand of Hidalgo's fold. With news of this tragedy many enraged poor of the land sprang forth from their slums, spreading blood and hate in all directions about the geographical center of Mexico. Clearly outnumbering the colonists in most of their encounters, the revolutionary army (which at times is thought to have numbered close to 100,000) fell before the withering fire and calvary tactics of the disciplined loyalist soldiers. Hidalgo's hordes retaliated in a fashion that historians do not easily vindicate. Nearly everyone not openly sympathetic to the revolutionary cause was put to the sword or torch. Multitudes thus perished, most of them innocent, in what clearly had become a fanatic uprising of the Indian and mestizo poor against the dominant upper classes. But the Hidalgo revolt was short-lived. On January 17, 1811, the volunteer army faced a highly skilled force of vastly lesser numbers near Río Lerma. The loyalist army under the superior direction of General Félix María Calleja, himself possessed by a blind fury of revenge against the insurrectionists, ordered wholesale massacres of the revolutionists who in turn fled Guadalajara leaving Hidalgo and his immediate staff as victims of imminent capture.

Hidalgo was defrocked, disgraced, and executed by the Spanish authorities. Thereafter the charge passed to the more able and temperate hands of another priest, José María Morelos, who earlier had been commissioned by Hidalgo to undertake responsibility for an uprising in the south. Morelos' superiority to his mentor was both tactical and intellectual. He did not attempt to control more men than was humanly possible and his well-disciplined insurgent units seldom were guilty of wantonness, terror, or outright atrocities. Ideologically, Morelos did not urge vengeance generally upon the non-mestizo. This, in part, had been Hidalgo's tactical error, for in creating an unbridgeable gulf between the Indian-mestizo masses and the creole colonists, he had failed in his opportunity to unite many creoles to his cause. Morelos tried to cajole the creoles but failed beneath the stigma of horror he had inherited. Morelos called for abolition of religious privileges, for division of land, and, most important of all, he launched a positive appeal for Mexican independence as a general cause; thus Morelos fought *for* a free Mexico, and not merely *against* Spain. In 1813 he convened a revolutionary convention at Chilpancingo representing the various southern territories still under his control. Out of this meeting emerged Mexico's first revolutionary constitution, which was promulgated at Apatzingán in 1814. Morelos and his supporters carried the haunting specter of Hidalgo's ignominious defeat within their hearts until December of 1815. Pursued by the same General Calleja who had ruined Hidalgo, the Morelos movement was gradually driven into the clandestine reaches of the forests and back streets. Forces led by Agustín de Iturbide ultimately captured the rebel priest and later defrocked him. But he could not be made to recant as had Hidalgo. Morelos gave his life as the first real cornerstone of independence, one which could be embraced symbolically and revered without the stigma of treasonable disgrace.

By the year 1819 only two of Morelos' regional chieftains still operated in defiance of the loyalists. One of them, Guadalupe Victoria, more popularly known as Félix Fernández, was driven to become a mountain cave-dwelling recluse, later to become the object of considerable folklore enchantment. The other, the stubborn and ingenuous Vicente Guerrero, continued to fight alone. His guerrillas took a toll of loyalist troops which shocked the viceroy and made it increasingly difficult to maintain publicly that the revolution unleashed by the "mad priest" of Dolores had come to nought. However, if the Querétaro Club of 1810 had provided a catalyst for revolution, the insurgent wrath of Vicente Guerrero one decade later gave it a final spark. Lamentably, when the spark produced independence it was hardly of the variety envisoned by Hidalgo, Allende, Aldama, and Morelos.

Early in 1820 the government of Spain fell into the control of those who said they favored government by constitution rather than by monarch. The loyalists in Mexico feared that news of this turn would initiate a new wave of independence-minded terrorism by the small remaining patriot forces. The menace of Vicente Guerrero lived on and with it the figures of Hidalgo et al. continued to tower menacingly from the past. Viceroy Apodaca commissioned the man who had overcome Morelos, Agustín de Iturbide, to exterminate Vicente Guerrero. He tried and failed. Indeed, he tried many times, to the extent of proving that Guerrero was unquestionably the better of the two men on the field of battle. Then, after stealing money from the loyalists who paid him to eliminate Guerrero, Iturbide launched the Mexican people upon a narrow ideological course whose norm is yet a lingering pestilence to this very day: he became a traitor and sold out compatriots and friends. At his headquarters in Iguala, Iturbide invited Vicente Guerrero to the conference table; this was decidedly not the latter's preferred field of battle. When Guerrero agreed to the *Plan de Iguala* on February 24, 1821 he sincerely thought he had won a victory; in fact, all Mexico had lost.

Incredibly, the Iturbide-Guerrero accord won support of most of the remaining Morelos chieftains; even Guadalupe Victoria came out of hiding to champion the cause of independence. Creoles too joined the groundswell and on September 27, 1821, Agustín de Iturbide marched confidently into the capital city flanked by Vicente Guerrero and Guadalupe Victoria. A change in government had taken place to be sure, but it was not accompanied by the social and economic reforms envisoned by Morelos. The man who was to rule Mexico briefly as emperor was motivated primarily by personal greed. After all, it was Iturbide who, as military commandant of the agriculture-rich Valle del Bajío, had instituted the insidious practice of monopolizing the sale of grain (and thereby multiplying the numbers of ill-fed and starving in the very midst of plenty) for an attractive personal profit. He undertook to govern the new "nation" in much the same fashion, naturally to the chagrin of Guadalupe Victoria and Vicente Guerrero. When his congress refused to approve financial measures needed to support his military establishment Iturbide simply suspended the legislature and ruled openly as a dictator. Putting an army into the field, Iturbide succeeded temporarily in declaring an extension of his empire as far south as what is now the northern half of El Salvador, but was forced to withdraw in the face of republican opposition throughout what later became known as the United Provinces of Central America. The short-lived empire netted only the southern territory known as Chiapas, a matter still in dispute by Guatemala although it was incorporated as a piece of Mexico at that time.

Iturbide proved to be a traitor in every sense, even to the point of neglecting his military. Unpaid, and seething with discontent, factions of the military united behind the commander of Veracruz to depose him.

The Age of Santa Anna

Iturbide's final act was fully as treacherous as had been his first. He accepted payment and agreed to leave the country forever. Thus, in February of 1823, Mexico entered upon the disastrous era marked by Antonio López de Santa Anna who had learned his style well under Iturbide, and saw to it that his mentor was promptly executed when he attempted to return to Mexican soil in violation of the agreement under which Iturbide had been exiled. From his estate in Veracruz, known as Manga de Clavo, Santa Anna ruled his nation for virtually thirty years. The era was punctuated by numerous rebellions, interim presidents, and frequent exiles of Santa Anna himself, but until the traumatic end it was a bitter epoch which bore the stamp of a single hand.

Guadalupe Victoria and not Santa Anna became Mexico's first president. He sought to rule under an absurd constitution patterned after that of the United States which assumed degrees of political socialization and responsibility nonexistent among the then untutored population. Victoria was opposed by the Scottish-rite Masons as well as by the York-rite Masons. The latter, deeply involved in political intrigues with the American ambassador Joel Poinsett, caused the first republican government of Mexico to be rendered financially impotent.[1] In 1828 when the conservative Scottish-rite Masons succeeded in electing General Manuel Gómez Pedraza to the presidency Vicente Guerrero rose in arms against the regime. Santa Anna pronounced in favor of Guerrero and thus in 1829 Victoria turned the reins of government over to his former revolutionary partner. The turmoil, and the atrophy of drives toward needed reforms, surrounding these and succeeding events have filled many historical treatises. Their outcome was, unhappily, not one of social progress.

Throughout these events Santa Anna remained in the background. He was soon to emerge as a hero in defending Mexico against an abortive Spanish effort to regain its lost colony and then subsequently came out in defense of President Guerrero who was overthrown by

---

[1] One of the political curiosities in Mexico's early years of independence was the prominent role of Masonic groups, particularly the Scottish and York rites. One version of their presence in Mexico is that they came around 1815 to combat the insurrection that had been created by Hidalgo and Morelos. But whereas they may have begun as philanthropic institutions they soon were converted into warring political factions in the struggle for power. In Mexico at that time there were no political organizations and it is not surprising that the lodges with their organizational skills should have become the basis for the creation of political parties. The Scottish-rite Masons became identified with the maintenance of socioeconomic privilege and with support for some political dependence upon the Spanish Crown. The York-rite Masons, for the most part, championed political independence and democratic institutions. Thus York-rite came to represent socioeconomic liberation (to which they devoted more word-service than actions) and Scottish-rite came to personify conservatism.

The Masonic lodges became virtual political parties during the early years of Mexican independence: in Oaxaca, for instance, the York-rite Masons were called *"aceites"* (oil) and the Scottish-rite Masons were called *"vinagres"* (vinegar). Mexico's early political socialization was accomplished in this polarized way which, not surprisingly, left the great masses abandoned and uninvolved. The Scottish-rite called for the abolition of all secret societies in its Plan of Montano in December of 1827 (despite the fact that it was one itself) and demanded the expulsion of United States Ambassador Joel Poinsett who was widely believed (probably unfairly) to be responsible for the militancy of York-rite Masons and, indeed, their founder in Mexico.

a military coup in 1830 led by Anastasio Bustamante, a mere puppet for conservative boss Lucas Alamán. The latter was a survivor of the massacre of Guanajuato and personified the oligarchic reaction against what Hidalgo and all subsequent revolutionaries had stood for. After two years of military dictatorship and unrest Santa Anna was finally chosen president; but he cleverly chose to allow his vice president, Valentín Gómez Farías, to rule in his stead. Not proving sufficiently reactionary to satisfy the military and the clergy, Gómez Farías was ousted with the treasonable assent of Santa Anna, who had placed him in power. Santa Anna wanted to be cajoled into office so as to more easily justify assumption of absolute dictatorial powers. Nevertheless, he continued to allow the actual governance of Mexico to be handled by lesser figures, all the while remaining in defensive isolation at his Veracruz estate.

The first great challenge to Santa Anna's cunning began to emerge in 1830 when the question of American settlers in the northern Texas territory generated concern among Mexican nationalists. American ambassador Joel Poinsett had explored the possibility of purchasing the territory. To unsettle matters further, Stephen Austin was temporarily jailed in Mexico City after attempting to secure independent statehood for Texas—but as a Mexican state—from a hostile Mexican congress. In 1836 Santa Anna led an army north to reaffirm Mexican sovereignty over the territory. After overcoming the dramatic stand of a handful of Texas settlers at the San Antonio mission known as the Alamo, Santa Anna's ill-trained forces were routed near San Jacinto by well-trained American volunteers under Sam Houston. Spared the ignominy of imprisonment upon his capture, Santa Anna was taken to Washington to confer with President Andrew Jackson and made to promise guarantees for the safety of the Texas settlers in return for an American promise not to annex the territory. By returning Santa Anna to Mexico the United States had committed the first in a series of "unpardonable acts" against her southern neighbor.

By 1845, the attitude of the United States government had changed from one of hands off Texas (originally dictated by the fear of a new slave state) to one of annexation under Manifest Destiny (in competition with gestures of acquisition on the part of Great Britain). A mission headed by the American diplomat John Slidell, which can best be described as an attempt at international bribery, was sent by

President Polk to Mexico City and was rejected promptly by the proudly nationalistic president Joaquín Herrera. The Mexicans then began massing troops in the north to defend their territory and in April of 1846 the United States declared war. The design of President Polk was more the conquest of California than Texas but one could not be had without the other. Border incidents used to justify the war declaration are considered by some historians to be of questionable authenticity. When the war had ended, Santa Anna had been exiled to Jamaica, thousands of Mexicans had perished, the Mexican treasury had been paid fifteen million dollars for the loss of Texas, and Mexico had for all practical purposes lost the most valuable half of its national territory. This was formalized on March 10, 1848, by the treaty of Guadalupe Hidalgo. The irony of this document is that its American negotiator, Nicholas Trist, had previously been fired by Washington for incompetence and at the time of the agreement he was acting without portfolio. The American congress swallowed its "pride" and ratified the treaty.

In most nations peopled by proud human beings the end of the war with the United States would most surely have been the end of a dictator such as Santa Anna. That it was not, testifies to the deplorable status of political democracy in Mexico around the middle of the nineteenth century. The presidency fell into the hands of a succession of political adventurers, and, however shocking, it is not surprising, that the old dictator, now boasting a wooden leg, should be called once again from exile in 1853 to try to impose order upon the resulting chaos. When shortly thereafter Lucas Alamán died, Santa Anna saw no reason to honor the trust of the conservatives who had returned him to power and proceeded to loot the treasury mercilessly. He climaxed the era that bears his name with the epitome of treacherous acts: he sold a piece of Mexico's territory to the United States. The Gadsden Purchase of 1853 gave the United States a right of way along the southern Arizona border for railroad construction and it gave Santa Anna funds with which to sustain his caprice for another two years. By that time, the remnants of the Morelos movement had regrouped into a truly liberal opposition determined not only to get rid of Santa Anna but to wipe out the landed and clerical oligarchy once and for all. The Liberals proclaimed their *Plan de Ayutla* in 1854 and the following year Santa Anna left for South America. His era of rapine had ended.

La Reforma

The Liberal forces under Juan Álvarez, which occupied the capital city following the exit of Santa Anna, brought with them Melchor Ocampo, Miguel Lerdo de Tejada, and, most prominently, the Indian leader from Oaxaca, Benito Juárez. The Liberals were unable to hold the capital permanently and provisional governments were established in the regional centers of Michoacán and Veracruz. The famous Liberal Constitution promulgated in 1857 gave official impetus to the War of the Reform. It soon became a religious war against the Church and its legion of socioeconomic privileges. The Constitution embraced the earlier *Ley Juárez* and *Ley Lerdo* whose joint effect was to deny the Church all but its purely ecclesiastical functions within a very narrow definition. Marriage was made a civil function, monasteries and other Church properties were confiscated, priests and nuns were proscribed from wearing their habits in public and denied the right to engage in public education. Juárez acquiesced when his followers murdered priests and desecrated altars, but never allowed the carnage to grow totally out of control as it had in the years following 1810. He occupied the important port of Veracruz and began wearing the conservative forces down by denying them foreign commerce and customs revenues. With the help of an able general, Porfirio Diaz, the conservative armies in the south crumbled as had those in the north earlier, and on New Year's day, 1861, Juárez' army seized Mexico City. The war had been won but the reforms had yet to be institutionalized.

To Mexico, the combined cost of the Age of Santa Anna and the Reform was enormous. Although the United States had favored Juárez with guns and financial aid the European nations and Great Britain now demanded reparation payments for losses incurred by their nationals. Both liberals and conservatives had appropriated to their pocketbooks the valuables of foreigners, and to make matters worse, the Civil War in the United States made it impossible for Abraham Lincoln to continue to bolster Juárez logistically. Then in the early part of 1862 England, France, and Spain threatened the port of Veracruz in an effort to collect their losses by force. When it became apparent that France, then under Napoleon III, really intended to establish an empire in the western hemisphere the British and Spanish withdrew, leaving Veracruz in French military possession. Although the invaders were temporarily routed at Puebla on May 5, 1862, the invasion continued and President Juárez was forced to move his capital north to Monterrey. Mexican clericals and conservative oligarchs returned from their Paris exile hoping to carry on in the tradition of Lucas Alamán but were shocked to find the French busily taking over lands under provisions of the Lerdo Law and the Constitution of 1857; and to make the pill yet more bitter to swallow, Napoleon had in the spring of 1864 imposed the Austrian archduke Maximilian and the Belgian princess Carlotta on the Mexican "throne." Their blindness was twice that of Napoleon III who knew the Mexicans would not love their new royalty but hoped to maintain them by force of arms while the quest went on for the treasures of the Guanajuato gold and diamond mines. These mines, largely ruined and abandoned by fifty years of plunder and abuse, proved to be almost worthless. Maximilian and Carlotta believed that the people would love them and that great treasures were to be uncovered. When both proved to be false hopes, the French withdrew, leaving Maximilian to face a firing squad of Juárez' army, on a hill overlooking, appropriately, Querétaro; Carlotta was abandoned to a European exile and eventually to insanity.

Seldom had two cultures met in so irreconcilable a clash. When Juárez reentered the capital city in 1867 the power of the clerics and landed oligarchs appeared broken and aid from the United States again began to trickle in, but he ruled a nation bled of its human and material wealth. It is hard for North Americans to imagine how so much misfortune could be continually visited upon the same nation, and that it should still exist.

The Pax Porfiriana

Desparately lacking in financial resources Juárez commenced at once to rebuild his ravaged nation. He constructed schools, encouraged railroad development, and sought credits abroad. He was reelected twice to office and seemed to enjoy the confidence of the masses. Notwithstanding, former soldiers turned bandits plagued the nation and often intruded into the political arena via attempted coups against state and municipal governments. Increasingly the people looked for a leader, other than Benito Juárez, to bring security to the troubled land. In the elections of 1871 attention turned to one of Juárez' most valuable field commanders in the War of the Reform and in the campaign against the French occupation, General Porfirio Díaz. Since no candidate received a majority of votes the congress returned Juárez to office over the objections of Diaz, who had campaigned on the pledge of "effective suffrage and no reelection." Tragically for Mexico, Juárez died in 1872 before his new term had hardly begun. Congress replaced him with Sebastián Lerdo de Tejada who could not quell growing unrest and who fell ultimately to a military coup led by Porfirio Díaz in 1876. At that point, Latin America's longest single dictatorship began.

It has been said that Porfirio Díaz was at once Mexico's most ruthless and productive president. He governed for thirty-four years, occasionally stepping out of office to allow a puppet to take over out of "deference" to his campaign pledge. He cleaned up the violence in the countryside via a commissioned militia of mercenary rogues who tried and shot "criminals" summarily and guaranteed the security of the vast legion of foreign investments that now poured into Mexico. In this way Díaz built a gigantic railroad and highway system, thus providing the basic infra-structure the country so badly needed to industrialize. This is the great Díaz legacy to twentieth-century Mexico. As could be expected, it was accomplished with a full measure of blood and brutality, and at the almost total expense of political freedoms and individual guarantees for the masses.

Across the traumatic sweep of nineteenth-century Mexico a collectivity of forces had gathered that would oppose Díaz just as they had fought Iturbide, Santa Anna, and the interim conservative oligarchs. Among the most dedicated foes of the Díaz regime was the Liberal party, a regrouping of previous reformist movements now under the leadership of Ricardo Flores Magón. Toward the end of the Pax Porfiriana Flores Magón's publication *Regeneración* had become a troublesome thorn in the side of the Díaz oligarchy. In 1906 the Liberal party, largely forced into exile in various cities of the United States, issued a program that was directed against a legion of abuses committed by the Díaz government. The liberals demanded that Díaz honor his commitment to no reelection, the abolition of military conscription, restoration of freedom of the press, increased budgetary outlays for education and school construction, enforcement of the

anticlerical provisions of the Constitution of 1857, radical land reforms, and generally, the disestablishment of the wealthy oligarchy.
Not unexpectedly, such entreaties fell on deaf ears in the national
government. Although Flores Magón pretended to be heir to the
Liberal tradition of Juárez, he was much more radical than the
Zapotec Indian from Oaxaca; Flores was bent upon the total destruction of Mexico's socioeconomic fabric, in the fervent belief that a new
ideological consensus would somehow be forthcoming. Violent strikes
against an American-owned copper company at Cananea and the
famous Río Blanco strike of January 1907 brought federal troops into
play against the Liberal insurgents and revealed the butchery of
which Porfirio Díaz was capable when he felt pressed. Ricardo
Flores Magón, at first exiled in Los Angeles, California, then in other
United States cities, imprisoned while in exile, hounded by the
American "yellow" and "jingo" press of William Randolph Hearst
(himself the owner of valuable property in Mexico), ultimately became a dedicated anarchist. Flores Magón's writings breathed a spirit
of beauty into the violence which he came to worship as a goal of
life, whereas formerly it had only been a means to secure justice.

Irony was a lingering trait of Mexican political development.
So it was that when true revolution came (not a resignation of cabinet
or president, or even a widespread insurgency of national proportions, but rather an uprising that produced lasting and profound
socioeconomic change) it was fronted by a meek little man who did
not drink or violate women, seldom ate meat, and was not as virile
(*macho*) as most leaders of the Mexican stripe were expected to be.
It was not Flores Magón who visited revolution upon his populace
but the innocuous aristocrat from Coahuila, Francisco Ignacio
Madero. Madero's timid manner belied many of his great skills, but
the art of politics was not among them. He had been an early contributor to the Flores Magón movement but broke this tie when it
became certain that the Liberals sought carnage first and democracy
second. Madero was first and foremost a champion of democracy, as
he indicated in his mild-sounding treatise *The Presidential Sucession
of 1910* in which he suggested that Mexicans ought to be free to
choose their own vice president if not the first magistrate himself.

Interestingly, Madero did not write this treatise via the spontaneous
outpouring of his soul as Flores Magón had done. Rather he wrote it
after being prodded by an influence from the United States: the publi-

cation in March 1908 of an interview by James Creelman held weeks earlier with Porfirio Díaz in which the aging dictator allegedly stated that he would welcome the rise of an opposition (loyal) political movement in Mexico as a measure of the nation's growing political maturity. With this apparent invitation, numerous factions (including Madero's and the followers of Flores Magón) began to declare their candidacies for the approaching elections. Díaz and his brain trust (the scientists led by José Yves Limantour) felt uncomfortable. Theirs was a natural reaction. Following publication of the Creelman interview in the Mexican press, a somewhat embellished version to be sure, Francisco Madero announced formation of his Anti-Reelectionist Party whose motto also became "effective suffrage and no reelection." Madero demanded that the choice of his party's candidate be made in an open convention and made a speaking tour of the country in which he emphasized that he did not seek to impose himself on the people.

Not only did Madero win his party's nomination, he attracted enough of a following so that in June of 1910 a threatened Díaz government had him arrested on false charges of sedition. Later that month the election results were declared to have been overwhelmingly in favor of returning Díaz to the presidency. Madero's family arranged a bribe to free him from prison under his agreement to remain out of the capital city. He honored this pledge, while all the time gathering evidence (it was abundant) that Díaz' election had been fraudulent. On October 25, 1910, Madero and his swelling ranks of supporters issued the famous *Plan de San Luis Potosí* whose effect was a declaration of war against the Díaz regime: on Sunday, November 20, 1910, all Mexicans were urged to rebel. Madero by this time was enjoying unofficial sympathy from Washington, and logistic support for his uprising began to cross the Río Grande. The United States was infuriated with Díaz' apparent favoritism toward European oil concessionaires and annoyed by his aid to José Santos Zelaya, the yankee-baiting president of Nicaragua.

From exile in Texas Madero sought to mold United States public opinion while at once attempting to lend direction to the now incipient revolution which was bursting forth in Chihuahua and Coahuila under the leadership of such guerrilla fighters as Doroteo Arango (better known as Francisco "Pancho" Villa) and Pascual

Orozco. In February of 1911 Madero crossed the Rio Grande and shortly thereafter made his famous assault (unsuccessfully) on the town of Casas Grandes. He emerged from the encounter as a man of courage if not of military talent. News came that in the state of Morelos to the south Juan Andreu Almazán and Emiliano Zapata had risen in arms in support of Madero's cause. Venustiano Carranza assumed leadership of the revolutionary forces in Madero's home state of Coahuila. In May, 1911, the frontier city of Juárez fell to Madero's forces. The federal armies, alleged to be some 40,000 strong, were in fact no larger than 15,000 due to the prevalence of a curious greed syndrome developed earlier by Iturbide: the padding of payroll budgets with fictitious names whose salaries went into the pockets of greedy officers. When it came to battle, the payroll list of fake soldiers was an empty resource. Shortly after occupying Juarez, Madero faced an open confrontation with Orozco and Villa, both intent upon assuming command of the revolutionary movement, and the mild-tempered vegetarian once again proved himself to be a man of courage. Thus his charisma and popular following continued to grow. City by city the country was falling to the revolutionaries, and on May 21, 1911 representatives of Díaz and Madero signed a treaty at Juárez providing for the dictator's immediate abdication.

The Great Revolution

Díaz, however, balked at resigning. Late in May, crowds that had gathered outside the national congress building in response to rumors that the dictator was about to abdicate were disappointed and moved on the Zócalo where they were charged by Díaz' palace guard. Before the melee was over several hundred Mexican citizens had been machinegunned, enough to convince Diaz it was time to resign. By the end of May 1911 Díaz was aboard a German ship bound for Europe and his Minister of Foreign Relations, Francisco León de la Barra had become interim president, with the promise that he would conduct new presidential elections in the fall and that he himself would not be a candidate. Here was where Madero probably made a serious mistake, one that his country was to pay for dearly and in blood. According to one analyst of the period:

There would have been no hindrance if Madero had seen fit to declare himself President immediately. He might have saved both himself and Mexico much trouble had he done so. Taking power at the high tide of his popularity might have brought peace and stability.[2]

By insisting upon a strict adherance to constitutionality in the succession Madero gave ample opportunity for separationists within his own ranks, like the Flores Magón group now centered in Baja California, to vie for place and power. To complicate the matter further, Madero naïvely expected not only de la Barra but the entire federal bureaucracy and army to become loyal to his movement overnight. Compounding the risk, Madero disbanded many of his revolutionary troops, thus denying them a greater share in the spoils of victory and disarming himself of their protection. Many of these disappointed troops became followers of Zapata who openly rebelled against Madero, charging that the process of agrarian reform was going too slowly. Old followers of Porfirio like Bernardo Reyes revived their power ambitions.

With chaos threatening from all sides, interim president de la Barra turned over the reins of government to Francisco Madero several weeks early on November 6, 1911. By this time Emiliano Zapata had openly broken with Madero over the failure of the land reform program. Indeed the followers of Zapata had charged Madero with treason:

Mexicanos: considerad que la astucia y la mala fe de un hombre están derramando sangre de una manera escandalosa por ser incapaz de gobernar; . . . las (armas) volvemos contra el por haber traicionado a la Revolución . . . (Emiliano Zapata et al., *Plan de Ayala,* 1911.) [3]

Mexican citizens: because of the cunning and bad faith of one man blood is being spilled in a scandalous manner; . . . because he is incapable of governing we will take up arms against him for he has become a traitor to the Revolution.

From there on until the end of the first year of Madero's administration the story, albeit rich in complicated details, can be put briefly.

---

[2] William Weber Johnson, *Heroic Mexico* (New York: Doubleday, 1968), p. 73.

[3] As quoted in Heriberto García Rivas, *Breve historia de la revolución mexicana* (Mexico: Editorial Diana, 1964), p. 112.

Three major uprisings threatened: that of Zapata in Morelos, Orozco in Chihuahua, and Felix Díaz (nephew of the exiled dictator) in Veracruz. Madero's Constitutional Progressive Party, now headed by his brother Gustavo, sought to cultivate popular loyalty and tolerance, but by this time Francisco's charisma had worn thin. Francisco Madero was honest, and brave, but more than that was needed to rule Mexico. Perhaps what was needed was a skilled impostor such as Rodolfo Usigli was later to describe in a brilliant play whose insight into the psychology of Mexican politics was keenly penetrating. But this was not Madero; he simply lacked the strength of his opponents. He would lie to no one; he deceived only himself.

Again, briefly and in deliberate sacrifice of the richness of detail that abounds in numerous historical sources, the story of Madero's demise unfolds from the fateful trust he placed in General Victoriano Huerta, one of Porfirio Díaz' trusted chieftains who had personally escorted the fleeing dictator aboard his Europe-bound vessel. In February, 1913, Huerta undertook to do battle in the center of Mexico City with the forces of Félix Díaz, now stockaded inside an old military arsenal known as the *Ciudadela*. Ostensibly Huerta was to smash this rebellion against the constitutional government but it is now believed that the action, known as the Tragic Ten Days, was a façade for a pact being arranged between the two men, with the fighting designed, cynically, to decimate the ranks of the government troops. Students of the Mexican Revolution should acquire some feeling for the pathos generated by these legendary moments of the Revolution. Its cruel barbarity has been shown brilliantly by William Weber Johnson, who described the Revolution's birth pains in *The Tragic Ten*:

As a battle it was spurious, fraudulent, a grand deception—like the strategy of a pickpocket who jostles a victim from one side to distract his attention and then picks the pocket from the other side. The purpose, which did not become immediately apparent, was to create a scene of such havoc and frightfulness that any solution, no matter how dishonorable, would become preferable to present horror.

Corpses lay in the street where they fell, bloating in the February sun. Persons dying of natural causes could not be buried; their bodies lay in the gutters, putrefying along with the battle victims. Government troops tried to collect the corpses. Some were loaded on two-wheeled carts, taken to Balbuena Park, piled in huge mounds and burned. Others were doused with kerosene where they lay and burned in the street. Still they accumulated faster than these primitive methods could dispose of them. Garbage was piled on the sidewalks. All city services had ceased. No food supplies came into the city and people barricaded in their homes were starving. Electric lines came down in the cannonading and the nights were dark and terrifying, lighted only by the funeral fires and the flames from houses set ablaze by looters or vandals. On the the night of the 14th the Madero home in the Calle Liverpool was put to the torch by a group of "aristocratic cretins" as one commentator described them. The Madero family, except for the President, who was in the National Palace, took refuge in the Japanese legation.[4]

When the slaughter ended Madero and his brother Gustavo were prisoners. The president had tried to repeat the success of the personal confrontation he had had with the rebels Orozco and Villa who earlier sought to depose him at El Paso. This time, his defiance failed; the magic of his charisma had waned.

Then came the nadir of shame in the history of Mexican-United States relations. Our ambassador, Henry Lane Wilson, acting apparently without the knowledge of the President of the United States, offered the United States Embassy as the stage from which Huerta and Díaz (the supposed enemies to the death) could proclaim their infamous *Pact of the Ciudadela.* Huerta would become interim president and in exchange Díaz would be guaranteed the support of Huerta to succeed him via the next "election." Nor did the odious story end there. After Madero and his vice president José María Pino Suárez were forced to sign resignations, they were both murdered under mysterious circumstances while being transported in the "safe custody" of their military captors. The ultraconservative American ambassador, who was slavishly loyal to North American business interests and who viewed Madero's reformist bent with alarm, was inescapably involved in the tragic affair.

American students who ponder the fact that many Mexican intellectuals today dislike us should remember this salient fact: no later than 1913 the United States had succeeded in taking by force the most valuable half of Mexico's terrain, purchased a collateral piece of the national patrimony, and had then sought to ingratiate itself further by presiding over the assassination of the father of Mexico's (and indeed Latin America's) first true revolution. That is

[4] Johnson, op. cit., p. 101.

a melancholy and sobering truth with which we must live and which our Mexican neighbors cannot forget.

The regime of Victoriano Huerta was foredoomed by the very personality of the man who headed it. Huerta was the most inept of dictators. He alienated such regional chieftains as Venustiano Carranza, Pancho Villa, and Emiliano Zapata, who now rose in arms against the Mexico City government. To make matters worse, Huerta began an exchange of insults with President Wilson, after which American marines were ordered to seize Veracruz in April 1914. War between the two countries was barely averted through the good offices of the foreign ministers of Argentina, Brazil, and Chile. In 1914 Huerta resigned and fled to Europe with a generous array of loot taken from the Mexican Treasury. In August of that year, he was succeeded by General Carranza, who became a de facto President and was later recognized as such by President Wilson. Carranza was forced to flee the capital by an invasion of forces under Pancho Villa and Eulalio Gutiérrez, but returned safely after a major triumph by his trusted general, one of Mexico's truly great military figures, Alvaro Obregón. Carranza sought to repair the injured relations between his nation and the United States, a task made difficult by the border raids of the Mexican "Robin Hood," Pancho Villa, during 1916.

This period, often referred to as "the storm," is probably the most critical point in the growth of Mexican nationhood. Her political and military leaders now grew aware that the social fabric of the country was almost in tatters. The chronicle of the events which led to the month of December 1916 tells little or nothing of the apathy, the naked despair, of the people of Mexico during this horrendous six-year period. The novel Los de abajo by Mariano Azuela tells this story in the poignant words of a disillusioned revolutionary who was caught up in the anarchy which swept across the countryside like a plague in the aftermath of the revolution. Perhaps it was the pitiful blindness of those who fought onward to their destruction which ultimately produced a vision of lasting order and the conviction needed to make that vision real. Order was the determination of Venustiano Carranza when he called a Constitutional Assembly into session at Querétaro at the end of 1916. The following February the Assembly promulgated a document which has provided the basic governing format of Mexico to this day.

Institutionalizing the Revolution

The Constitution of 1917 embraced most of the Liberal principles of the Juárez-Ocampo-Lerdo Constitution of 1857. The four key features of the new Constitution were the following: 1) Article 3 prohibited clerics from participating in public educational instruction and severely limited the political rights of relgous groups. Specifically, the article proscribed the use of religious titles in the names of political parties and endorsements by religious groups of political parties; 2) Article 27 deprived the Church and foreigners of landholding and subsoil rights throughout the Republic; 3) Article 33 opened the door for the Mexican President to expel foreign companies and personnel from the land; 4) Article 123 endorsed the principle of collective bargaining, recognized the right of workers to organize into unions, and enumerated principles for land distribution and reform. It would be an enormous understatement to say that Mexicans of 1917 were ready for such measures as these.

Carranza recognized the need for the reforms defined in the Constitution of 1917, but he was not eager to enforce them. His own cronies and followers participated generously in the booty that issued from the Presidency, but little filtered down to the masses. Thus the populace again came to wonder whether the revolution had been for nought, since it resulted in merely a paper document of reform. Pancho Villa's forces in Chihuahua and those of Zapata in Morelos and Guerrero still opposed Carranza's rule. Ignominously—and, it is suspected, with the blessing of Carranza—the legendary Zapata was assassinated in 1919, and thus a revolutionary of wide popular following became a martyr. But Zapata, posthumously, may have had his own requital. The following year Carranza himself was assassinated while attempting to flee the country by way of Tampico. Carranza had refused to honor his 1917 pledge of "no re-election" and in April 1920 had used federal troops to interfere with a Sonora strike involving Luis Morones' newly formed CROM, the Regional Confederation of Mexican Workers. With organized labor and the followers of Zapata still against him, Carranza recognized the precariousness of his situation and abdicated, only to lose his life in attempted flight.

General Obregón was proclaimed President for a four-year term in 1920. He tried to implement the land-reform promises of the Constitution, as his predecessor had failed to do, and carried out an ambitious program of public education under the brilliant guidance of the philosopher, José Vasconcelos. Despite an attempted coup by Adolfo de la Huerta, Obregón turned the Presidency over to Plutarco Elías Calles, the constitutional President-elect, in 1924. Whereas Obregon had begun educational and land reforms pursuant to the Constitution of 1917, Calles considered as his special province the implementation of the anticlerical provisions of the Constitution. To this end he confiscated Church lands, abolished religious instruction in public schools, deported priests, forbade the wearing of religious habits in public, and in general waged a Kulturkampf against religious privilege in all its protean forms. A counterrevolution of Rightists and clerical fanatics, under the banner of the *cristeros*, or defenders of Christ, erupted in defiance of Calles. Despite the shock felt by foreigners over Calles' treatment of the Church, Mexico's relations improved with the United States, largely because of the adept qualities of Ambassador Dwight Morrow, who sympathetically understood the Mexican dilemma and sought constructive channels to aid it.

Once again, in 1928, the question of the presidential succession threatened to visit another bloodbath upon Mexico, with rival factions of the military seeking to impose their favored candidates. In open contempt of the constitutional prohibition of re-election, Obregon's supporters successfully imposed his candidacy upon the electorate in an election of questionable honesty, as were many of the following elections. Before he could take office, the President-elect was assassinated by a religious fanatic who, anachronistically, was allegedly one of the defenders of Christ working in the employ of Calles. So vigorously did Calles denounce the affair, however, and so determined was his appeal for government by law rather than by passion, that violence of major proportions was avoided. Calles, like other contemporary leaders, was not above enriching himself at the public trough, but he exhibited moments of progressive conviction, as had Carranza and Obregón, which allowed the revolution's "paper gains" to inch forward toward realization.

Congress named Emilio Portes Gil, an intimate and supporter of Obregón, to be provisional President for fourteen months. During this time Calles and his group, which now included Luis Morones, formed Mexico's first revolutionary political party, the PNR, or National Revolutionary Party, which held its first convention in 1929 and nominated Pascual Ortiz Rubio to succeed Portes Gil. The latter, in his *Quince años de política mexicana*, described Ortiz Rubio's defeat of José Vasconcelos in a bitter electoral struggle which pitted the reformist thrust of the revolution squarely against the Conservative forces of clerical reaction. Not only was Ortiz Rubio a puppet for Calles, he was also a poor risk. The Congress challenged the President's budget, and during the ensuing controversy, Ortiz Rubio saw fit to fire several pro-Calles members of his own Cabinet. To this gesture of contempt Calles, the great cacique, retaliated and forced Ortiz Rubio's resignation, replacing him with a wealthy militarist and landowner from Baja California. Abelardo Rodríguez finished the term faithfully in service to his chief. The elections of 1934 saw the left wing of the PNR erupt in disgust with a situation in which the Mexican presidency was obviously being run by Calles from his villa in Cuernavaca. The new revolutionaries were able to impose upon Calles their own favored candidate for the Presidency, General Lázaro Cárdenas, who was promptly elected and assumed office. That Calles had underestimated the General as a potential puppet became swiftly obvious. Soon Calles was in exile in the United States, marveling at the socioeconomic reforms which began to sweep the Republic.

Cárdenas: Toward Economic Independence

The Cárdenas era (1934–1940) was the "take off" stage of the Mexican Revolution during the post-violence period. Casting aside all remnants of bondage to the Calles machine, Lázaro Cárdenas distributed agrarian lands to peasants more generously than had any other previous Chief Executive. He did so via the usufructuary device of *ejidos*, or collective farms, regulated by the State. He sought political change internally by scrapping Calles' old PRN in favor of a new party, the PRM, or Mexican Revolutionary Party. At the same time the old CROM of Luis Morones was replaced with the CTM, the Mexican Confederation of Workers, which came under the new and vigorous leadership of Vicente Lombardo Toledano. With both Calles and Morones exiled to the United States, Cárdenas governed without serious opposition. His support rested squarely on a broadly based configuration of peasantry, urban labor, and the armed forces. Among Mexico's true revolutionaries, that is, leaders who were instrumental in bringing about concrete change, Lázaro Cárdenas merits a special place in his nation's quest for the benefits of socio-economic-political modernity. Not only did Cárdenas refuse to become a puppet for Calles' political machine, he was opposed to the exaggerated religious persecution that had led to the *cristero* crisis. Cárdenas was, to be sure, unsympathetic with fanatic clerics who sought to enslave ignorant peoples via superstition and witchcraft and he lent government support to community reformers who fought to secularize public education; but he would not be a party to extermination of the clergy. To this end he ordered an end to the dissemination of anti-religious propaganda in the classroom and encouraged Mexican families to come together around a nucleus of Christian values and practices. In making a limited peace with the Church, Cárdenas had done much to pacify and to stabilize Mexico politically. However, this should not be taken to imply that the anticlerical reprisals of the Calles period were without justification. Organized Roman Catholics had emerged from the great Revolution clinging tenaciously to a myriad of nefarious economic practices and social evils. The dilemma facing Cárdenas was how to keep a just retribution from becoming ecclesiastical genocide.

Although Cárdenas' quelling of the church-state dilemma was only to be temporary, it was nonetheless an important achievement. He sought to accomplish an even greater step toward modernity however in his attack upon the agrarian and land-use structure of Mexico. Upon taking office in 1934 it was painfully clear that previous efforts toward land reform had improved living standards for really very few persons. Cárdenas is said to have spent more time traveling about the country listening to the complaints of the poor and landless than he did in his capital city office. He knew the imperative need for land reform and, perhaps naively and within a somewhat Marxist intellectual framework, believed that redistribution of land would assuage the nation's ills. A vigorously extended and reorganized program of state farms was to be part of his panacea. Cárdenas superintended the reform personally and often from the actual site of a given land distribution. Mexicans have never forgotten this; indeed they should not, for Lázaro Cárdenas, his naïve Marxism and simplistic "populism" notwithstanding, conquered the hearts of his people, as Madero could not do, for long enough to institutionalize a stable regime. The people loved Cárdenas while the bureaucrats often hated him:

He created administrative chaos, but he distributed land. In his first three years he doubled the number of heads of family with land to work and the amount of land available to *ejidatarios*. By the end of his term he had expropriated and distributed over 17 million hectares to nearly 8000 new villages in which over two million people lived. As a result of his efforts and those of his predecessors, by 1941 nearly 15,000 villages accounting for a quarter of the total population enjoyed the use of slightly less than half the crop land and about one-fifth the total land. Twenty-five years earlier almost none of these people had land they could call their own.[5]

At the end of Cárdenas' term the nation was experiencing a somewhat better distribution of wealth than that which existed at the advent of Madero's effort to front the Mexican Revolution. But the large landowners, despite all of their egaliterian shortcomings, still were able to demonstrate that private enterprise could produce more food than socialized enterprise. The distribution of the food and its financial earnings was another matter, one that Mexico still must solve. A central, and remaining, fact in this dilemma was that the government bureaucrats appointed to redistribute land, hence wealth, ultimately became a sort of special interest group in themselves, and much of the redistributed land is known to have landed in their hands.

By the year 1921, Mexico produced nearly one-fourth of the world's supply of oil. This part of the territory the Americans had neglected to conquer in the 1840's. The Constitution of 1917 gave the Mexican nation exclusive rights to subsoil minerals. During the *Pax Porfiriana* subsoil rights were sold profitably to foreigners. Despite the lip service given to nationalization, little concrete action had really been taken to assure that profits from subsoil exploitation would even in part be reinvested in the Mexican nation or redistributed to her nationals. On March 18, 1938, President Lázaro Cárdenas signed a decree intended to rectify this imbalance. The overall result of his action, in long-range terms, is still a moot issue. What is clear is that before 1938 the majority of Mexico's oil production was destined for foreign consumption. Low salaries and poor living conditions aggra-

[5] Charles C. Cumberland, *Mexico: The Struggle for Modernity* (New York: Oxford, 1968), p. 299.

vated the complaints of Mexican workers who were forced to labor in the employ of foreign concerns. After Cárdenas expropriated the oil, that is up until about 1951, the quantity of petroleum production destined for local markets almost tripled and thereafter Mexican petroleum products continued to play an important role in the domestic economy (favored, of course, by protective legislation). In this writer's opinion, reached after considerable discussion with informed Mexicans both supportive of the national petroleum firm PEMEX and with some who vehemently oppose it, it is difficult to state categorically that the expropriation has been a success economically. But politically PEMEX, i.e. Lázaro Cárdenas et al., has been a gigantic domestic success, one that will seldom, if ever, be equaled during the second half of the twentieth century.

Lázaro Cárdenas' reform era was anathema to the forces of the Mexican oligarchy, the same powerful upper class against which all previous reformers had struggled. Wearing modern attire of the twentieth century, the oligarchs arrayed against the reforms were still essentially the same as earlier, but now they were joined by foreign oil companies and other commercial newcomers (such as American-owned grain farms in Sonora's Yaqui Valley). In his drive for a progressive liberalism, Cárdenas entered into the lineage of Juárez, Morelos, Madero, and Zapata. Probably more than any other figure, Cárdenas shaped the image of his Revolutionary party (PRM) as an organized spokesman for popular distress. He instilled securely the notion of public entrepreneurship as a co-partner with the private sector in his nation's development and institutionalized the psychology of being "revolutionary" as a credential of legitimacy (a concept to which we will return at various times throughout this book). It is fair to say that Lázaro Cárdenas, while a disappointment to Calles, proved to be a delight to the Mexican populace. He combined Juárez' ideological commitment to concrete change with Zapata's ability to reach the common people. He accomplished this without being deposed or exiled as was Juárez and without falling victim to his own violence as did Zapata. At the moment of this writing the late Cárdenas' mystique still inspires the Mexican people; he is, in a very real sense, the father of the contemporary Mexican political system.

In 1940 Cárdenas gracefully stepped aside and was succeeded by General Manuel Ávila Camacho, who carried on, though with less urgency, many of the Cárdenas reform programs. Ávila Camacho was matched against the candidacy of General Juan Andreu Almazán whose support came from a number of splinter parties including PAN, the Party of National Action, which foreshadowed the growth of a permanent political opposition in contemporary Mexico.

The elections of 1946 and 1952 were tranquil compared to the rest of Mexican experience in the twentieth century. The official party, PRM, became the PRI, the Revolutionary Institutional party, during the regime of President Ávila Camacho; and this party supported the successive regimes of Miguel Alemán Valdés and Adolfo Ruiz Cortines. Alemán Valdés' rise to fame set a pattern which was soon to be repeated in Mexican political life. He rose from governor of a major state, Veracruz, to campaign manager for Ávila Camacho in 1940, and from that position to *Secretario de Gobernación* (Secretary of the Interior) in the President's Cabinet. With the end of World War II, it was felt that Mexico needed a president somewhat to the political right of the Cárdenas tradition who would promote commercial and industrial development. Miguel Alemán Valdés became one of Mexico's most entrepreneurial presidents. During his regime the nation's industrial economy surged forward toward maturity.

The selection of Adolfo Ruiz Cortines as the PRI standard-bearer in 1952 represented only a mild reaction to the conservatism of the Alemán administration. This selection is somewhat paradoxical inasmuch as Ruiz Cortines was one of the more trusted Alemán followers who had pursued exactly the same route of ascent as had his predecessor and mentor. Ruiz had always been distinguished, even within Alemán's orbit, as being impeccably honest, and Alemán is known to have assigned to Ruiz certain financial custodial tasks which Alemán did not even trust to himself. Under Ruiz Cortines, Mexico's public administration was purged of many of its former objectionable practices, and definite strides were taken to expand the state farm program, public welfare, and other needed social reforms.

In 1958, Adolfo López Mateos brought to the Presidency a distinguished background as a labor mediator and organizer. His service as Secretary of Labor in the Ruiz Cortines Cabinet and earlier as a troubleshooter for the Mexican Treasury had attracted the admiration of ex-President Cárdenas which, coupled with López Mateos' long-standing friendship with Miguel Alemán, served ideally in fitting López for the PRI candidacy. He was unusual in that he enjoyed the unanimous support of not only the three principal emeritus figures in Mexican politics at the time, but also the unqualified support of most businessmen, of organized labor, and of the military establishment.

The election of Adolfo López Mateos in 1958 was significant in several respects. It was the first time in Mexican history that the franchise had been extended to women. Moreover, part of the PRI's campaign pledge was the institution of a sweeping program of socialized medicine, medical and dental clinics, and maternity care centers intended particularly for rural and depressed urban neighborhoods. López Mateos generally made good this pledge and thereby endeared himself to many Mexicans who otherwise might have remained apathetically on the edge of their national political life. The 1958 presidential campaign was one of the most determined, indeed violent, campaigns since the religious riots of the 1920s. The opposition candidate endorsed by PAN, the National Action Party, was Luis H. Álvarez, an elite-born firebrand who saw Mexico slipping into an abyss of Marxian socialism and ultimately Communist dictatorship. Álvarez was openly the spokesman for clerical interests and for some members of the financial aristocracy.

Political stability was the hallmark of López Mateos' regime. This stability did exist despite several naval and border skirmishes with Guatemala, international friction over relations with Castro's Cuba, and the problem of the salinity in the Colorado River water coming from the United States. Even though Mexico remained a country in which misery and injustice were still widespread, her booming economy, her aggressive trade unionism, the broad range of her social welfare services, her public education system, and her generally enlightened leadership all combined to make Mexico an example of success in terms of the usual consequences of revolutionary violence, for the rest of Latin America.

Díaz Ordaz: The Declining Revolutionary Axis

Today, there are evidences pointing to what I have chosen to term the declining axis of revolutionary politics. Certainly, as the decade of the 1970's opens no one can be secure in his prognosis of the direction in which change will occur in the revolutionary system. Since a prognosis occupies major sections of this work, any detailed examination of recent events will be deferred until later chapters. It is clear, however, that the system President Díaz Ordaz inherited from López Mateos in 1964 had critical elements that might be labeled entropy, disruptive forces tending to produce dysfunctional behavior and to tear the system apart, to produce disequilibrium. A later chapter examines the thesis that these forces existed during the previous revolutionary regimes (including that of Cárdenas) and that the catalytic element which, combined with other factors, held the system together was in large part the personality of the incumbent president. This, it may be argued, has been true throughout Mexican history. If the president lacked the personality to either electrify the masses, or pacify (or deceive) the oligarchies as well as the masses, his tenure of office was gravely insecure. This surely was the lesson of Francisco I. Madero's downfall. Díaz Ordaz, it is felt by many well placed Mexicans, has an aloofness about him, much as if he were the director of a large bureaucracy in which there was little need to reach out to the "operatives" at the grass roots level.

Mexico, like all Latin American (indeed all western) nations, suffers the baneful consequences of a severe generation gap between the young and old. The most serious manifestation of this gulf occurred during the student riots in Mexico City in 1968 (see Chapter 5). Pressures of the young, the poor and wretched, and the internal politics of a giant organism itself forced Díaz Ordaz into defensive actions which former presidents with other personality structures might have been able to obviate. It is critical to point out that President López Mateos was widely loved and was regarded as a great compromiser. He was a popular figure despite the fact of his being widely rumored to be involved with narcotics, to have a teenage mistress, to have lined his pockets handsomely from the public trough; but these *macho* traits also meant that many powerful figures were in his debt. He knew how to compromise and often did so. Conversely, Díaz Ordaz is widely said to lead an exemplary personal life (as did Francisco I. Madero) and to be honest. But he does not compromise well and he does not communicate skillfully enough to make the power contenders about him feel that compromise is even viable.

Events during the first two years of his administration speak partially for themselves. Following an armed clash between members of rival factions of the CNC (*Confederación Nacional Campesina*) or National Peasants Confederation, on August 20, 1965 which left upwards of thirty workers dead, the head of the Confederation, Amador Hernández, resigned under pressure from Díaz Ordaz. The conflict dramatized growing cleavage high up in the national power structure and Díaz Ordaz saw expulsion as more feasible than a negotiated compromise. The reform minded mayor of the Federal District, Ernesto T. Uruchurtu was fired in the wake of a controversy over his campaign to eliminate vice and corruption. Carlos A. Madrazo (to whose case we shall return variously throughout this book) was ousted in a direct confrontation with Díaz Ordaz over a question of democratizing local elections. Madrazo, as president of the PRI, had been in effect Mexico's second most powerful political figure. Governor Enrique D. Ceniceros of Durango was fired for his "incompetent" handling of a student strike against foreign mining interests. Saltiel Alatriste, director of Mexico's Social Security System was fired in the midst of an anti-corruption campaign he had launched. Ignacio Chávez, chancellor of the National University of Mexico, was forced to resign for his "excessive tolerance" of student demonstrations on campus (at one point students had forced him into submitting a resignation with a knife to his throat).

In 1967 and 1968 student protests against fraudulent elections in Yucatán, Villa Hermosa, Hermosillo, and what amounted to an unmasked electoral fraud in Baja California testified to the determination of the Díaz Ordaz-steered Revolutionary party to perpetuate itself at practically all costs. The greatest evidence of the declining Axis of the Revolutionary system came in August and September of 1968 when the police and military brutalized student protesters in a sequence of violence that was described as the worst since the downfall of Madero. Tragically, and perhaps ironically, ex-president López Mateos, whose skills might have been invoked to restore peace, had himself been removed as national chairman of the forthcoming Olympic games; he was slowly dying in a coma with brain damage and complications following surgery.

Folklore has it that Porfirio Díaz once admonished the aspiring Francisco I. Madero that a man would need to be much more than honest to govern Mexico. It was the same Díaz who had allowed the satrap Antonio López de Santa Anna to return home, ignominiously but quietly, to die. As the term of President Díaz Ordaz draws to a close it is unclear whether he will have achieved either sufficient wisdom or pragmatic awareness to enter history's pages as a bulwark of the revolutionary axis: or if instead he will have been the critical point at which it broke. As the final chapters in this book will show, the regime of Luis Echeverría Álvarez, under whose aegis Mexico now enters the decade of the 1970's, does not promise to be more supple in its approach to an increasingly antagonistic political arena.[6]

[6] This chapter purports to be no more than the author's synthesis of existing secondary source material and is, at best, a political scientist's view of the major figures, currents, and epochs in the development of the Mexican political system. For the reader with more scholarly historical interests the following bibliography is offered.

Alba, Victor. *Las ideas sociales contemporáneas en México.* Mexico: Fondo de Cultura Económica, 1960.

Araquistain, Luis. *La Revolución Mexicana, sus orígenes, sus hombres, su obra.* Madrid: Renacimiento, 1929.

Beals, Carleton. *Porfirio Díaz: Dictator of Mexico.* Philadelphia: Lippincott, 1932.

Clendenen, Clarence C. *The United States and Pancho Villa.* Ithica, N.Y.: Cornell, 1961.

Cockcroft, James D. *Intellectual Precursors of the Mexican Revolution 1900–1913* Austin: University of Texas, 1968.

Cosió Villegas, Daniel, ed. *Historia moderna de México.* 8 volumes. Mexico: Editorial Hermes, 1948–1965.

Mancisidor, José. *La Revolución Mexicana.* Mexico: Ediciones El Gusano de Luz, 1958.

Quirk, Robert E. *The Mexican Revolution, 1914–1915: The Convention of Aguascalientes.* New York: Citadel Press, 1963.

Simpson, Lesley Byrd. *Many Mexicos.* Berkeley: University of California, 1960.

Tannenbaum, Frank. *Peace by Revolution—An Interpretation of Mexico.* New York: Columbia University, 1933.

Vernon, Raymond. *The Dilemma of Mexico's Development.* Cambridge: Harvard University, 1963.

Womack, John. *Zapata and the Mexican Revolution.* New York: Knopf, 1968.

2
Visions of Mexican Political Life

Legitimacy is a jealously guarded political attribute in Mexico, an esoteric quality to which only members of an exclusive and large political "family" have priority rights. Where legitimacy is esoteric, illegitimacy tends to be exoteric as applied to those who either have wandered from the sanctioned path or who were never admitted to it in the first place. The honored political "family" PRI holds authoritative sanctions over the admission of new power contenders to its membership. This book takes as its primary focus the ramifications of the gulf that separates the "legitimate in-groups" from the "out-groups." Across this gulf lies a vast and uncertain panorama of political change. One of the principal reasons for the existence of such a gulf is the relevance of public policy and the performance of governmental entities.

This chapter will treat three separate dimensions or visions of the dynamic flow of Mexican politics. I choose to call them national pride, practical politics, and literary insights: one may easily (albeit superficially) reduce this to the honorific, the pejorative, and the aesthetic. There are many other dimensions that will be examined throughout the book, but the present triad is offered for the heuristic purposes of the classroom and because this approach seems to be a useful conceptual scheme for viewing contemporary Mexico as it enters the throes of a political renaissance during the closing years of the 1960's and the opening decade of the 1970's.

Roots and Symbols of National Pride

A statue of General Emiliano Zapata at the entrance to the urban district of Cuernavaca in the state of Morelos bears an inscription honoring a man of humble Indian birth who rose to fame and greatness as a champion of the common folk. Zapata supported the insurrection against Porfirio Díaz in 1910 that brought to a close Latin America's longest political tyranny. But Zapata ultimately broke with the Revolution's father, Francisco I. Madero, over the latter's inability to see the treachery about him that threatened to sacrifice the very goals of the resistance to the Porfirio followers. Madero, the intellectual architect of the Revolution, was murdered in 1912 by men in whom he had unwisely placed his trust. Zapata, the violent instrument of the Revolution, was himself assassinated in 1919 by an act which punctuated that era of rapine and ushered in the start of institution-building and a drive toward political socialization. Today, nearly every town in Mexico has streets and monuments to the honor of Madero and Zapata. All Mexican school children read of their triumphs. Through these and other charismatic figures Mexicans have come to honor their national heritage. They have been taught to revere the honors of battle, and manly courage, and to respect the traumata of human life ebbing from a bloody sword.

It has been variously written that Francisco I. Madero's personal tragedy was in the fact that he was born at the wrong time in history and lived in the wrong country as well.[1] In contrast Zapata's behavioral style was surely more the order of that day. In calling the constitutional convention at Querétaro in December 1916 Carranza sought to create institutions that would at once internalize the spirit of Madero and reduce political reliance upon the action styles of Zapata. But what was accomplished on paper was honored as much in the breach as in the observance. Zapata's aggressive primacy of individual values has remained the behavioral norm of political action throughout all levels of government in Mexico to this day. That value syndrome, not uncommon in other Latin American countries, has been one of the principal barriers to overall national development.

[1] See, for instance, William Weber Johnson's comment in *Heroic Mexico* (New York: Doubleday, 1968), p. 92.

The astonishing thing about Mexico, all of the difficulties notwithstanding, is that her institutions have become relatively sound and stable when compared with the experiences of most of her Latin American neighbors. The Mexican Revolution, even with its horrendous bloodletting, was not fought in vain. Mexico today enjoys many benefits of socio-economic political modernity; and to the extent that she does, we may say that her people boast genuine symbols of group attachment and national pride whose cultural roots are firmly anchored.

Compared with many Latin American countries, Mexico has been able to achieve a measure of political stability that has honored the growth of visible educational, social, and economic benefits. Countering unemployment, a chronic problem in most Latin American countries, is an active system of social security and welfare that is constantly being extended to serve more and more people. Leading sector industries and their smaller service-function partners offer steady sources of employment. Although salaries (especially for women) leave much to be desired, Mexicans are visibly better off than many of their Latin American neighbors. Mexican newspapers devote headlines, for example, to a new shipment of locally built electric motors bound for Chile. The nation is frequently lauded both for its drive toward industrial maturity and for the extent to which it has translated business expansion into employment opportunity. One of Mexico's leading industries is tourism. Her proximity to the United States favors tourism as do the many attractions of her natural beauty. The government operated (and subsidized) airline, *Aeronaves de México*, mounts an aggressive worldwide campaign to attract tourists. Long known as intellectual centers, Mexico City and Guadalajara offer an impressive array of cultural attractions. Historic and archeological sites abound from the aqueducts and castles of Guanajuato to the pyramids and volcanoes that are variously scattered through the region to the south. The colorful historic richness of the entire nation does much to invite scholars and travelers from around the globe. Internationally, the *Ballet Folklórico de México* has been a magnificent cultural showpiece for the nation's indigenous achievement. During 1968 Mexico City hosted the Olympic Games, a monumental undertaking in itself. All of this, in one way or another, is a source of Mexican pride. It is also a measure of her potential greatness. There is no denying credit to her principal governing institution

PRI (*Partido Revolucionario Institutional*) for much of this great success. But, there is more!

The triumphs of Mexico's Revolutionary system are more readily visible at the gross or aggregate level than in terms of measurable betterments in the livelihood of any social sector in particular. Perhaps most obvious in this instance is the fact of the strength and prestige of the Mexican peso. The peso is among the world's thirteen most stable currencies as rated by the International Monetary Fund in 1968, and Mexico shares this honor only with Venezuela among the Latin American community of nations. When French President DeGaulle initiated a policy of attack on the US dollar during 1967 and 1968 it was gallant Mexico and her distinguished Minister of Treasury, Antonio Ortiz Mena, who came to the defense of the dollar by offering to sell large quantities of Mexico's gold reserves as a confidence gesture. Not many Americans appreciate the courage of this move and probably few Americans or Mexicans even knew of it. Part of the strength of the peso is due to the stability of Mexico's political system, the relative historical absence of public violence since 1917, and to the effective combination of state investment capitalism via a government development bank and private banking institutions. Mexico *reputedly* is less plagued with flight capital than are other Latin American nations. Her savings bonds paid nine percent interest in 1968 and were an attractive inducement for capital to remain within the nation. Because there is more money in circulation and more private initiative there is also more competition. The price benefits of a competitive system are obviously favorable to the Mexican consumer. For contrast, one has only to travel south to neighboring Guatemala to see the dire impact of a monopolized commerce in terms of consumer prices.

Despite government controls on the importation of newsprint, Mexico has maintained a relative freedom of the press. An active underground and clandestine press is in operation and one may be informed about the pros and cons of public affairs if he so wishes. Articulation of disagreement with the government is both possible and feasible without serious personal risk to the individual, providing he does not become violent or "anti-social." The greatest constraint on governmental criticism comes in the form of political and economic sanctions that may be brought against a person who strays too far from the Revolutionary fold. This was one of the lessons in the case of former president of the PRI, Carlos A. Madrazo, whose exit from Revolutionary power is mentioned elsewhere.

Mexican political instutions, while far from being objects of great admiration by all her people, have generated a set of popular symbols of group attachment in which many take pride. The ability of the Mexican people to experience in common the ongoing thrust of their environmental history, and to derive satisfaction therefrom, is a hallmark of the process of nation building. Mexico is one of few Latin American societies in which this process has reached out widely so as to embrace nearly all major population segments. Mexicans see their government as the embodiment of the state. The people constitute the nation. Although Anglo-Saxon cultures may have succeeded in obliterating the distinction between the two concepts (state and nation) the dichotomy remains meaningful to most Mexicans. The point is, the Mexican nation is a great ubiquitous collectivity of symbols that provide for common foci of affection and attachment among some 50 million people. The state, on the other hand, and the way it is staffed and managed, frequently serves as a divisive factor among groups and between regions. The term nationalism must then be understood in a very special context of the allegiance of a people to itself, its legends, heroes, values, and only incidentally to the incumbent government that stewards the ongoing affairs of the dynamic society. Nationalism and operative political values may, at a given moment, be quite distinct characteristics. While Mexicans love their nation they often disparage the state.

Mexicanismo is seen by most Mexicans as a unique process of recent history beginning with the Revolution of 1910–17. They are wont to eschew any notion that theirs is a parasite or hybrid culture in the sense of depending upon foreign ideological transfusions. They consider themselves the result of a unique and locally indigenous process. They owe no foreign allegiance. Mexico's federalized educational system helps to inculcate the symbols of national pride from the primary level of education on up. It is an effective and far reaching process.

What are Mexicans most proud of? A legion of answers would be needed to do justice to the question. But here is a partial list: they are proud of their Aztec heritage which makes Mexicans practically unique in the hemisphere, names like Cuauhtémoc, Ixtlizóchitl, Netzahualcóyotl, Anáhuac, and Moctezuma; they are proud of having had Latin America's first social revolution; they are proud of their material progress and of the fact that tourists from about the world consider Mexico a truly desirable place to visit. Their capital city has monuments, golden angels, lighted pyramids, skyscrapers, international cuisine, all of which holds up to the world the fact that Mexico has a rich culture and that she is modernizing at a rapid pace.

Each of these elements of national pride has roots that are in some manner traceable directly to the institutions that grew out of the great Revolution. As principal heir to this tradition, the PRI claims honorific status as Mexico's primary instrument of progress. While this book devotes attention to the structures and programs created under the PRI aegis, and does so in the sincere effort to give PRI its full due, it is also the intention herein to tell part of the story of those who are dissatisfied with the direction the Revolution has taken "institutionally" and who have forged themselves into parties and pressure groups dedicated to winning access to high circles of power and decision-making. From these groups will come the new Mexico of the 1970's and 1980's. It may be a vastly changed Mexico in which the political organization PRI does not even exist or PRI may have merely changed its name to pacify its challengers and to lull them into the false conviction that reform has finally taken place. It may also be a Mexico living under a newly reformed PRI. If so, there will have been strong reasons why.

Popular Alienation and Political Power

Some expressions of "everyday people" who know and feel the impact of political life in a nation where legitimacy is an officially guarded fetish are: "politics is whatever the government dictates," "it rains only on election day or when old folks get married," and "in the land of the blind the one-eyed-jack is king." There is indeed a cynicism about the way in which many Mexicans talk about their politics and government, i.e., the symbolic distinction between state and nation mentioned above. Almost any taxi driver will refer to the traffic police as vultures and crooks and will look toward a state government palace saying "the same gang of theives." A Chihuahua newspaper once published a cartoon showing the dead carcass of the people of that state being devoured by a pack of wolves representing the various levels of state and local government.[2] The opposition party

[2] *Indice*, 3 de febrero 1962, p. 1.

PAN (*Partido Acción Nacional*) published that same year a photographic exposé of how electoral fraud was accomplished.[3] Publication of a documentary monograph *La grieta en el yugo* provoked violent reprisals by the state police in the state of San Luis Potosí.[4] Sonora and Baja California have been the scene of recent electoral scandals. The 1968 Olympic games were for a time threatened by thousands of students who surged through Mexico City's streets chanting "death to Díaz Ordaz." Mexico's world renowned painter, David Alfaro Siqueiros, was imprisoned during much of the term of Adolfo López Mateos for a sedition conviction whose process and sentence were seriously open to question in the eyes of many. There is no limit to the anecdotes we could list here to demonstrate a simple point: despite the great pride Mexicans have in their nation, there is much of which they are deeply ashamed.

There is a familiar expression, subject to a legion of variations, that perhaps capsulizes one practical key to political power in Mexico of the late 1960's. It frequently runs something like this:

Se necesitaría vivir fuera de México para ignorar que aquí el que tiene el poder tiene la sartén por el mango, y que por medio de ese mango se consigue la "lana." Es rara avis el que, habiendo ocupado un puesto público, no lo aprovecha para enriquecerse.[5]

One would have to live outside of Mexico to ignore the fact that here he who has power has the "frying-pan by the handle" and by means of this "fruit" one gets rich. It is indeed a rare "bird" who occupies a public post and does not take advantage of his position in order to become wealthy.

In effect, it says that he who has his hand firmly in command of a situation, by any means available, is most certain to emerge victorious and proud. He who has a public position, and to a somewhat lesser extent a private one, is expected to enrich himself out of communal funds. Rare is he who fails to do so, for indeed this is a norm of expectation. In Mexico if one has a skirmish with the police he offers a polite gratuity in return for having the affair "fixed." If a serious crime is involved, then it is necessary to pay a large "bite." A person embroiled in a serious police or administrative matter at nearly any

[3] *La Nación*, 13 de abril 1962, p. 18.

[4] Antonio Estrada M. *La grieta en el yugo* (San Luis Potosí, 1963).

[5] Taken from *Sucesos*, 6 julio 1968, p. 22.

level of Mexican government can expect grave consequences if he does not carry the proper "influence credentials" in terms of working relationships and friendships or, worse, if he is unable to secure them with money. A poor or ignorant person is almost certain to be the victim of police fury. Much more grave is the case of a defenseless woman who is often violated by the "officers of the law" who apprehend her.[6] Everything has its price, everything is an object for negotiation in Mexico. The traffic police view their role not as accident prevention but rather as a personal sinecure which carries its own commercial prerogatives.

Although the ruling party PRI claims great accomplishments for its social security institutes and medical programs, these are seldom adequately staffed and the average Mexican will often prefer to consult a pharmacist, homeopathic doctor, or a quack before waiting in long lines and subjecting himself to the brusk and frequently crude treatment that will be forthcoming if he seeks help via an official agency. The Mexican of average social position has grown accustomed to being maltreated, to being pushed aside, and stepped upon.

The government, created by PRI, has arrayed against its citizens an overwhelming bureaucracy. All of the bureaucrats call themselves "Revolutionaries" and this is a central fact of the PRI mystique, the inarticulate major premise that controls when a question of citizen versus state arises. The prerogative of a bureaucrat usually takes precedence over those of a common citizen. The average Mexican has, in general terms, "lost his civic spirit and only murmurs, but does not protest; more certain, is that for the most part he has no one to protest to."[7] The authorities often abuse the people to hold them in line. The people endure this stoically, and if a mere citizen should dare to bring charges against an official, he is rapidly and skillfully transformed into the accused who must himself stand trial. The status quo now enjoyed by PRI depends in no small measure upon the continued acquiescence of the populace in this power system. It depends upon the sustained unwillingness of the people to invoke methods of relief now available to them. The dilemma facing PRI today is that many Mexicans have awakened to these shortcomings and are transferring their loyalty to groups that demand reform of the country's overall governing system.

6 Ibid.

7 Ibid., p. 23.

A knowledgeable and high ranking official of the PRI confided to me during the summer of 1968 that a scandal had occurred at a high enough level of Mexican government to bring down the presidency of most nations including the United States. Briefly, the confidential source related, a new port facility and ocean breakwater had been constructed at a given location on the Caribbean coast of the Yucatán peninsula. The engineering survey was conducted without an adequate oceanographic study. When billions of pesos had been spent on an attractive looking facility, it was discovered that coral reefs at the entrance prohibited the entry of any vessel except those too small to need such an elaborate port. At that time it appeared questionable that the facility could ever be made operational. The source also told me that the director of the harbor authority in question was a personal friend of President Díaz Ordaz, a medical doctor by profession, who was in no way an expert on maritime engineering or international commerce. This is a true story. But there are hundreds more like it. Suffice it to add that many Mexicans in high and low places today are severely disturbed at what they see.

Ironically, no one in Mexico could agree more strongly with the latter proposition than the former president of the PRI's National Executive Committee Lic. Carlos A. Madrazo. In December of 1965 Madrazo faced a showdown with President Díaz Ordaz over the question of who was to be the dominant figure in the national power structure. The President of the Republic won. In substance the test evolved around Madrazo's demand that the PRI honor its 1964 campaign pledge of democratizing all of Mexican politics and admitting a greater number of power contenders into the favored light of "official respectability." Ostensibly, a series of proportional representation electoral reforms[8] enacted prior to that campaign were intended to spur the democratization process. Madrazo's proposal had been modest indeed. He wanted to begin by requiring local committees of the PRI to choose their municipal candidates in a sort of primary election in which the grass roots would determine the nominating process instead of the local caciques. His proposal was anathema to PRI bosses throughout the countryside. How could the former governor of Tabasco turn his back on the very avenues that had led to

---

[8] The reforms made it possible for political parties (officially recognized ones) to win deputies both on the basis of formal districts and under a special quota system (see Chapter 3).

his own rise to power? Madrazo himself told me that his career had been marred with various political "skeletons in closets" for which he had publicly repented many times. He said he was prepared to redo the very system that had made his own political success possible.

But Madrazo's quest for democracy reflected other considerations that tell much of the pejorative side of Mexican politics. As governor of his native state he was profoundly shocked at the inability (or unwillingness) of all levels of government to correct the glaring deficiencies of urban life. Only if the urban people had a greater voice (and pressure) in their political system could the squatter colonies and prostitution zones with their violence and disease be eradicated. He related to me his concern (while governor of Tabasco) over the inherent inability (and inactivity) of the state in helping people of both rural and urban vintage to escape the ravages of a hostile environment. He remembered the village folk of neighboring Chiapas who often had to be rescued from floods by state agents of Tabasco because of the disinterested attitude of their own state's governor. He described the need for urbanites all over Mexico to carry arms for defense against paid state and local policemen who often worked as highwaymen and night attackers.

Carlos Madrazo did not abandon his status as a true "Revolutionary" for that would have disarmed him of access to the only effectively organized arena for political competition. Madrazo's tactic was to discredit the incumbent PRI leadership, those who had campaigned on the López Mateos regime's promise of free and honest elections with open political participation to follow. He sought to undo the existing power structure and to replace it eventually with one of his own making. It was in some respects a tactic similar to that employed several years earlier in 1963 when ex-president Cárdenas founded his *Movimiento de Liberación Nacional* (MLN) and ex-president Alemán founded a countervailing group on the right, the *Frente Cívico Mexicano de Afirmación Renovadora* (FCMAR). Madrazo's ideas were not even so reactionary as to include rapproachement with PAN, a group he continued to regard with bitter disdain. The only reason, Madrazo told me, why voters support PAN is because of the failure of the PRI to honor its revolutionary commitments. The justification for this charge is, according to Madrazo (and I would agree), most poignantly visible at the urban level. Following the ideals of Zapata, PRI may have won some "land and liberty" in the countryside but, anachronistically, the nation has moved toward becoming predominantly urban and the cry of "food and social welfare" is a crescendo that now drowns out the rural themes. Madrazo heard this cry and acted upon it. His reward, dismissal, was consistent with contemporary behavioral norms. Madrazo, thus, became another piece in the growing mosaic of Mexico's political discontent.

Internal conflict is clearly visible within PRI at the moment of this writing. Protests by students, workers, peasants, and PRI stalwarts themselves have occurred with increasing frequency during the past several years throughout Mexico. Especially bitter have been incidents in Sonora and Yucatán in 1967, and incidents in Tabasco, Puebla and Baja California Norte in 1968. The latter case, (the state and municipal elections in Baja California Norte on June 2, 1968) dramatized an entire range of problems which local PRI dominated governments must face and, even more, showed how the PRI can front an aggressively voracious entrepreneurial role on the part of key members of its elite with a consequent jeopardizing of the party's own power structure. Baja California, perhaps as much as any other state, reflects the traumata of contemporary Mexican political change and will receive special treatment later as will the bitter Yucatán electoral crisis of 1969.

Whether one chooses to focus attention upon police corruption, administrative malfeasance at any level of government, tolerance and exploitation of vice, narcotics, and prostitution, electoral fraud, or roadblocks that defeat the efforts of political reformers, we still come back to a common point of focus: Mexico's esoteric democracy is failing to meet the needs of too many of her people. Increasingly, major socioeconomic aggregates within the population find cause to express alienated sentiments. Population increase without a concomitant expansion of job opportunities has fed the fires of lower class resentment against the ruling class, the Mexican socioeconomic elite and its international friends. When only one party governs, it, of course, can take credit for the good things which happen to its nation. At the same time, however, it cannot escape responsibility for the failures. Wealth is poorly distributed in Mexico, a fact which renders impressive GNP figures practically meaningless in terms of their potential for creating *supportive* political attitudes among the masses.[9]

---

[9] See figures given in Chapter 7.

This is the inescapable and melancholy fact of life in Mexico for easily more than half of the population: they are poorly fed, housed, clothed, socioeconomic mobility is stultified, the government seems unresponsive to their plight and whatever programs of assistance are available are lacking in the reassuring warmth of genuine concern. I am told on good authority that the average university graduate in Mexico today (a tiny percentage of the population) who becomes a *licenciado* (between the US AB and MA) can rarely expect to earn as much as $160 dollars per month. That in itself is a salary of hunger and the majority who get less have to live on salaries of despair. Mexico's burgeoning youth groups have cause for alarm at the short-comings of their political system. Their voices herald an incipient crisis.

Literary Glimpses and Philosophic Overviews[10]

Mexico has generated a great and scholarly humanistic literature. She has poets, philosophers, and novelists of whom any nation could be justly proud. They have told much of the story of how Mexican man sees his sociopolitical environment. Tragically, they have written about the plights and destinies of those who, in all reasonable proba-bility, would never read the pages that were written sympathetically in their cause. Most poor Mexicans who wish for a better way of life have likely never heard of Octavio Paz, Carlos Fuentes, Juan Rulfo, or Rodolfo Usigli. But the university students have. Their clamor for a revitalized Mexico may sometimes be interpreted as an exposé of scandal; but more hopefully, it can be seen as a positive sign that political maturity has grown and is making the Revolution become a self improving reality.

The political values of Mexico must be viewed in several different strata and according to intellectual sectors of the society. Let us con-sider first the ideas of two of Mexico's best known sociopolitical phi-losophers, José Vasconcelos and Octavio Paz. Their works shed light upon such questions as: the broad values of the society, the best or optimum relationship between the individual and the State, and the generally preferred form of government.

---

[10] I am grateful to one of my graduate students Mr. Raoul Isais, who assisted in preparing parts of this section.

The Mexican philosopher José Vasconcelos saw political change more as a function of ethnic or racial evolution. In his *La raza cósmica*, 1925, Vasconcelos outlined a theory of four basic human species and corresponding cycles of power operative throughout time. He feels an intense necessity to enoble and glorify the brown or mestizo classes.

Thus we have the four stages and the four racial types: the black, the Indian, the Mongol, and the white. The last of these, upon organizing itself in Europe, has become the invader of the world and has proclaimed itself the master of all peoples as did previous races each at the height of its power.[11]

Vasconcelos believed that domination of the world by the white race would be transitory and ought to be judged in terms of its cultural legacy. The whites have had a different mission from their predecessors and have created a technology necessary for socioeconomic development. The white and Indian races are destined to pass through a period of miscegenation, out of which will emerge a new fifth race. This race will be the final stage of the ethnic dialetic and will apply the technology created by whites. Thus, the white race will have made possible the final development of mankind, which is cultural union in a fifth or cosmic race. *"El fin ulterior de la Historia . . . es lograr la fusión de los pueblos y las culturas.*[12] In the final race Vasconcelos saw the "ultimate idea" of human reward, not unlike Hegel's "march of God across the earth."

At one point, Vasconcelos outlines a law of three stages, the *ley del gusto*, which is operative throughout history. The three stages are the material, or warrior stage, the intellectual, or political, and the spiritual, or aesthetic. In the first stage material wants and values are the goals of human behavior. The second finds reason prevailing over the human appetite for force and violence. The final period, yet to come, will see reason replaced as the sole arbiter of men's lives by a constant aesthetic inspiration.

One would not look for the merit of an action in its immediate result, as was done in the first period, nor should one adopt hard rules of pure reason; the same ethical imperative will be surpassed and beyond good and bad, in

---

[11] José Vasconcelos, *La raza cósmica* (México: Austral, 1948), p. 16.

[12] Ibid., p. 27. "The ultimate goal of history is to achieve the fusion of the peoples and cultures."

the world of aesthetic pathos ·nothing will be important except that an act should result in beauty. . . . To live in the happiness of love is the third stage.[13]

La raza cósmica was written during the period when Vasconcelos served as Minister of Education in Mexico under President Alvaro Obregón (1921–25), one of the most productive and satisfying periods in the author's life. The work is a serious and determined intellectual formulation seeking to find hope in the midst of an unjust social order. It is an optimistic call to faith which its contemporary social and political events did not always justify. In the ethnic dialectic Vasconcelos offered Mexicans a cause for renewed confidence in the future of their Revolutionary State.

A more contemporary Mexican writer, Octavio Paz, told an immensely different, albeit complementary tale of Mexican man vis-à-vis his sociopolitical environment. He wrote that solitude, the condition of thinking and feeling oneself alone, is the essence of the human condition. Solitude underlies man's natural state of change, which consists in aspiring to be what one is not, to capture the spirit of one's future self. This concept is the foundation of an important essay, El laberinto de la soledad, 1947, in which the Mexican writer interprets life as flowing toward loneliness and away from life's external chaos immediately upon birth. To live is to separate ourselves from what we were in order to enter into what we are going to be. Alone in the phenomenal world, man toils laboriously to steel himself against the fact of his isolation. In self-defense he creates artifacts, one of which is the contractual concept of marriage, a co-operative human effort to defeat loneliness through love.

Love is one of the clearest examples of this double instinct which leads us to withdraw and find refuge within ourselves, and at the same time, to go beyond ourselves for self-realization in another form: death and recreation, solitude and communion.[14]

In his Labyrinth of Solitude, Octavio Paz has gathered together a soul-searching perception of the Mexican man. In a section entitled "The Mexican Masks," he defines his view of the Mexican's existential

---

[13] Ibid., p. 40.

[14] Octavio Paz, El laberinto de la soledad (México: Fondo de Cultura Económica, 1959), p. 182.

being. He sees the Mexican as a refugee with a mask hiding in the shadowy twilight of solitude. The man envisions himself alone, alienated from society and the artificial universe. It is his fear of spiritual pain that forces him to use a mask. His mask is a facade of indifference and remoteness from the mundane life. His most prominent character traits are withdrawal in the midst of his forced conformity to outward norms. For the Mexican, time has little value, for death and life are a continuous cycle within the universe. Life and death are mere punctuation marks of fate.

The Mexican defines his existence in terms of a number of cults: that of the *"macho,"* of the Virgin of the Guadalupe, and of Cuauhtémoc. All serve as masks. Paz analyzes the phrase *"hijos de la chingada."* The last word gives the impression of failure, of being made a fool. But the final impression is the idea of violent aggression. As Paz puts it, "The verb denotes violence, an emergence from oneself to penetrate another by force. It also means to injure, to lacerate, to violate bodies, souls, objects and to destroy."[15] The *macho* and the *chingon* are the same, aggressive, insensitive and invulnerable. The cult of the young redeemer is always the picture of a suffering, humiliated Christ, condemned by soldiers and judges.

Also Cuauhtémoc, the young Aztec ruler who was tortured by the Spaniards becomes the fallen hero meeting death and awaiting resurrection. The final cult and probably the most important is that of Guadalupe, the Indian virgin, the fertility goddess. She is the protecting mother. She is not only the protectress of the suffering Christ, but also of the suffering Indian. She is strength incarnate.

In sum, she is the Mother of Orphans. All men are born disinherited, and their true condition is orphanhood, but this is particularly true among the Indians and the poor in Mexico. The cult of the Virgin reflects not only the general condition of man but also a concrete historical situation in both the spiritual and material realms. In addition, the virgin—the Universal Mother —is also the intermediary, the messenger, between disinherited man and the unknown, inscrutable power: the strange![16]

The above descriptions of the thought of two key Mexican sociopolitical philosophers yield much insight into the values and attitudes of what we might term the Mexican intelligentsia. Although both

[15] Ibid., p. 76.
[16] Ibid., p. 85.

Vasconcelos and Paz wrote about the dilemmas of the common man (as each saw him) and were intimately concerned with interpreting his plight, neither author depicted the totality of life; neither achieved personal acclaim among the masses. Their works have been, for the most part, destined for intellectual consumption.

The common Mexican man does not elaborate his *weltanschauung* in the systematic terms of Vasconcelos and Paz but has, nonetheless, a world view of his own. The problem is that of sampling and reflecting his vision of political life. Let us attempt this through the eyes and works of an American anthropologist, Oscar Lewis, whose name has been synonymous with studies of the "culture of poverty." It is to be understood that Lewis sought to reflect the values of typical Mexicans without being deliberately perjorative or laudatory. To this end he used tape recordings and detailed interview notes with an eye towards scientific accuracy (the controversy now going on in anthropological circles as to the adequacy of his method is a topic quite beyond the scope of this chapter). My own field experience gives me confidence that Lewis has made an accurate reflection of much that goes on in the mind and life of the common lower-class Mexican that is relevant to the study of his political outlook. Let us consider only two of Lewis' anthropological pictures, that of Pedro Martínez and of the Sánchez Family.

In *Pedro Martínez*, Lewis describes the life of a poor Indian family living at a subsistence level in a rural Mexican village. Pedro Martínez, the head of the household, is an older generation Mexican Indian who, within his lifetime, has changed from an Indian to a *mestizo* way of life. He now speaks Spanish rather than his native Nahuatl. At one time, he was active in village politics. He has undergone many personal uncertainties which, however, have complicated his basic quest for a purpose in life. Emotional conflicts have exacerbated the problems of political identification which afflict those caught in the midst of cultural change. Pedro's life has been a search for ideals and causes with which to identify: Catholicism, *Zapatismo*, village politics, education and religious evangelism. He tried to find identity in them all but because of fear of the world about him he was unable to integrate these symbols effectively into his life. Like most peasants Pedro needs guidance; he is fatalistic, suspicious and concrete-minded. He stays on the fringe of politics or out of it completely.

Pedro's first contact with the national political life was by fighting in the Revolution of 1910. In the 1920's following the Revolution, Pedro returned to his village of Azteca and became active in village politics. The people, still filled with the spirit of the revolution, formed community action committees to help improve the welfare of the village. Streets were paved and fountains were built. Eventually, however, the commitees came into conflict with the old caciques who still held considerable power in the village. Peaceful politics turned to violent politics and Pedro, along with other community organizers, was forced to flee the village temporarily. Esperanza, Pedro's wife, did not approve of her husband's political activities. She wanted him alive and safe rather than politically successful. This is a common fear of lower class men and women in Mexico today who seek to challenge the powers of local or village political structures.

The people would say to me, "why does he keep mixing in politics? Now the children are alone, poor innocent ones, with nothing to eat. Tell your husband he has nothing to win by it, only jail sentences and his family's ruin. He might even get killed. They are being used as instruments; the politicians make promises and they stupidly follow. The politicians enter it because they have enough to eat, but the others have nothing; they are poor and ruined."[17]

Pedro after being jailed twice and having his life threatened, suddenly came to the "realization" that those who were not mixed up in politics were indeed the very ones who lived peacefully. He vowed that he was through with politics and would spend the rest of his life as an ordinary citizen. He had become disillusioned once again. He was a part of the alienated mass, but safely so.

The family life of the Martínez' reflects a common Mexican pattern of acquiescence in authoritarianism. Pedro's contacts with his children are very reserved and characterized by a considerable social distance. In order to gain a measure of security, Pedro maintains a relationship of fear and respect between his wife and children and himself. This relationship is especially significant in the father-son relations of the Martínez family. It is similar to the awe he feels toward his government. There are many Pedros in today's Mexico and their burgeoning number increasingly threatens to undermine the status quo.

[17] Oscar Lewis, *Pedro Martínez* (New York: Vintage Books, 1964), p. 159.

In the book *The Children of Sánchez*, Lewis examined a poor urban family in Mexico City. Jesús Sánchez and his four children Manuel, Roberto, Consuelo and Marta live in a slum known as Casa Grande. The urban environment is very different from the rural one of Pedro Martínez but most of the basic rural values are carried into the city by the migratory peasants. In many cases the traditional culture of the peasants is dramatized by its conflict with some of the more modern values of an urban culture. The large family which may have limited feasibility in the countryside is a socioeconomic disaster in a Mexican City slum. According to Lewis the urban milieu is marked by such attitudes as "a strong orientation toward the present time with little ability to defer gratification and plan for the future, a sense of resignation and fatalism based upon the realities of their difficult life situation, a belief in male superiority which reaches its crystallization in *machismo*, or the cult of masculinity, a corresponding martyr complex among women and a high tolerance for psychological pathology of all sorts."[18]

The authoritarian trait is often just as dominant in the urban environment as it is in the rural. Jesús rules over his family with an iron fist. The fear and respect that he demands and the effect of this on his children is well illustrated by a portion of Manuel's monologue:

Whenever I tried to speak out to my father, something stopped me. With others I had more than enough words. But with him something formed in my throat and didn't let me speak. I don't know whether it was profound respect I felt for him or whether it was fear. Perhaps that is why I preferred to live my life apart from my father, and from the rest of my family, too. There was a gulf between us, a disunity, and although I respected them, and was hurt to see what was happening to them, I shut myself off.[19]

In Casa Grande about a fourth of the families were related by blood ties and about a fourth by marriages and compaternity (the extended family). It is around these primary groupings that most interpersonal relations are formed. While the children seem to have some sense of community and form friendships and gangs, the adults tend to "go their own way" and maintain their own privacy. Visiting other families is not common among adults, and intimate contacts are generally made only with relatives and special friends. The importance

18 Ibid., p. xxvi–xxvii.
19 Ibid., p. 34.

that is placed on distrust is illustrated by the advice that Jesús' father gave to him on his death bed.

When I came, my father was still alive, and I saw him die. He told me "I'm not leaving you anything, but I will give you a piece of advice. Don't get mixed up with friends. It's better to go your own way alone." And that's what I have done all my life.[20]

As far as direct contact with the political system and attitudes concerning politics, there is very little among the Children of Sanchez. The poor urban Mexican is concerned more with where his next meal is coming from than with the functioning of the political system. Jesús has little knowledge of or use for politics.

I don't know potatoes about politics. I read one or two paragraphs in the newspapers, but I don't take it seriously. Nothing in the news is important to me. A few days ago I read something about the leftists. But I don't know what is the left and what is the right, or what is Communism. I am interested in only one thing . . . to get money to cover my expenses and to see that my family is more or less well.[21]

Unfortunately for today's Mexico, the attitudes of Jesús tell much of the picture of political alienation that separates the masses from the ruling elites. The imperative for keeping one's stomach full has, in the past, kept much potential alienation from being translated into dysfunctional anomic behavior. Hungry peasants and slum dwellers simply cannot sustain themselves long in a major riot or demonstration against a powerfully entrenched status quo. Yet, the culture of poverty looms menacingly in the background of Mexico's contemporary political life as the student disorders of 1968 so well demonstrated. In attitudenal terms, Oscar Lewis has summarized the case well:

A critical attitude toward some of the values and institutions of the dominant classes, hatred of the police, mistrust of government, and a cynicism which extends even to the Church gives the culture of poverty a counter quality and a potential for being used in political movements aimed against the existing social order.[22]

[20] Ibid., p. 6.

[21] Ibid., p. 424.

[22] Oscar Lewis, *The Children of Sánchez* (New York: Random House, 1961), p. xxvii.

Inescapably, there is an incipient breach among rulers and followers which poses the most critical political crisis which the Revolutionary system has yet had to face. The socioeconomic plight of the Mexican masses figures prominently in the direction from which change will come and, if it does, will endure. Behind all of this is a basic value anomaly. That too must be resolved. If it is not, the Mexican masses will increasingly begin to disagree with Jesús Sánchez; they will and are beginning to care more about politics.

The tragedy of today's Mexico is that people like Jesús Sánchez have existed for decades and their numbers continue to multiply. Mexico's own humanist intellectuals have frequently echoed their cause. One distinguished voice among the many was Rodolfo Usigli who, as early as 1937, expressed what is probably the psychological synopsis which explains much of the value crisis facing Mexican political life in the twentieth century. Usigli created in his play *El gesticulador* a history professor, César Rubio, whose namesake was a famous Revolutionary general believed to have died under mysterious circumstances years before. A naïve American historian gave César the notion of pretending that he himself was the famed hero still living in a self imposed exile. At one point the Mexican professor, caught up in his own greed for power, is forced to explain this impersonation to members of his own family:

Todo el mundo aquí vive de apariencias, de gestos, Yo he dicho que soy el otro César Rubio . . . a quién perjudica eso? Mira a los que llevan águila de general sin haber peleado en una batalla; a los que se dicen amigos del pueblo y lo roban; a los demagogos que agitan a los obreros y los llaman camaradas sin haber trabajado en su vida con sus manos; a los profesores que no saben enseñar, a los estudiantes que no estudian. . . .[23]

Everyone here lives by appearances, by gestures. I have said that I am the other César Rubio. . . . who is hurt by this? Look at those who wear the general's eagle having never fought a battle; at those who call themselves friends of the people but who rob them just the same; at the demagogues who stir up the workers and who call them comrades having never worked with their hands; at the professors who do not know how to teach and the students who do not study. . . .

Seen through the eyes of a native Mexican humanist as quoted above, the North American scholar is able to grasp important clues

---

[23] Rodolfo Usigli, *El gesticulador* (New York: Appleton-Century-Crofts, 1963 edition (first published 1937), p. 46.

to the psychological nub of Mexico's political dilemma. It is a statement of an ominous behavioral norm, one that threatens now as it did during the earlier decades of the revolutionary system's formation when it was written. Importantly, Usigli's voice was raised against officialdom at a time when the Cárdenas era reforms were supposed to be carrying Mexico toward the "modernizing" goals of political socialization and administrative accountability. Usigli's voice was not alone.

The novelist J. Rubén Romero in his work *La vida inútil de Pito Pérez*, 1938, captured more of the political drift that Mexico would be taking. The life of Pito Pérez is one of cynical contempt for the "paper triumphs" of Mexican politics:

Pobres de los pobres! Yo les aconsejo que respeten siempre la ley, y que la cumplan, pero que se orinen en sus representantes.[24]

Poor poor people! I advise them to always respect the law, and to obey it, but that they should urinate on their representatives.

It also reveals the hopeless plight, then in the 1930's as today in the 1970's, of the individual before an omnipotent state:

Repórtese usted, Pito Pérez, y ni en la hora de su muerte se atreva a opinar en contra del Supremo Gobierno—que no se equivoca nunca—porque todo el rigor de la ley caerá sobre su cabeza. Además, pondría usted en peligro la salvación de su alma.[25]

Report, Pito Perez, and do not dare even on your death bed to speak against the government—which is never in the wrong—because all the force of the law will descend upon you. Besides, you could put yourself in danger of losing the salvation of your soul.

Thus you have the aesthetic dimension of the many visions of Mexican political life. That the aesthetic has more in common with the pejorative than with the honorific is a fact that will not have escaped the reader. Within the esoteric democratic system there are cer-

[24] J. Rubén Romero, *La vida inútil de Pito Pérez* (México: Editorial Porrua, 1969 edition), p. 86.

[25] Ibid., p. 227.

tain structural features which explain the prevalence of such political attitudes in Mexico today. We will next examine some of those features.[26]

[26] In the background of any consideration of attitudes in Mexico one must remember that her political ideologues do not enjoy legitimate freedom of the press. Newsprint is government controlled and a hostile journal can be threatened or suppressed by cutting its access to paper. The journal *Por Que* has been especially hard hit by this tactic during recent years.

3
The Structure of Mexico's Esoteric Democratic System

Political power in Mexico is exercised via a pyramid-shaped hierarchy of command at whose apex stands the President of the Republic. Professor Frank Brandenburg in an especially revealing chapter has termed the presidency and its subordinate system the "Liberal Machiavellian."[1] He writes:

Dictatorship of the Diaz variety has slowly given way to six-year authoritarianism of the Revolutionary variety, directed by executives of relatively liberal mold dedicated to the broad lines of the Revolutionary Creed. Within the Mexican milieu, the political sun rises and sets every six years on the presidency, and in identical cycles on gubernatorial offices. Mexicans avoid personal dictatorship by retiring their dictators every six years.[2]

Ostensibly a benevolent authoritarian, the President of the Republic must still rely upon an extensive security network for the exercise of intelligence functions and for applying coercive sanctions. The President has at his disposal a well-trained and disciplined army and a secret police organization whose services can, and frequently are, invoked when needed (see Chapter 5). In this chapter we will consider only those instruments of power that may be considered political (in the sense of nonviolent) aspects of the human process whereby events are influenced and values allocated. We will examine both the formal

---

[1] Frank Brandenburg, *The Making of Modern Mexico* (Englewood Cliffs: Prentice-Hall, 1964), pp. 141–165.

[2] Ibid., p. 141.

structure of power and some of the informal relationships that give it meaning.

There is some disagreement among both Mexican and North American scholars as to just how the presidential succession is accomplished in Mexico. Brandenburg's excellent study contains a series of steps that seem to have taken place in the past. One thing is very clear: the incumbent president has much to say about his successor who in turn controls the vast machinery that is the revolutionary coalition.

PRI: The Structure of the Dominant Class

During the decade of the 1960's the *Partido Revolucionario Institucional* had ceased to be a distinct political party that could be treated analytically as a homogeneous ideological group. It was more accurate to call PRI an *organized dominant class*, having at its apex an official family or coterie of privileged elites. At its base PRI had some ten million members and many more sympathizers and fair weather friends. Party stalwarts fanned out their influence, patronage, and coercion via a complicated network of organizational linkages which can be called the formal structure of esoteric democracy in Mexico. Beneath President Díaz Ordaz in the political hierarchy was an organism known as CEN (*Comité Ejecutivo Nacional*). Presiding over CEN was Alfonso Martínez Domínguez who, beginning in 1968, had a direct wire to the Presidency of the Republic. He would not make the mistake of Carlos A. Madrazo and attempt to steer an independent course; nor would he forget the dictum "*el que se separa o aspira a hacer política por su cuenta, corre el peligro de degollarse en un suicidio inútil*" (he who departs or seeks an independent political course runs the risk of killing himself in a useless suicide).

I have embraced the terms *organized dominant class* to characterize and conceptualize the PRI. To view the PRI as a single monolith glosses over a legion of organisms, structures, arenas, and even certain defiantly independent participant movements, that cluster, often precariously, under the ever expanding revolutionary aegis. That PRI has been able to command as many loyalties for over half a century and with so relatively few defections is a remarkable accomplishment in itself. It is possible for workers and peasants to move up (and down) the socioeconomic hierarchy via participation in the PRI. If one stays in good graces with his benefactors he may greatly improve his material circumstances.

Most Latin American nations offer certain avenues of succor and reward but what is strikingly unique about Mexico is the breadth of coverage and the popular availability of such participatory incentive. The PRI has created a "trickle up and trickle down" system whose benefits are shared on a remarkably wide basis (relative to most Latin American political systems). Whether Mexico's political system can generate sufficient quantities of such material rewards to forestall a repetition of the chaos of the summer of 1968 is yet another question.

There is impressive evidence that PRI dominated governments are increasingly unable to meet the socioeconomic demands of a population now nearing the fifty million mark in a nation already unable to feed at least thirty percent of its population in a satisfactory (by World Health Organization standards) way. What will this pressure do to the PRI? Already it has forced many of its former affiliates into the ranks (and often reluctantly) of *Acción Nacional* and the *Partido Popular Socialista*. More critical are the numbers of *priista* (PRI followers) Mexicans who now lend their bodies and voices to the radical and violence-prone movements which will be discussed in a later chapter. There is a crisis of legitimacy facing the PRI and it is one to which Alfonso Martínez Domínguez and his successors will be forced to assign a high priority or face certain disaster. Mexico's PRI faces a decade of severe test in the 1970's. Let us consider here the formal organisms it has created to perpetuate itself as a dominant class and, hopefully, to guide Mexico toward a progressive future.

Since 1946 when the old PRM of Lázaro Cárdenas was renamed PRI there has been a continuing domination of the party by the Presidency of the Republic. However in formal terms the National Assembly is the most authoritative collective organ of the party. Its primary function is the selection of candidates for President of the Republic. The National Assembly is charged with creating rules for membership and conduct and has a lesser function of ratifying occasional policy stands that the party wishes to express outside of the congress.

Also, the National Assembly ratifies the party president who presides over the CEN. A second national organ of the PRI is its National

Council or Grand Commission. This body is intended to represent the party organizations of the twenty-nine states and gives representation to special delegates selected from each of PRI's basic membership sectors, labor, agrarian, and popular. The National Council differs from the National Assembly in that it represents regional and functional groups while the latter is meant to represent the people, albeit on a state-by-state basis. Finally, there is the PRI's National Executive Committee (CEN) which, along with the National Council, is expected to perform a sort of watchdog function on an interim basis between meetings of the National Assembly. The CEN exercises influence in state party affairs via the National Council and it is this nexus that often gives the PRI the appearance of a tightly knit monolith.

The CEN is clearly the most powerful of the three national organs of the PRI and is instrumental in the overall party control exercised by the President of the Republic. The CEN convokes meetings of the National Assembly and controls the admission of delegates to such meetings. The description which follows of the succession from Lauro Ortega to Martínez Domínguez as CEN president would benefit from a more exact knowledge of delegate selection to the special National Assembly convocation in 1968, but these facts tread intimately upon the informal vestiges of PRI power and are hard to ascertain on a precise basis. Among the functions that go to make Martínez Domínguez and his successors among Mexico's most powerful men are the following CEN prerogatives: party discipline on a personal and group basis, special investigations, control over state and municipal party-nominating conventions, power to intervene in the affairs of state and municipal party organizations including the power to remove members of these organizations (the power to remove elected state and local officials belongs formally to the President of the Republic), and responsibility for propaganda and recruitment to expand PRI ranks and socialize the people politically into PRI participation. In the above mentioned list of powers, the control over the municipal party organizations became critical in 1965 when CEN president Carlos A. Madrazo campaigned for local party primaries in which the choice of party delegates and candidates for public office would be democratized and not dictated from above as had been traditional throughout the PRI. Madrazo, in effect, sought to weaken the powerful CEN over which he presided and, as we saw earlier, he was fired for this by President Diaz Ordaz late in 1965.

The CEN president calls meetings of that body along with those of the National Council and is the presiding officer in each case. He controls the CEN budget (which is known to be considerable) and names, with approval of the National Assembly, a general secretary for the party. This subsidiary, although powerful, position was one of the "plums" which Lauro Ortega reputedly offered to Martínez Domínguez in return for the latter's withdrawal from the race for the presidency of the CEN in 1968. The general secretary has control over important channels of information and his nomination is an important patronage device for the president of the CEN. There are seven members of the CEN: president, general secretary, and secretaries for agrarian affairs, labor, popular action, political action representing the national Senate, and political action representing the national Chamber of Deputies. Key posts in the CEN are those of labor, agrarian affairs and popular action which usually are held respectively by top leaders of the PRI's labor sector (CTM), its agrarian sector (CNC), and the popular sector (CNOP). Whereas the primary function of the National Assembly (perhaps in a ritual sense) is the representation of the people, and that of the National Council is representation of local and regional party organizations, the primary function of the CEN is representation of the PRI's functional sectors (discussed below) and the PRI's congressional delegation. Since CEN virtually controls the National Council, its powers over the grass roots are enhanced significantly. Clearly, the CEN stands at the apex of Mexican *priista* power and pays homage only to the Presidency of the Republic itself.

Central to the power of the CEN is its control over finances which are destined for informational (propaganda) and educational functions and which may be used to promote individual candidacies of PRI leaders in the various states and localities. It is said that the CEN funds come largely from dues-paying members of the rank and file but informed sources have told this writer that generous subventions come from the federal government. Withholding of these monies prefaced the downfall of CEN president Carlos A. Madrazo's campaign for democratization of local elections. This had the side effect of forcing the CEN president to rely more heavily upon state and local membership contributions which, in turn, was sure to lead to friction between the CEN and its regional affiliates.

With its own funds CEN is able to assist candidates for office in the poorer districts where local sources of financing may be severely limited. This often has a curious side effect that is unfavorable to opposition parties and is cleverly exploited by the PRI, namely, the opposition is often forced to choose a wealthy candidate who can afford to put up a campaign against the local *priista* who enjoys the support of "foreign" funds. This has produced an especially anomalous position for the opposition left whose candidates are frequently taunted as rich marxists. An example of this same dilemma but on the right of the opposition spectrum is the PAN deputy from Celaya, Guanajuato, Ricardo Chaurand Concha, who is known to be several times a millionaire and is one of few persons living in that relatively poor community whose financial strength would allow him to mount an election campaign against the PRI. Skillfully, thus, PRI often forces its opposition into the image of a privileged elite while PRI masquerades as a "movement of the people." The financial prerogatives of the CEN are of critical importance in this process. The rules within which these prerogatives can be exercised are fluid and when written are still subject to liberal interpretation.

Surrounding the party structure discussed above, the the three broad membership sectors of the PRI: labor, agrarian, and popular. The labor sector is integrated around the giant CTM or Mexican Workers Confederation, itself divided into regional and local components. The CTM may be considered a functional group specializing in organizing and promoting the cause of labor. Frequently, labor leaders hold at the same time a party office and an elective public office. Such an arrangement makes possible attractive opportunities for duplication of reward and serves the cause of intra-party discipline, especially at the state and local levels. The CTM has a long tradition of involvement at all levels of Mexican politics. Its roots go back to the original CROM (Regional Confederation of Mexican Workers) founded during the Calles period of the 1920's by Luis Morones. The CTM received international stimulus and recognition when its general secretary, the marxist intellectual, Vicente Lombardo Toledano, became instrumental in the creation of the Latin American Workers Confederation CTAL in 1938. Labor disputes have recurred and renegade groups have splintered away, but the CTM continues to be the most powerful voice of organized labor in Mexico today and, as such, is a major bulwark of the PRI. During the 1960's the CTM sought to extend its influence by drawing about itself a number of splinter unions in a formation known as BUO, the United Workers

Bloc. BUO was opposed by the CROC (a workers central that is associated with, but less tightly wed to, the PRI) and a number of other splinter unions that grouped together to form the CNTM, National Confederation of Mexican Workers.

Under the regime of President Lázaro Cárdenas (1934–40), the second basic sector of functional membership was created within the PRI. The agrarian sector took shape around the CNC or National Confederation of Farmers and Peasants. Organizationally, the CNC is easily as complex as the labor sector with its grass roots support originating in a myriad of peasant and rural labor leagues that are frequently integrated with the state farm program. The CNC is charged with mobilization of rural support for the PRI and represents itself as a defender of the interests of rural folk vis-à-vis the government and large private landholders. That it has been unsuccessful in the last mentioned role is evidenced by the rise of anomic protest movements of rural farmers and peasants against governmental and private land tenure patterns. Movements such as the UGOCM of Jacinto López, whose squatter-invaders have invaded large landowner properties throughout northern Mexico, dramatize growing discontent within the official agrarian sector. Nevertheless, the CNC has made many Mexican peasants into something that they had never been historically, i.e., a political force to be reckoned with. Not unexpectedly, splinter movements have broken with the mother body. Even within the CNC, conflict has at times been severe. Witness the slaughter of some 40 cocoa workers near Acapulco in 1968 as a result of a conflict involving not only the agrarian sector but labor and members of the national congress as well. Formally at least the CNC is expected to represent its constituents before such organs of government as the Ejido Bank (intended to finance the agricultural development of the state farms) and the Department of Agrarian Affairs and Colonization, DAAC.

Padgett has written extensively on the capacity of the Mexican peasants, the state farm leagues, and groups of farmers to make themselves felt within the agrarian sector of the PRI[3] and of the corruption in local agrarian politics that frequently causes unrest about the countryside. In 1963 a new association of offshoot peasant leagues

[3] L. Vincent Padgett, *The Mexican Political System* (Boston: Houghton Mifflin Co., 1966), pp. 185–201.

was formed calling itself the Independent Peasant Confederation (CCI). At the time it claimed the titular leadership, often more pretended than real, of former president Lázaro Cárdenas (who opposed the formation at first) and since then has associated itself variously with the amorphous political group MLN (National Liberation Movement). At the moment of this writing CCI is felt to be seriously divided and in search of unifying leadership. It is questionable whether PRI dominated governments will continue to tolerate a major threat to their official agrarian sector (i.e. the CNC) should CCI acquire real power and take a genuinely competitive stance.

The final and perhaps most amorphous sector of the PRI is the popular sector whose principal integrating device is the CNOP, National Confederation of Popular Organizations. Whereas in the cases of the labor and agrarian sectors there is a legally prescribed relationship and control between the national government and those sectoral organizations, the CNOP has been allowed to develop with relative independence since the group was founded in 1943. (PRI's former military sector was abolished in 1944 and an effort was made to blend its membership with the newly created CNOP). Nearly all Mexican communities have a municipal CNOP affiliate that participates in a statewide league and ultimately with a national organization. Like the labor and agrarian sectors, CNOP is represented on the PRI's CEN via the secretary for popular action. Also attached to CNOP are organizations of small private farmers small businessmen, professional and social organizations, skilled workers (not usually affiliated with CTM or its components), teachers and public service employees. The merger of such diverse groupings gives CNOP its heterogeneous character. This "umbrella" experiment has worked well and relatively few splinter movements have occurred to seriously challenge CNOP leadership and hegemony. Indeed, in recent decades, CNOP has tended to grow in power and prestige while the labor and agrarian sectors were experiencing discord. CNOP claims the federal bureaucrats union, FSTSE (Federation of Syndicates of Workers in the Service of the State), and is believed to command the allegiance of most of Mexico's organized teachers and professors. This gives CNOP an intellectual and middle-class aura that is conspicuously absent in the other sectors. Lacking a specific functional orientation that is directly rooted in a policy area (e.g. such as labor or agrarian affairs), the CNOP is first and foremost a political movement and as such is one of the principal support-mobilizing arms of the PRI. CNOP banners are conspicuously displayed at all official party celebrations, often in greater abundance than those of other sectors. Some observers of Mexican officialdom comment that CNOP holds the potential for becoming a separate political party were it not so closely wed to PRI and therefore subservient to it.

Two cardinal facts distinguish the CNOP from the other sectoral nucleus groups. First, because unlike the labor and agrarian sectors, membership in the CNOP or its subdivisions is not controlled by federal law, its members must be continually courted and cajoled into allegiance. This gives a premium to the political skills of the CNOP leadership and creates pressures for efficiency and effectiveness that often are missing in the other sectors. Second, because of the relatively high politicization of the CNOP (via its key role in the CEN) it has become a recruiting ground for high public office at the ministerial and congressional levels. Of all three sectors, CNOP probably has the greatest access to the top levels of planning and decision-making in the federal government. The following story of Alfonso Martínez Domínguez' rise to the presidency of the CEN tends to support this contention.

The Camarilla or Political Clique

Inside the auditorium there was scarcely room for a hatpin to be squeezed into an aisle, and much less so for additional spectators to the unveiling of Mexico's newest "grey eminence." It was 1968 and the principal national organ of the PRI, the National Assembly, had just proclaimed a new successor to the presidency of the party's executive organ known as CEN, the National Executive Committee. The president of this body is considered to be the second most powerful man within the PRI monolith and is probably one of the most influential figures throughout the republic. Lauro Ortega was the outgoing provisional president of the CEN. He succeeded Carlos A. Madrazo who had been fired by President Díaz Ordaz in 1966. Ortega smiled weakly as he prepared to surrender his shortlived power to the man who would replace him the following day. Fresh in his ears were the plaudits of the previous day's demonstrations by youth groups of the PRI's Revolutionary Youth Movement, seeking to assuage through a kind of planned effervescence the sorrow that one must feel when a temporary political power fails to transform itself into a permanent one.

Ortega's close friend, the labor leader Fidel Velásquez, had failed to keep Ortega at the head of the CEN. Ironically, one of Velásquez' own labor rivals, Francisco Pérez Ríos of the electrical workers, had placed in nomination the name of the man who would become the new CEN president. That man was Alfonso Martínez Domínguez. He had been a compromise candidate agreed upon via the National Assembly's informal power mechanisms. Martínez Domínguez' formal nomination went unchallenged (as had also been agreed) and then began the formal rituals of acclamation. The PRI had unveiled a new strongman.

For many years Alfonso Martínez Domínguez had cultivated his own *camarilla* or political clique from which the political roots of national power could spring. His antecedents tell much of the story of how a competent politician may gain ascendency within the revolutionary coalition. For many years Martínez Domínguez was an obscure politician holding varying bureaucratic appointments at lower echelons in the government and in the PRI. Here it is critical to state that government positions frequently go to persons whose principal role is political and limited to the PRI, and who rarely are expected to perform in a bureaucratic role although they are ostensibly being paid to do so (a latinized version of the Anglo-American sinecure). Martínez Domínguez first gained national attention as part of the political clique of Lic. Adolfo López Mateos who was a leader of the public bureaucrats union FSTSE in the early 1950's. Following the inauguration of Adolfo Ruiz Cortínez as President of the Republic in 1952, López Mateos was named Secretary of Labor and all the members of his clique including Martínez Domínguez were generously rewarded with government sinecures. When López Mateos became President of the Republic in 1958 Alfonso Martínez Domínguez was accelerated abruptly to the prestigeful position of Secretary General of the CNOP (*Confederación Nacional de Organizaciones Populares*), one of the most powerful mainstays of the PRI.

At this point it is correct to say that Alfonso Martínez Domínguez had graduated from membership in the clique of López Mateos and began to form one of his own. Once in command of the CNOP his chief dedication was the placing of his own people in key positions throughout the party and governmental structures. One of these appointments was Pedro Luis Bartilotti, a talented and aggressive right hand man of Martínez Domínguez. With the support of the people he had placed in key positions, the political star of Martínez Domínguez continued to grow, first as a national deputy under the new regime of President Díaz Ordaz and shortly thereafter as floor leader of the PRI delegation in the Chamber of Deputies, a position considered to be equivalent to cabinet membership. From there Martínez Domínguez built an even greater base of power by promoting the loyal Pedro Luis Bartilotti to the rank of federal deputy (ostensibly via the electoral process but one in which nomination is tantamount to winning) and ultimately to coveted membership on the National Executive Committee CEN.

The political trajectory of Alfonso Martínez Domínguez was calculated and progressively upward, conspicuously unsullied by the scars and smears of public scandal or malfeasance of duty. His story exemplifies one of the keys to *personal political power* in Mexico: he had cultivated a faithful coterie of friends who stuck by him through the recurring uncertainties of the political game in which positions and offers were bartered and exchanged like grab bag prizes. Martínez Domínguez had even been offered the secretariat of the party by Lauro Ortega in exchange for the latter's continuation as head of the CEN (or so this author was informed by usually reliable sources). But surrender to the then provisional president of the CEN would have severely restrained Martínez Domínguez from achieving future mobility so he made the calculated risk of holding out for all or nothing within the National Assembly. This was a considerable gamble because Lauro Ortega, the principal challenger, enjoyed the powerful support of labor leader Fidel Velázquez. It was said that if Lauro Ortega had convened the special session of the National Assembly one year earlier he might have been able to command a sufficient majority to win the informal power struggle, but this was impossible for reasons of party discipline. By delaying the National Assembly, the Martínez Domínguez clique had time to consolidate its forces and recruit external support for their chief. When the informal power struggle had been resolved, staff members of the Presidency of the Republic began to "leak out" rumors of a great wave of popular support for Martínez Domínguez and that the CNOP leadership had gone to his side. This was a typical, and fruitful, machination of political power within the higher echelon of the revolutionary coalition.

Alfonso Martínez Domínguez assumed the reins of the PRI at a time when the entire revolutionary party structure was suffering from multiple ailments: the desertion of the intellectuals, the abandonment of the young, and the increasing alienation of patriotic egalitarian citizen groups who saw PRI as an exclusive, albeit gigantic club, that formed an avenue toward elite privilege. When the National Assembly met in 1968, PRI had two recent thorns in its side: the municipal victories of the opposition party PAN in Hermosillo (Sonora) and Mérida (Yucatan), both of which dramatized the popular decline of confidence in the PRI as a mechanism for articulating demands for change. The PRI was still a party open to workers and peasants as Martínez Domínguez took command. The officially sponsored CTM and CNC were effectively organized to give the common masses a broad appearance of political belonging. Martínez Domínguez told the Assembly that the PRI would continue to oppose the privileged status of elites (despite the obvious fact that he himself belonged to one). But he had no plan for the burgeoning middle class, estimated at around thirty percent in 1968, that was producing leaders of satellite movements opposed to the PRI. This tendency toward atrophy and related anomic political reactions against PRI would constitute the greatest challenge of Martínez Domínguez' political career.[4]

The *camarilla* or political clique is central to understanding the creation, maintenance, and transfer of power within Mexico's PRI. The case of Martínez Domínguez is one of thousands whose mosaic of linkages constitutes the broad network of power which is the PRI. There is, of course, a formal power structure in terms of those who have the ability to allocate values, influence events, and bring to bear a near monopoly of coercive pressure upon those who *appear* to be violating formal dicta for political behavior. The formal structure operates, or breaks down, according to the functioning of the political brotherhoods that lie at the heart of Mexico's esoteric democracy. If Mexico differs from countries outside the Latin American political tradition in this respect, it is probably because in the Anglo-American tradition it is probable that formal rules serve to channel and coerce political behavior; whereas, in Mexico's esoteric democracy the in-

---

[4] The description of the succession to Martínez Domínguez and of his career development is based on confidential interviews by the author.

formal structures are likely to take priority over legal strictures. Throughout the development of the contemporary Mexican political system, the creation of pressure groups of one sort or another has been crucial to the exercise of power. Whether we refer to them in English as cliques or brotherhoods is unimportant if it is understood that we refer to tightly knit nuclei of loyalty and influence, usually founded about the power of a given individual whose ability to control behavior and allocate rewards makes him the catalyst which gives the group a singularity of purpose, and an informal web that can perhaps be called a latent structure.

The beginnings of Mexico's political life may be traced to the gigantic "super-camarilla" that formed around first the towering figure of Plutarco Elías Calles and second his intended protégé Lázaro Cárdenas del Río. From his villa in Cuernavaca Calles controlled the destinies of Mexican politics for over ten years, both from within and from outside the presidency. This he accomplished by means of a well "heeled" brotherhood of patronage and influence. Violent coercion was always a useful tool of "recourse." In the shadow of the relatively uncultured but charismatic personality of General Calles a series of lesser, but potentially great, personalities was nurtured: Emilio Portes Gil, Abelardo Rodríguez, Pascual Ortiz Rubio, and Lázaro Cárdenas del Río . . . all became presidents of Mexico, and all were from the original clique of Plutarco Elías Calles.

During the provisional presidency of Emilio Portes Gil (1928–1929) the PNR, (*Partido Nacional Revolucionario*), emerged from the "super clique" of Calles and was the precursor of today's PRI. Indeed, to some extent this clique was itself the genesis of the contemporary Mexican political system. President Portes Gil acted early in his term to make the PNR an official party, thereby drawing party and government apparatus tightly together. According to the Mexican historian Jorge Vera Estañol it was Portes Gil who ordered that all public employees be deducted the equivalent of one week's pay in order to support the new political organization.[5] Still, the man who controlled the purse and pulled the strings of power in Mexico was Calles. Portes Gil admits as much in his book *Quince años de política mexicana* with this self quotation: "General, I want us to speak frankly as always. I realize, as does everyone in the country, that it is you who resolves

[5] Jorge Vera Estañol, *La revolución mexicana* (Mexico: Editorial Porrúa, 1957), p. 630.

the problems of government. I want you to hear me for a few moments so that I may tell you how I think and feel. That is why I came to see you."[6]

Then Lázaro Cárdenas joined the brotherhood. At the onset of the Revolution in 1910 he had been first a follower of Zapata, then of Pancho Villa, and later supported Carranza. In 1920 he found a marriage of convenience with Calles and joined the "super clique." In 1933 Calles designated Cárdenas candidate of the PNR hoping to place another cooperative and obedient puppet in the Presidency. Calles did not know the private ambitions of Cárdenas. The latter began silently creating his own group out of the newer generations who saw their future success in terms of a new clique that would be free from the tutelage of the aging strong man from Cuernavaca. Mentor and protégé were destined to collide and when they did in 1936, it was the elder Calles who was expelled ignominiously from his land along with labor leader Luis Morones and other key figures of Calles' entourage. At this point a new and lasting rule of the Mexican political game was implanted: Mexicans do not follow ideas, nor movements; they follow men. From then on there would be no "super clique" that would be immune from challenge. Mexico's democracy would be esoteric, but among competing pressure groups there would still be a measure of democracy in the sense of freedom to compete for power. From Cárdenas to the present moment the competition among such groups has been a way of life in Mexican politics. *The nation's relative political stability, when compared with the experiences of other Latin American nations, is due in no small part to the institutionalization of this competitive process. Despite all the other limitations of the revolutionary coalition that are dwelt upon throughout this book, Mexico's esoteric democracy has been a gigantic success when viewed in comparative terms about the hemisphere.*

How do these political cliques operate. Already we have considered the example of how one was formed, i.e., the case of Alfonso Martínez Domínguez. The clique is a political brotherhood and it is also a political family, having multiple linkages and interdependencies with other subgroups of its ilk. These groups become a circular system in the sense of their competitive interaction with the revolu-

---

[6] Emilio Portes Gil, *Quince años de política mexicana* (México: Ed. Botas, 1954), p. 467.

tionary coalition (PRI). But within themselves they have an additional circular aspect. There is an original boss who normally will be someone with a known reputation for political and economic power. Following him, immediately below, are collaborating members of the inner circle who are tied to the boss for reasons of "political godfathership" or personal intimacy on a social or economic basis. Here, as in all political systems, the kinds of socioeconomic ties that form the bases of political power must be legion and practically unknowable. Later the group splits into two circles of intimacy which may multiply. Each of the circles extends its sphere of influences via the location of key persons in places of responsibility among the syndicates, the professional associations, and within the ranks of formal party organs that belong to and depend upon the PRI. As spheres of influence extend, a broader "subcircle" of influence comes into being and is held together by the common fabric of desire, on the part of individual ideologues, to better their station in life via the rewards that come from support of the next echelon upward. Surrounding them is a periphery of anomic and diverse groups which can hardly be called brotherhoods. They are the aspirant satellite groups which seek to become cliques; their membership is fluid as is the changing pattern of their ideologies. They are looking for attachment to a boss just as Alfonso Martínez Domínguez did in attaching himself to the clique of López Mateos.

Camarillas as Circles of Intimacy: The Spectrum of Influence

We have seen how the formal structure of the PRI is given impetus and meaning by the underlying informal system of *camarillas*. These groups sometimes become coalitions that constitute party wings in the face of major issues affecting the entire revolutionary coalition (like the municipal reform issue or the question of student violence). Internally, however, the quest for mobility is most likely to see these political cliques as relatively discrete actors within the more restricted sense of the term given earlier. This generalization applies not only to the formal party hierarchy (i.e. CEN, National Council, National Assembly, but also to the functional organizations that make up the three PRI membership sectors. Taking the party hierarchy and the sectoral organizations for the moment and grouping them under the general rubric revolutionary coalition, which is to say the PRI, it is possible to isolate the following as major cliques within the *internal spectrum of influence*: a) the Miguel Alemán clique frequently called the conservative "wing" of the PRI; and that of the late Lázaro Cárdenas frequently called the left wing of the PRI; b) between and beneath these two circles of intimacy are a range of cliques which cannot realistically be labelled according to the liberal-conservative continuum, but which function around the key personalities of Lic. Luis Echeverría, former Secretary of Interior, Lic. Emilio Martínez Manatou, Secretary of the Presidency of the Republic; Prof. Juan Gil Preciado, former governor of the state of Jalisco and Secretary of Agriculture; Lic. Antonio Ortiz Mena, Secretary of the Treasury; and Gen. Alfonso Corona del Rosal, Governor of the Federal District. Not surprisingly, each of these political figures was mentioned as the PRI candidate for the Presidency of the Republic who was to be unveiled in November, 1969. Aspiring neophytes who enter Mexico's political arena in search of upward socioeconomic mobility are, at least at the moment of this writing, well-advised to attach themselves to one of the above groups via the various *subcamarillas* which collectively go to make up broader circles of political intimacy.

Beyond the PRI hierarchy and its sectoral organizations there is an *external spectrum of influence*. Its circles of intimacy are legion and form a tangled mosaic that no serious scholar would attempt to describe exhaustively for the practical limitations of time and space. Let us consider several of the principal components of this external spectrum.

The Mexican press forms an influence component whose power to criticize, hence to curtail, is considerable in many cases. Probably the most influential press organ in the nation is the daily *Excelsior* which operates a number of smaller daily and weekly subpublications of its own. *Excelsior* is controlled by a *camarilla* to the left fringe of the PRI and in recent months has opposed the revolutionary coalition quite openly. Its leader is Julio Scherer García, director of *Excelsior* and a personal enemy of President Díaz Ordaz. Prior to 1964 *Excelsior* was the center of a more acquiescent brotherhood vis-à-vis the PRI. Another important press *camarilla* centers about the dedicated editor José Pagés Ilergo and his semiofficial weekly journal *Siempre*. This publication features a familiar series of names with each publication

(Mario Monteforte Toledo, Renato Leduc, Antonio Vargas Mac Donald, and many others) and often appears to be the opponent of PRI dominated regimes. Its slings and arrows are carefully directed, however, and the PRI usually comes off with a "respectable" chastisement. A favorite pastime of *Siempre* is the denegration and excoriation of all things "USA" and through the technique of making the PRI appear to champion the masses vis-à-vis the United States, the journal renders a valuable image-building service to the revolutionary coalition. Many fellow, and aspirant, ideologues of the Cárdenas circle of intimacy have made their reputations by way of the journalistic cult of "boss" Pagés, as the director of *Siempre* is commonly known.

Both *Excelsior* and *Siempre* constitute influence sets that are critical of the PRI but are not at war with it. Significantly, they fall to the revolutionary left of the spectrum of groups and influences attached to the PRI. I do not know of a single major press organ of the political right which both opposes the PRI and is, nevertheless, blessed by it. There are other opponents on the left which are barely tolerated by the PRI but without subsidy and with only the most fragile of blessings. Among these is the review *Sucesos*, which formerly opposed the PRI under the direction of Mario Menéndez Rodríguez, but which now receives a subsidy from the Cuban Embassy in Mexico City and often lauds PRI accomplishments, especially if they can be made to sound anti-North American.

Apart from the press cliques, the most prominent influence sets that impinge directly upon the exercise of governmental power are the consortiums of commerce and industry. Again, these power complexes belong to the external spectrum of influence, and merge with the various levels of the revolutionary coalition in a myriad of ways that defies exhaustive description. Prominent among these is the "Monterrey Group" centered in the capital city of Nuevo León which is a conservative, often reactionary, voice that cannot easily be ignored in Mexico City. The "Monterrey Group" has made its influence felt both within the PRI and at times via the opposition party PAN. Principal industrial components include much of the glass-producing industry, the automobile assembly plants, a number of iron and steel foundaries, and related commercial service firms. The "Monterrey Group" is known for its laissez faire capitalist orientation and opposition to government controls as well as to corporate state capitalism. In this regard many PRI sponsored enterprises such as PEMEX (*Petróleos*

Mexicanos) are anathema to the "Monterrey Group." Originally in 1939 the consortium that now constitutes the "Monterrey Group" sponsored PAN hoping to turn it into a puppet for its reactionary philosophy. But PAN was not that easily bought out, contrary to popular anecdotes told by supporters of Mexican officialdom, and the consortium turned to the right wing of the PRI, i.e. the *camarilla* Miguel Alemán. Beneath the often veiled blessing of this sector, the "Monterrey Group" built what is perhaps Mexico's best technical school, the Technological Institute of Monterrey, which, aside from its pedagogical function, often serves as a vehicle for bridging the gap between the right wing of the PRI and the far reactionary right which falls into the satellite system of opposition parties and out-groups.

The "Monterrey Group" is torn by this dilemma: much of its membership is opposed to the excessive state capitalism that the revolutionary coalition sponsors. But it cannot afford an open breach with officialdom because of its strong working relationships and socioeconomic ties with the PRI. The existence of officially-sponsored national chambers of commerce and industry (like CONCANACO and CONCAMIN) that are governed by federal law, and in which membership is obligatory for most businesses of any size at all, means that the "Monterrey Group" has obligations toward officialdom which it must satisfy whether it cares to do so or not. It is rumored that discontent among the "Monterrey Group" has sponsored such clandestine terrorist organizations as MURO (*Movimiento Universitario de Renovadora Orientación*) and financed the journal *Resumen*, nationally known for its Social Darwinist orientation.

An exhaustive discussion of the spectrum of political influence groups and *camarillas* that surround the PRI would be impossible. The press cliques of the left and the economic ones of the right mentioned above, serve only to illustrate the ties of influence between officialdom and the satellite system of groups that are basically external to the revolutionary coalition. One could attempt to conceptualize the Mexican spectrum of political influence in terms of three partially overlapping circles representing a spectrum of left to right with PRI holding down the ideological center. Over this schema one would have to superimpose the national university UNAM, its components, and the legion of private and state schools which make up Mexico's system of higher education, in itself a giant spawning ground for these political cliques.

Intercepting the Spectrum of Influence: An Anecdote

Lic. Manuel de la Isla has helped me to construct an anecdote, or if you prefer, a simulation, of the road to power within the revolutionary coalition for one who is a relative unknown. This is a true story and we have omitted names for reasons that should be obvious to the reader. The case is one of a young Mexican who aspires to a career in his country's political life. Like many Mexicans he is basically supportive of the revolutionary coalition although he is aware of many of its failings. As they do to most Mexicans, the accoutrements of a political career seem attractive to our neophyte, especially money, power, public honors, and social deference. But the young man lacks family or primary group ties on which to base his rise to fame; he needs a formula. Here, then, is a likely series of steps that he must follow to arrive at his goal.

1) He should join the PRI. This is indispensable.

2) He must participate in party affairs, beginning at the "grass roots" level, and above all he must attach himself to the coat tails of some prominent politician whose orbit of success is already firmly established.

3) In making this attachment he will have joined a clique. This is a point of some considerable risk for should the clique fail to grow in power and wealth our young aspirant will have to seek admission to another clique and this could be both embarassing and costly. The cliques combat each other and the young man and his colleagues must become vehement loyalists to the clique and its leader if they are to confront their competition. The leader's cause becomes that of the group.

4) Once a final choice of clique is made, the young political hopeful must direct himself to carrying out a legion of mundane and highly pedestrian tasks for his group and for the PRI at large, e.g., arranging youth meetings, distributing propaganda, answering correspondence, all of which can be done in his spare time and without pay. Our political neophyte has yet to be permitted "to live from his politics."

5) If our hypothetical candidate is intelligent, capable and performs his tasks well, his immediate boss will most likely reward him

with a better spot, perhaps that of private secretary to a deputy who belongs to the same clique. This will be a full time paid job in which the neophyte will learn how to resolve minor political problems and will undertake special missions about the Republic in connection with electoral plans and propaganda. He will undoubtedly be handed the task of writing minor political speeches, and in general he will have become "initiated" into Mexican politics.

6) Having shown promise in this role for several years the young politician (probably living on a salary of around 200 dollars per month) will naturally aspire to greater position; that, after all, was why he entered the arena in the first place. At this point he must pass successfully the tortuous throes of a crucial series of ordeals; he must "keep himself on ice" cautiously and patiently; he must perform a range of trying but essential ritual functions varying from political breakfasts to greeting party dignitaries, all the while molding an image favorable to his "silent candidacy" for greater fame and higher place. Playing this game skillfully results in his being elevated to the role of Secretary for Political Action within the Youth Committee of the PRI for the Federal District. This is a test of his political "sensitivity" and an important one. Unfortunately, this position is only honorific, not remunerative, and he must arrange another salary to sustain himself. This, he finds, can be accomplished by means of a special sinecure which is little more than a fake salary paid to our young politician for work he does not do in an office that he seldom or never visits. This is not unusual, for among the "in-group" of the Revolutionary Coalition (PRI) there are many persons who receive five or six sinecures of this sort. In this way the PRI can subsidize its political figures with salaries from the public budget while leaving them maximum freedom to work full time for the party.

7) As Secretary of Political Action in the Youth Committee our young man performs well and wins for his clique certain honors that qualify him for two more fake salaries and the promise of more to come.

8) At this juncture the young politician has become somewhat "seasoned" and, feeling secure, he begins gradually to form his own political clique. He enjoys having younger men look up to him in terms of future reward. His power is limited but he has some of it nonetheless. He can, for example, recommend a young aspirant of his own clique for a special although minor post; he can convene special "political meetings" based upon his own new circle and can begin to

attract a following by doing a legion of minor favors for friends and acquaintances. He is beginning to be successful in the game of politics. By this time he receives a salary of around one thousand dollars per month (thanks to his several sinecure paychecks) and has his own loyal constituency whose members obey his every command. His supporters want him to rise, as the coat tails effect of this will surely benefit them when the power and related largesse are distributed.

9) Our hypothetical politican still has not taken over as head of the larger clique which he joined originally at the grass roots. But he remains in the good graces of the man who is still "boss" and thereby it is arranged that our politician is named alternate deputy for the PRI in the Federal District. This is a second-rank post as positions of federal power go, but it carries its privileges and credentials which enable one to jump from stone to stone in the upward spiral of trials which constitute the quest for national power in the Republic of Mexico.

10) As an alternate deputy in the Federal District our aspirant welds a series of providential relationships in the upper circles of the federal government. He gains favor with the PRI's top echelon, the CEN (*Comité Ejecutivo Nacional*) which in turn names him Electoral Delegate for the State of Guanjuato. He must travel there to represent CEN on the official team in the PRI's coming campaign for governor of that state. It becomes our man's personal charge to appoint special CEN representatives in the various electoral committees about Guanajuato for purposes of liaison with the national party organs. First and foremost in his portfolio, however, is the imperative that the PRI win in Guanajuato, preferably by legal means, but in the last analysis by any means at all. These he is free to invent.

11) Here is where our politicians's career is sullied by partial defeat and considerable disgrace. PRI wins the elections in Guanajuato to be sure, but at the expense of being caught with an impressive cache of false ballots which incident the opposition is able to inflate into proportions of national scandal. The national press carries the story in detail and federal executive power is necessary to quiet the public storm via the promise of an "investigation." Our political hero is blamed by the opposition press for the fraud and his own superiors chastize him for ineptitude. This is a setback and he will have to wait for an opportunity to overcome it.

12) As a result, not unexpectedly, of his failure in Guanajuato, our "exemplary" politician loses favor with his former boss (of the

clique) and his political privileges and salaries remain frozen for a time. Nonetheless, he continues to work quietly, organizing a special student group inside the National University and in this endeavor he makes good use of his own small clique which is still together. He knows that the University will be a fertile breeding ground in which to reingratiate himself with his "boss."

13) For a considerable time the name of our hypothetical politician remains forgotten in the spiderwebs. Then one day in the very bosom of the University a serious conflict explodes, one which the government fears it will not be able to control. The PRI and the "government" are one and the same vis-à-vis a common helplessness of not knowing how to proceed.

14) It is then, during these moments of crisis, that our disguised personality becomes suddenly very optimistic and ventures to tell his boss: "I can control these students by way of my movement and the extreme loyalty they feel for me. But there is a price tag. The government and the PRI will have to: 1) name me as principal candidate for federal deputy in the next elections; 2) assign several of my followers to positions within the Youth Committee of the PRI." Here he is placing members of his clique as an insurance factor.

15) This offer is accepted. With government backing our politician and his clique succeed in stultifying the student effervescence that surely would have led to a University-government conflict. Out of such a test of strength no one could possibly win, but the PRI would be a sure loser. The conflict dies and our man is named candidate for deputy along with new positions for his followers. His name has been cleared, the stains of the Guanajuato campaign are forgotten. He has achieved success, he is invited to political breakfasts, and the press begins to laud him. (Its members form lines to receive their *embute*, a monthly gratuity paid to reporters in exchange for their efforts to create a favorable public image for a given person.) At the top level of the PRI our man is now being discussed for assignment to the CEN. He has made it from the unknown to a high place in the PRI.

Self Preservation: The Handling of Deviant Charisma

Mexico's esoteric democracy is led by a dominant class formed out of circles of intimacy which in turn stem from a number of political cliques that are the basic membership units of power. The principal dilemma of the esoteric system is that its self perpetuation becomes increasingly stymied by the financial and political ties the PRI is forced to accept, as its principal cliques have multiplied and overlapped with groups whose ideological base may be hostile to the revolutionary coalition. The premium placed upon maximizing individual values fosters the proliferation of cliques and tends to dilute the power of the PRI's national organs; at the same time, however, this proliferation is a means of political socialization. On the success of this process much depends. It has certain critical implications that we must mention here.

One of these relates to the ability of the PRI to contain the phenomenon that I will term deviant charisma and which is inevitably generated by the *camarilla*-based structure of power. As the foregoing anecdote illustrates, a premium is paid for the aggressive, but dutiful, promotion of one's image as a true revolutionary within the PRI. This requires the neophyte to run certain risks and rewards him for a behavioral style that is commonly described as *machismo*, the aggressive instinct of the male for conquest. It has been suggested by one analyst that the PRI "with its hierarchical structure and its virtual monopoly of effective political activity, its overwhelming victories at the polls and its control of elective and appointive offices, provides an emotionally satisfying symbol of masculine aggressiveness and omnipotence."[7] The secret to the PRI's inner psychology would be, therefore, that it allows the participant to indulge his need for *macho* satisfactions politically speaking while still making it possible to carry on certain other compromise-dependent functions that the society requires and by non-*macho* styles of behavior, i.e. "the current practices of 'petitioning' and maneuvering behind the scenes would seem to display characteristics of what is regarded as feminine behavior."[8]

Following his ouster as president of the CEN in 1966, Carlos A. Madrazo confronted the PRI in a belligerent style strongly resembling the *macho* behavior described above. In May of 1968 he issued a confidential letter to political functionaries of the PRI and other parties who were generally below the level of a nationally known political reputation. He asked them to state which they would prefer,

[7] Evelyn P. Stevens, "Mexican Machismo: Politics and Value Orientations," *The Western Political Quarterly*, December 1965, p. 853.

[8] Ibid.

a national front composed of existing parties and groups (basically within the revolutionary coalition), or a totally new party (presumably to be headed by Madrazo) as the solution to the list (which Madrazo presented) of critical problems then afflicting Mexico. The latter option, a totally new party, would have been a radical gesture meaning a closing of the doors to the present revolutionary coalition and denouncing its leadership as petrified conservatives. The national front proposal, however, admitted of an internal restructuring and revamping of the PRI. It was a compromise which Madrazo seemed to favor while still holding out the possibility of a total split with tradition, thus bringing the crisis of legitimacy directly to a head.[9] Certainly no Mexican politician of the aggressive stripe of Carlos A. Madrazo would admit to being anything less than totally *macho*; but here was a crossroads situation in which criteria more rational than *machismo* were needed to avoid what could very well have become a disastrous collision.

I interviewed Madrazo at some length in June of 1968 following the issue of the confidential letter. He expressed hope that the revolutionary coalition could be saved but stated emphatically his disposition to bolt the PRI and to try to regroup the satellite left about his leadership in a new party were there no other way. Madrazo's tragic death one year later leaves in doubt the direction in which he would have resolved his unavoidable decision. But this much is clear: Madrazo frightened officialdom, he frightened them into blaming him for the Mexico City riots of 1968 and even, it has been argued, into ordering his assassination via the airplane accident of June, 1969.[10] In short, Madrazo tested the reconciliation capacity of the PRI, perhaps as it had never been tested before.

[9] The confidential Madrazo letter (a copy of which is in my possession) carries with it a slip to be filled out and returned to Madrazo by the given respondent. The required information was the person's preference for a *frente* or a *partido* and then personal data and group affiliation. The slip was to be signed by the respondent thus giving Madrazo a de facto pledge of support under one of the two alternatives. The third alternative of continuing the status quo was, of course, not included.

[10] There are several discussions in the clandestine press of the alleged assassination of Madrazo. Although the present author is unprepared at the moment to take sides in the controversy, the reader's attention is called to one of the more lucid articles that appears in the June 25, 1969 edition of *Voz Nacional*, especially page 5. It should be noted that at the time of this writing no major public attention had been given to investigating the crash of a Mexicana de Aviación jet near Monterrey which claimed the life of Madrazo along with a number of lesser public figures.

Deviant charisma of the Madrazo variety tests the ability of the PRI to reconcile (reconciliation system) a breach between itself and an individual renegade. PRI is also called upon to be a cooptation system as described in another analysis published shortly after the election of 1964.[11] Included is an especially good discussion of the experience of the CCI (*Central Campesina Independiente*), which challenged the PRI's agrarian sector during the early 1960's. Although CCI factions split over the very issue of cooptation, i.e. collaboration with the PRI, and rebel leader Danzós Palomino was imprisoned in the ensuing discord, it is argued that PRI essentially "coopted" the CCI into the revolutionary coalition. It is certainly true that Vicente Lombardo Toledano, then titular leader of the *Partido Popular Socialista* and intellectual mentor of the CCI, was coopted as was the firebrand peasant leader Jacinto López whose squatter-invader movement variously known as UGOCM suffered organizational chaos when Díaz Ordaz took office in 1964. The authors noted an important principle: "if cooptation of dissident groups fails, then repression is likely to occur."[12] It is crucial here to recognize that Lombardo and López fell into severe disrepute with a large majority of their followers for having joined the PRI. Danzós Palomino, on the other hand, became a popular hero and his prolonged encarceration at the moment of this writing lends to his revolutionary mystique. Lombardo and López are seen outside the revolutionary coalition as sellouts. Within the PRI there is evidence that López (Lombardo has now passed away) is distrusted for his earlier counterrevolutionary activity. Reconciliation and cooptation may appear to be the same process where individual leaders are concerned, but no matter which term is used, the process may win over leaders and alienate vast masses. My own interviews with popular leaders strongly support this contention.

I would stipulate that the process of cooptation, if indeed this is the best label for the capacity of the revolutionary coalition to stultify its opposition, is intimately related to the cliques as functional nuclei of power that give meaning to the PRI's structural forms. This is to say that for dissident groups to be integrated (coopted) into the PRI, there must be at least one clique of significant prestige that is

---

[11] Bo Anderson and James D. Cockcroft, "Control and Cooptation in Mexican Politics," in Horowitz, ed. *Latin American Radicalism* (New York: Vintage, 1969), pp. 366–389.

[12] Ibid., p. 380.

willing to grant them membership. The same must hold true for the reconciliation of individuals like Madrazo who are deviant charismatics. Both Lombardo Toledano and Jacinto López had group ties allowing for cooptation. Madrazo had his own clique which was large and powerful enough to make him a prize sought after by many elements of the revolutionary coalition. Danzós Palomino, the ex-rural school teacher, had few such ties. He was a dogmatic ideologue who would not compromise his revolutionary marxism and was repressed coercively. Other dissidents who could not be coopted have gone full turn from right to left but always in dedicated opposition to the PRI. Lic. Raúl Ugalde whose political career began as a militant juvenile leader of the PAN, abandoned this for a brief flirtation with the PPS, and ultimately helped to found the marxist and violence-oriented MRP (*Movimiento Revolucionario del Pueblo*). I interviewed Ugalde in the spring of 1969, shortly after his release from prison. He is truly a deviant charismatic from whom Mexico may hear much in years to come. Suffice it to say for now that his testimony, and that of his supporters, casts valuable light on the cooptation thesis as applied to the revolutionary coalition. It is likely that the political costs of self preservation are on the increase in Mexico. The PRI may well reconsider the implications of its own power system of cliques and it may ask itself how many more traumatas of the Madrazo variety are likely to result and how many of these it can really afford.[13]

---

[13] It is critical that scholars recognize the real basis of power within Mexico's esoteric democratic system, i.e., the linkages among the *camarillas* which are based upon informal working relationships, family ties, economic sanctions, and financial largesse. The basis of PRI power is not the electoral process as some North American scholars are prone to believe. Such assumptions lead to highly superficial analyses. See for instance the article by Barry Ames, "Bases of Support for Mexico's Dominant Party," the *American Political Science Review*, March 1970, in which the author postulates that Mexico is "modernizing" politically, that the PRI shows no loss of support (formally), and that elections in Mexico are significant parts of the political process. He says that since the winner in Mexico is never in doubt in most elections, and "because elections in Mexico usually indicate political skill and regime legitimacy, the number of people turning out on election day may be as interesting as the direction of the vote" (op. cit., p. 154). This study shows its author to be most concerned with the niceties of quantitative data analysis and much less concerned with the substantive anchoring which his analysis postulates. The presidential election of 1970 was widely seen in Mexico as a gigantic and costly ritual designed to mask the regime's very illegitimacy.

4
Governmental Performance and the Roots of Alienation

It is one thing to argue that Mexico's esoteric democracy affords itself the luxury of a cooptation process wherein dissident groups are cajoled into participation and would-be renegades are lulled into disgruntled acquiescense; it is quite another to allege that the sympathy of the Mexican people is similarly coopted by the output of government. Although for political purposes government and the PRI may be largely one and the same, it is critical to distinguish between the cooptation of key leaders and groups into the political clique system and popular satisfaction with governmental performance. The groups that lie at the heart of the official power structure contain only a tiny percentage of the population when contrasted with the millions of Mexicans who are affected by what the government does or fails to do. The people, ideologically fragmented and atomized though they may be, exhibit alienation toward their governmental output as a dominant and continuing characteristic. Viewed across the body politic, this alienation becomes a powder keg needing only a fuse and spark to ignite chaos and disaster (see Chapter 6 for a case study of exactly this eventuality).

One way to isolate the roots of political alienation in Mexico is to examine various key patterns of governmental performance as they come to bear directly on human life. As a preface to this, let us consider a provocative analysis of Mexico as a "politico-administrative system" by Professor Julio Fernández who writes:

The Mexican political system, through political socialization, has been able to obtain, at least for the present, a stable and workable balance between traditional and modern societal norms by capitalizing on the unifying symbolism of the revolutionary ideology and the Mexican political executive. In terms of the conversion of political inputs into governmental or administrative outputs, one could describe the Mexican political culture and political socialization experiences as subject and ambivalent in orientation. The notion of subject orientations is used specifically to refer to the tendency of the Mexican citizenry to identify largely with the outputs or policy-making side of the political system headed by the Mexican political executive.[1]

Now let us contrast Professor Fernández' contention with the more cryptic observation made recently by one of Mexico's most distinguished intellectuals, the author Carlos Fuentes. He says generally that presidential rhetoric and official propaganda are the bane of the people. Fuentes once angered Mexican officialdom by charging that the Mexican people are like the body of a crippled tiger which has had an overdose of pentothal but yet refuses to die. Fuentes defined the "pentothal" as the official rhetoric of the PRI and described the Mexican government as a hollow political system.[2] Repeating the contrast again, Professor Fernández writes that "a State of the Union message in Mexico is not mere pomp or an unrealistic statement of aspirations."[3] The differences apparent in the views of the two scholars dramatize the fact that it is quite possible to be sincerely knowledgeable about Mexican government and politics and still come to quite opposite conclusions.

From the above insights emerge several important questions. How do the people identify with the "outputs or policy making side" of what the executive does? Identification: to what extent does this mean supportive attitudes and to what extent hostility? Is executive prestige ascriptive in the popular mind because the man, whoever he happens to be, is the President of Mexico? Surely a corollary of this would be the question of the extent to which the vast organizational structure of the PRI is seen in ominous and coercive terms by the citizenry, or contemptuously and jealously viewed by the multitudes who are excluded from the largesse distributed via the cliques. Finally we must ask who is best qualified to interpret and reflect the popular mind in Mexico vis-à-vis governmental performance? In coming to

[1] Julio A. Fernández, *Political Administration in Mexico* (Boulder: Bureau of Governmental Research (University of Colorado), 1969, p. 39.

[2] *Visión*, March 28, 1969, p. 27.

[3] Fernández, op. cit., p. 51.

grips with the last question I will bring to bear the views of a range of Mexican observers, both supportive of and in opposition to the revolutionary coalition, with regard to the preceding issues that were raised. We will consider several public policy areas and key programs on which a partial evaluation of Mexico's governmental performance can be based.

The Dilemmas of Mexican Labor

An examination of Mexico's labor codes, beginning with Article 123 of the Constitution, makes impressive reading if one can also believe that the letter of the law is a living reality. Most of the guarantees available to laborers in the modern western world have been honored on paper in Mexico. Minimum wages, protection for women and children, prohibition of debt peonage and company stores, guarantees for collective bargaining, and work-hour limitations were among the contemporary features that received legal status. Not the least of these was the right to strike. A federal system of arbitration and conciliation was set up to adjudicate labor management disputes. In truth much of what appears on paper has become a reality. Compared with most of its neighboring republics in Central America, Mexico is a laboring man's paradise. There is an aggressive social security program and a chain of institutes called IMSS which dispense a variety of socialized medicine *to member participants.*

There are numerous government figures available as to how many hospitals, rooms, participant members, and doctors and nurses have been commissioned by the various recent regimes[4] as well as how many pesos have been invested. The surface result of all this is most impressive. Beginning with the regime of Adolfo López Mateos, there was a major effort made to provide medical service to expectant mothers, especially to those without husbands. On the basis of this writer's personal investigations it seems certain that the hearts of many Mexicans have been won via the latter program. This is a major credit to the PRI.

[4] A substantial amount of such information is available in L. Vincent Padgett, *The Mexican Political System* (Boston: Houghton Mifflin Co., 1966), pp. 167–170; see also a series of officially published works under the title *México: Cincuenta años de revolución* (México: Fondo de Cultura Económico, 1961), passim.

In addition to the welfare benefits that have just been mentioned, there has been a federal effort directed at the goal of profit sharing. One of the principal agencies of this policy is the National Commission for Profit Sharing (known as CNRU) which is frequently called a "company union" vis-à-vis PRI favored industries. Mexico's profit sharing laws provide sufficient loopholes to enable those who wish to escape the "spirit of the law" a great freedom in which to do just that. The dilemma of the worker who is in the employ of the government, or of one of its many state industries or companies (like PEMEX, Aeronaves de México, CONASUPO), is intensified even further by the fact that he owes his employment to the PRI. No matter what his union affiliation, he is a part of the revolutionary coalition; otherwise his bargaining power will be nil. We will see presently how the state owned industries and businesses in Mexico are a major source of both ideological capital for the PRI and political disaffection against it.

The real dilemma for the Mexican worker today is that outside of the formal organs of the revolutionary coalition he has little hope of what we in the United Sattes would call competitive unionism. Those who seek to rise above the laborer class must secure a university degree that will be accepted and respected. Despite official subsidies for students (which often amount to PRI recruitment funds) the acquisition of such a degree is impossible for all but a small handful of Mexicans (see Epilogue). The worker, therefore, becomes a potentially volatile mass whose stultified desire for mobility threatens the tenure of the revolutionary coalition.

A case in point that dramatizes the dilemma of Mexican labor centers around Demetrio Vallejo, a man who sought to challenge the status quo. Vallejo was a flamboyant leader of the railroad workers who promoted secessionist efforts against the CTM around the time that López Mateos became president in 1958. About this same time he associated himself with the Mexican Communist Party and President López Mateos offered him a truce and amnesty. There are conflicting reports as to precisely what led Vallejo to defy the president thereafter, but it is frequently argued that López Mateos had in fact tricked Vallejo in a time-buying effort, while behind the scenes reprisals were being carried out against the railroad workers. In any event Vallejo engineered a strike in 1959 which seriously paralyzed Mexico's railroads. It is often said also that Vallejo himself had been forced into the strike by pressure from the Mexican Communist Party. President López Mateos retaliated and crushed the strike by use of federal troops. Vallejo was condemned to twelve years in prison. While serving this term a fight occurred between Vallejo and a prison official in 1963 thus ruining his chances for an early parole. At the moment of this writing Vallejo has just been pardoned but his future is uncertain. To this extent some Mexican jurists argue that Vallejo has been deprived of constitutional rights and it is widely believed that this was done on high orders from the PRI.

In contrast, the world famous painter and self styled communist David Alfaro Siqueiros who was imprisoned subsequent to Vallejo, but for complicity in the same railroad strike, was pardoned by López Mateos following the presidential election of 1964. This occured presumably to spare Díaz Ordaz the embarrassment of inheriting a world respected artist as a living martyr (despite the fact that Siqueiros ran for the senate from his jail cell under the illegal banner of the FEP whose leader Danzós Palomino was jailed shortly thereafter for sedition).[5]

Agrarian Reform: Mexico's Other Face

Let us leave the question of labor policy, and glance in greater detail at Mexico's agrarian reform picture. Although the Wars of the Reform and the Revolution of 1910–17 were directed against existing monopolistic patterns of land tenure, it is clear that Mexico today still has a problem of landed estates. Although accurate figures are scarce it has been estimated by informal sources that around five percent of Mexico's total farms occupy nearly fifty percent of the usable agricultural land. Several years ago John Powelson contended that less than one percent of the farms contained nearly fifty percent of the private land.[6] From the years of Carranza until the "great step

[5] Movements like FEP and MLN have emphasized the plight of the working Mexican as an ideological theme. It is especially characteristic of the literature of protest such as Gilberto Balam's study *Tlatelolco*, Mexico, 1969 (by author) pp. 103–110. Despite the unofficial dialogue over collective bargaining and the right to strike, the basic fact remains that unionization continues to be an official prerogative in Mexico.

[6] John P. Powelson, *Latin America: Today's Economic and Social Revolution* (New York: McGraw-Hill, 1964), p. 37.

forward" of Lázaro Cárdenas, impressive figures have been quoted as to which president distributed the most land.[7] There is no doubt about the fact that land was indeed distributed. Padgett's study has done a commendable job of presenting the official sounding view of the dimensions of land reform;[8] but unfortunately the dimensions of rural neglect and the failure of the land reform program have gone relatively untreated in the English language. The DAAC (*Departamento de Asuntos Agrarios y Colonización*) is charged with administration of Mexico's "ongoing" land reform program. Specifically, it is intended to administer the program of *ejidos* (state supported collective farms) and to be the administrative instrument for rural development throughout Mexico. Because of the abundance of officialist oriented treatments of these farms and the DAAC, it is important to make known here several contentions that reflect another point of view.[9]

In a commentary on the state of Mexican agrarian reform, Rodrigo García Treviño has referred to the land reform period of 1920–50 as a premature nationalization of lands resulting in social maladjustment and a "new slavery." This, he says, consists in substituting for the old patron a greedy bureaucracy totally lacking adequate technical and managerial training.[10] The extensive reform bureaucracy allegedly has been in league with corrupt local politicians who are fleecing the farmers of their harvest profits. For many peasant farmers, of course, any profit earned is consumed by the non-producing members of his family which often means bank foreclosure on the state farm. Accordingly, the rapprochment of agrarian bureaucrats and local politicians underlies part of the rural-to-urban migration in Mexico because of frustrated economic expectations in the countryside. These allegations were supported in numerous interviews conducted among rural citizens by this author in 1962 and again in 1969 in various parts of the country. According to these sources,

[7] As an example see John Gerassi, *The Great Fear in Latin America* (New York: Collier, 1965), p. 102; also Pablo González Casanova, *La democracia en México*, 2d ed. (Mexico, ERA, 1965), p. 244.

[8] Padgett, op. cit., *passim*.

[9] For instance, see Howard Cline, *Mexico: Revolution to Evolution: 1940–1960* (New York: Oxford, 1963), pp. 209–221.

[10] Rodrigo Garcia Treviño, *Precios salarios y mordidas* (Mexico: Editorial América, 1953), p. 123.

farmers are often required to surrender such a high percentage of their harvest to corrupt bureaucats that even subsistence living is rendered difficult.

It was allegedly Zapata and his followers who coined the cry "land and liberty." It remains clear however that he had in mind not just "land" and, somehow miraculously, "liberty" thereafter, but quite precisely the liberty to acquire land. Zapata and his followers condemned Francisco I. Madero for treason to the land distribution cause, thereby helping to precipitate the fall of Mexico into the chaos of the Revolution. Article 2 of the Constitution provides for land distribution and presidents Obregón and Cárdenas did much to bring this goal to fruition. The usufructuary device of the state farm system has come to be a major ideological accoutrement which the contemporary revolutionary coalition uses to symbolize the reformist bent of the PRI. But every coin has two faces, and agrarian reform is the other face of Mexico. *Los Intocables,* or the untouchables, are those in Mexican agrarian affairs who have managed to escape the purview of Article 2. They are Mexico's large land owners, a lingering reminder that the *Pax Porfiriana* never ended completely. Witness this tale.

Some years ago, as the story goes, Anastasio Rodríguez and his common law wife Manuela Domínguez occupied a poor and de-deserted piece of land in the wilderness of Chihuahua and created a precarious life from practically nothing. They were destined to collide with Mexico's great landowners, the North American companies. and the Department of Agrarian Affairs and Colonization (DAAC). So begins a novel based on the real life experiences of Carlos Chavira Becerra, one time federal deputy from Chihuahua, who tells a bitter and empirically well-grounded account of the other face of Mexico, the realities of agrarian reform.[11]

A village was born in the desert rocks and mountains at a spot called *Cañón de la Madera,* a misnomer to be sure, for there was no wood in sight nor water to grow crops. The squatters carried in water, built miserable huts, and collected a few head of cattle and goats. Most of their income came from labor on nearby farms and in mines. At the onset, the squatters defended their tenancy under the legendary Decree of August 2, 1923, which all the rural poor knew how to

---

[11] Carlos Chavira, *La otra cara de México* (México: La Nación, 1966).

invoke by saying *"Pos yo estoy posiando aqui por el Decreto del dos de agosto."*[12] In reality no one knew how to define this decree. One day an engineer named Rivera came to survey lands near the old coal mine of Don Adolfo Orlich, a friend and benefactor of the squatters. From Rivera they learned of a way to constitute themselves legally as a state farm under the Agrarian Code. The squatters desig-nated Pedro Alvidres to go to the state capital and begin procedures for a state farm application. It was a difficult task for the illiterate Alvidres, but with help and advice from Rivera and Orlich the squatters finally received a large envelope with the national crest on it containing papers they could not read but which were interpreted to them as being a preliminary approval by the government's Agrarian Commission of their application for state farm status. It was a moment of great joy.

From that time on the residents of *Cañón de la Madera* were integrated politically into the CNC (*Confederación Nacional Campesina*) and received corresponding periodic instructions as to the intermittent formalities they must satisfy. Among these was the task of being brought like cattle in trucks to the municipal center called Manuel Benavídes to contribute their presence toward the appearance of popular adulation in favor of a PRI candidate for federal deputy. Once the candidate's presentation had ended, the squatters were herded rapidly back into the trucks and busses. Some-how no one remembered to pay them the five pesos they had been promised by CNC rural bosses for their participation.

Pedro Alvidres remembered quite seriously the lectures his village folk had received from CNC officials: if they did not go to vote on election day the reactionaries would come to power and take away their land.[13] But when they arrived to vote they were rudely cursed

[12] In colloquial Mexican Spanish: "Well I'm in possession here under the Decree of August the second." Apparently such a decree had historical significance and was handed down by word of mouth with embellishment sufficient to turn the original decree into a magic formula (in the minds of the squatter peasants) for the solution of nearly any rural land problem.

[13] The PRI conspicuously tries to convince the simple people that there are "reactionaries" who will swoop down upon them should the official party collapse. Anomalously, PRI politicians often seek to justify their official tenure by invoking this threat which they, in fact, became dependent upon. Mexican officials fre-quently use this same logic on the foreign scholar or visitor, e.g. "we are here to perpetuate the Revolution against the Church, the oligopolists, the landed gentry, etc. . . ."

by the polling place attendant for even showing up, thereby causing him the extra work of putting the electoral procedures in motion. All the time he had been marking ballots and stuffing the box in favor of the PRI. The peasants learned, although they did not thoroughly understand, that "the Party of the Government" had voted for them. Their bodies were needed; their minds and souls were superfluous. They had obeyed dutifully and expected their recompense. They wanted final title to their land. But the agrarian delegate for Chihuahua sought ways to prevent the state farm from gaining final legal status. Nevertheless, friends of the squatters prevailed. On November 30, 1933, the publication *Periódico Oficial del Estado de Chihuahua* contained a decree in which the governor gave (*dotaba*) the land including the *ejido Cañón de la Madera* to Pedro Alvidres and his peasant neighbors. The dotation was classified as provisional. Then, silently, a curious thing occurred. A certain engineer named Martínez was removed from the Chihuahua office of the Agrarian Commission (*Comisión Agraria Mixta*) for having disagreed with the national agrarian delegate for Chihuahua in the matter of the dotation. And thus a basis was laid whereby many years hence the land grant could be challenged by the untouchables, permanent enemies of agrarian reform, who considered Martínez' indiscretion to have been unpardonable.

The resolution of the governor was subject to final review in "second instance." Here an intricate web of power relationships unfolded. Licenciado Parrá of Chihuahua was legal council for a company of untouchables called *Compañía Ganadera del Norte* that was in the process of liquidating its lands via commercial sale but which had encountered the obstacle of several farms in "first instance" within its original terrain. The only way in which all of the original landed estates could be sold was by dissolution of these state farms and removal of the squatter peasants. That required a signed resolution from the President of the Republic. The key people were Licenciado Parrá and an obscure, but powerful, department chief in the Department of Agrarian Affairs and Colonization (DAAC) who saw to it (in return for a generous financial consideration) that when the president signed into law a number of resolutions during January of 1953 (and did so innocently and blindly) among them was a document whose effect was to disposses the residents of nearly every state farm in the municipality of Manuel Benavídes of the property they had cultivated and cared for during many years. This was to please the untouchables who sought to make a profit selling the land (and leasing it to North Americans) in small parcels. During these years the land values increased as the peasants had finally discovered water (via their own sweat and blood) and North American geological surveys indicated the presence of valuable minerals. Therefore, the poor but courageous peasants of *Cañón de la Madera* had to go; in this case the pretext was simple: when Pedro Alvidres and his farmers had made their initial solicitation they had presented thirty five names as parties to the petition . . . the law only required twenty signatures; the transaction was "obviously" fraudulent,[14] at least so reasoned the key figure of the DAAC and Licenciado Parrá.

An order was sent from Mexico City to a rural marshal known as Castro Carrillo telling him to dislodge the thirty-five peasant families from the land they believed to be theirs. Castro Carrillo was told to use the "federal force" to the extent he considered necessary. The pitiful spectre of this eviction is described by Carlos Chavira in his book and becomes in itself something of a study in bizarre administrative psychology at the government-to-people level. The peasants were taken to the municipality of Manuel Benavídes, tried and convicted by an illiterate justice of the peace, and then abandoned to die in the disease-ridden slums of this poor village. Their captor, Castro Carillo, told them to get out of his sight, to disappear; then he stole their livestock and left.

With the help of their old benefactor, Don Adolfo Orlich, a letter was written to the Presidency of the Republic asking for mercy and intervention. By the time a reply was received Pedro Alvidres and others were dead from disease and misfortune; but when the reply did come months later, it said only that the peasants' complaint had been turned over to the Department of Agrarian Affairs and Colonization, ironically, the very source of corruption in which the traumata of their displacement had begun. Then follows the poignant tale of the uprooted men who lacked the eight-hundred peso bribe needed to get a permit for work in the United States and whose already fragile health carried them to the dregs of a compassionless society and death. There is also the tale of the rural marshal Castro Carrillo whose biggest defeat was the indiscretion of getting caught accepting a bribe but who escaped punishment to retire gra-

14 Chavira op. cit., p. 146.

ciously on hacienda lands he had helped to "liberate" from peasant occupation.

A balance sheet on the *ejido Cañón de la Madera*, otherwise known as dotation number 826 in the municipality of Manuel Benavides, state of Chihuahua, reads as follows: a) peasants begin occupation of the land in question in 1924, b) they win provisional *ejido* title in 1934, c) a presidential resolution cancels their title in 1953; d) they are forcefully ejected from these lands in 1957. Carlos Chavira served as a PAN deputy in the federal Chamber of Deputies during the last years of the López Mateos regime. He tried repeatedly to secure administrative relief for peasant farm groups, like those of *Cañón de la Madera*, and sought unsuccessfully to gain an audience with the president himself on their behalf. Pressure from the untouchables of his state made it impossible for Chavira to gain a second term in office; the peasant evictions continued, and the profitable sale of Chihuahua land continued (notably to foreign groups like Menonites from the United States who could pay for the benefits of agrarian "reform").

The tragic character in this revealing novel is Pedro Alvidres who had been proudly chosen *Presidente Comisariado Ejidal* for the *ejido Cañón de la Madera* and whose badly disfigured body was found floating in the Rio Bravo del Norte (Rio Grande) shortly before the reply to the letter sent to the president of the Republic was received in his name. Pedro had become a "wetback" and crossed over into Texas to work in the melon fields in order to support his starving family; but lacking bribe money to purchase a work permit, and therefore without one, he was "caught by the law" as the poor Mexican's say and was executed. Unable to pay tribute to Mexican officialdom he paid with his life. Pedro was superstitious, yet religious, and held faith in witchcraft medicines and in mysterious revelations of divine truth. But, as Chavira writes, "Alvidres believed in things even more absurd than those":

creía, por ejemplo, en la honradez, en la justicia, en la integridad de los hombres, en el respeto a los derechos ajenos, en la decencia, en el amor, en el trabajo; creía, en fin, en una serie de utopías, tenía una inmensa fe de carbonero. Mas su creencia resultaba patológica al creer, y lo afirmaba muy en serio, en la vigencia y respeto de la ley, y ya en el franco camino de las entelequias, tenía fe también, una fe muy grande, una fe inmensa en la justicia del Señor Presidente de la República.

he believed, for example, in honor, justice, in human integrity and in respect for the rights of others, in decency, in love, in labor; he believed, ultimately, in a series of utopias, he had that great faith of the miner. But his belief was a pathology in itself, he was dead serious in putting it forth, serious in respecting the law that was in force, in giving an open road to nature's vital forces; he had faith also, an immense faith, in the benevolent justice of the President of the Republic.[15]

Perhaps the earlier quotation from Prof. Fernández now takes on additional meaning. "The notion of subject orientations is used specifically to refer to the tendency of the Mexican citizenry to identify with the outputs or policy-making side of the political system headed by the Mexican political executive." Fernández is correct; and Carlos Chavira is correct also. The ideological inconsistency which emerges from comparing their dictums is a clash that must claim a victim and he is Pedro Alvidres. In the "hollow political system" as Carlos Fuentes (also quoted earlier in this chapter) has termed it, such an anachronism is not only possible but is one to be expected. In the "hollow political system" no one cares if Pedro Alvidres is fed to the wolves so long as they are true "revolutionaries." Tragically, many Mexicans believe that Mr. President will save them from the "reactionaries" and from all other villains. Here is a basic grass roots breach in Mexico's esoteric democracy.

While civic moralists struggled against corrupt agrarian politics in Chihuahua (and elsewhere in Mexico), a related drama was being played out in the hills of Morelos (one hour by car southwest of Mexico City). Here another counterrevolutionary ideologue challenged the federal government's Department of Agrarian Affairs and Colonization (DAAC) and President López Mateos along with it. Rubén Jaramillo has come to symbolize Mexican agrarian resistance to authority in general and to the PRI's agrarian sector in particular. Jaramillo had reputedly served with Zapata's guerrillas both for and against Madero. After the Revolution Jaramillo continued to lead squatter movements against the remaining great landowners of which there were many. During the Cárdenas land distributions, Jaramillo suspended his more militant activities although it is said he never really believed that the reformist general-president would ever be anything but a puppet for Calles who had arranged his candidacy

---

[15] Ibid., p. 228 (translated).

in 1934. The regimes of Miguel Alemán and Ruiz Cortínes drove Jaramillo and his men into legendary exile where he remained, in the hills and mountains of Morelos, until President López Mateos offered him amnesty and a chance for peace following 1958. In fact, López Mateos met personally with Jaramillo in one of the century's most celebrated cases of a truce of convenience. Apparently the president promised the guerrilla chieftain many things, including considerable land for Jaramillo. But nothing happened and so Jaramillo's squatters began to occupy properties belonging to powerful friends of Morelos' governor Norberto López Avelar. For a brief time it looked as if the DAAC might support Jaramillo's plea that the unused land be given to his people under the agrarian reform laws.

Then, suddenly, the DAAC ordered Jaramillo's men to vacate the property. This coincided roughly with the announcement of plans to build a major hydroelectric project in the immediate area and on lands occupied in part by Jaramillo and his men. Here was another case in which private profits were to be made by claiming the abandoned land and by dispossessing the squatters. Apparently no offer was made to move the peasants to other lands of a comparable quality or to indemnify them for the loss that their eviction under "eminent domain" would produce. There are a number of versions in the popular folklore of what happened next and of who was responsible. The crude and bizarre fact of it is, explanations notwithstanding, that Rubén Jaramillo and his entire family were taken by force and machine gunned to death. Their bodies were found a short distance away on May 23, 1962. The government announced an investigation of the atrocity and President López Mateos had the officialist press carry the photos taken earlier of himself and Jaramillo making "cause," as Madero and Zapata had done in nearly the same political and geographic circumstances a half century earlier. It is significant to note that Jaramillo could not be coopted, although he was certainly disposed toward a dialogue with officialdom in the interest of progress. Folklore in Morelos blames Governor López Avelar. John Gerassi has cited impressive evidence that the Jaramillos were killed on top orders from the PRI.[16]

[16] Gerassi, op. cit., p. 107; see also Rubén M. Jarmillo and Froylán C. Manjarrez, *Rubén Jaramillo, Autobiografía y asesinato* (Mexico: Editorial Nuestro Tiempo, 1967).

Economic Paternalism: AUTOMEX and CONASUPO

A major tenet of the contemporary revolutionary mystique is national economic planning and state capitalism. By means of its principal development bank known as *Nacional Financiera* the Mexican government has accomplished the feat of an economic "take off" and more in the eyes of some scholars.[17] There are other agencies, such as the *Banco Hipotecario Nacional* (National Mortgage Bank) that contribute to Mexico's relatively high industrial growth. Overall responsibility for giving vitality and impulse to the economy rests with the SIC, Secretariat of Industry and Commerce. It is normally considered that industrial development and its attendent "spread effects" will combat political alienation by moving underdeveloped societies closer toward the western model of affluence and pacification. We will consider here two instances of industrial protectionism (or paternalism) in which the potential for generating political alienation is strong and which, at the same time, shed light upon Mexican policies of economic development.

According to this author's interviews and several published accounts,[18] the Ford Motor Company set up a small assembly plant in Mexico during 1925, marking the beginning of the nation's automobile industry. General Motors came in 1936 and Chrysler followed in 1938, the latter without its own assembly works but with a contract for auto assembly with a Mexican firm. This firm was known as Automex which had similar contracts with other foreign companies.

In 1959 Chrysler sought to increase its control over Automex by purchasing thirty percent of the stock. Three percent remained in the hands of Automex officials, around ten percent was sold publicly, and

[17] In addition to the works of Glade and Anderson that were cited earlier, see Ifigenia M. de Navarrete, *La distribución del ingreso y el desarrollo económico de México* (México: UNAM, 1960); and Paul Lamartine Yates, *El desarrollo regional de México* (México: Banco de México, 1962).

[18] This sequence on Automex is based largely upon confidential interviews but many of the factual data are taken from the publication *Voz Pública*, No. 2, April 1967 *passim*, which cites as a source for some of its information the North American publication *Car Life*, Vol. 14, No. 2, March, 1967.

approximately fifty-seven percent of the Automex stock remained in the hands of the powerful Azcárraga family and its associates. Although at this time the Mexican government pretended to have an open door policy toward foreign investment, it soon became obvious that if the automobile assembly industry was to generate new sources of employment it would be necessary to impose protective tariffs favoring cars assembled within Mexico. This was done but, in addition, the government decreed in 1962 that thereafter sixty percent of the parts on any automobile sold in Mexico would have to be manufactured within the country. This requirement was imposed on short notice and contained the proviso of an "auto czar" or high government functionary who would set production standards and quotas for the automobile manufacturers. From the standpoint of the automobile manufacturers, Mexico had welcomed them as a trick to induce large investments and then, once the assembly plants were established, the Mexican government said "now we will tell you how to run your business."

At the moment of this writing the man responsible for verifying standards and fixing quotas is Octaviano Campos Salas, the Secretary for Industry and Commerce. It is said that in recent years the firm Automex, which is to say Chrysler in Mexico, has received preferential treatment. It was alleged that for the year 1967 Automex had a permit to assemble and sell 28,000 vehicle units as compared with 20,000 for Ford and 20,000 for General Motors. This difference, along with projected quota increases designed to favor Automex, is attributed to the personal friendship and economic ties existing between Octaviano Campos Salas and Gastón Azcárraga, the first automobile magnate of Mexico. Here is an important point that relates to the previous chapter and will be taken up again later, namely, Automex is a political clique and the Secretary of Industry and Commerce is a member of it. The boss is Gastón Azcárraga. Although it is pretended that the favored quota for Automex is a nationalistic gesture in favor of a Mexican firm, the truth is that the financial structure of Automex makes it little more (except in name) Mexican than Ford and General Motors. Ties of personal influence, loyalty, and political power go much deeper than "nationalism" and lie at the bottom of the protectionism in favor of Automex. It is also known that little is done in Mexico to prevent the profits from Automex and like ventures from being shipped out of the country to accounts in "safe" banks.[19]

From the standpoint of the Mexican consumer, the decree of 1962 raised the costs of the average new automobile around thirty percent. Following the decree, Ford and General Motors claimed to have lost money in Mexico. Automex declared a modest profit. Today, on the average, any automobile purchased in Mexico will cost fifty to seventy percent more than would the same vehicle unit in the United States. The same holds true for the foreign cars, even the Borgward that is assembled on a modest basis in Monterrey in a factory that is partly a "home owned" industry of the Mexican government (despite official propaganda stressing the firm's ties with the former German concern). The government-owned company DINA produces the Renault automobile under special franchise. Previously, DINA had asked Automex to give up its contract to assemble the Italian Fiat so as to reduce competition against the government produced Renault. The *camarilla* ties between Campos Salas and Azcárraga were crucial in arranging this action in deliberate restraint of competitive trade. Now Automex assembles only the Chrysler line and, thanks to the protective custody of the Secretary of Industry and Commerce, enjoys a lucrative market. It is clear that such a rapprochement would set many industrialists against the government. This is part of the continued hostility of the "Monterrey group" toward the PRI. In addition, it weighs heavily upon the consumer. Ask any Mexican taxi driver, who is also the owner of his vehicle, for his opinion about the cost of replacement parts. You will most likely find that he blames the oligarchs and the government (probably he has heard of Automex only in passing and would be unable to name the Secretary of Industry and Commerce) whom he knows to be responsible for his unfortunate dilemma.

The case of Automex reflects certain economic aspects of the power nexus between government and industry. It is the case of an officially favored industrial enterprise which thrives beneath the political blessing of a highly influential clique; this is economic protectionism. Let us consider next an example of a state-owned and operated enterprise, one that is frequently held up as a showcase for revolutionary progress with which the PRI seeks to impress foreign dig-

[19] *Voz Pública*, op. cit.

nitaries. One such occasion was January 24, 1968, when the President of El Salvador, Fidel Sánchez Hernández, paid an official state visit to CONASUPO, the showcase organization in question. He said "we congratulate the Mexican people for achieving this level of perfection in an institution of such popular benefit."[20] Let us examine CONASUPO in the light of two perspectives, the official record and the criticism of a contemporary Mexican scholar.

WHAT CONASUPO INTENDS TO BE[21]

CONASUPO means *Compañia Nacional de Subsistencias Populares* which in a loose but equivalent English translation means *"Official Staple Commodities of Mexico Inc."* CONASUPO's administrative roots trace back to 1938 when an affiliate of the state-owned *Banco Nacional de Comercio Exterior* was transformed into the *Comité Regulador del Mercado de las Subsistencias* (Committee to Regulate the Market of Staple Goods). In 1941 this committee was converted into another organism (*Nacional Distribuidora y Reguladora, S.A. de C. V.*) that involved both governmental, private, and organized labor (practically the same as governmental) participation in a joint attempt to regulate prices of staple goods throughout Mexico. This became CEIMSA (*Compañia Exportadora e Importadora Mexicana S.A.*) in 1948. CEIMSA is well known in recent Mexican history as a programmatic bulwark of the PRI and can be translated loosely as Mexican National Import Export Company (colloquially it has been called the Mexican National Company for the Exploitation of Corn).

By 1952 CEIMSA was subsidizing the production and sale of corn, beans, eggs, and wheat throughout Mexico and had begun its own system of distribution of staple goods to poor people in depressed neighborhoods. A part of this program was a series of mobile vans which travelled to the various neighborhoods selling staple goods at

---

[20] From an official memorandum entitled *Declaración del Excmo. Señor Presidente de El Salvador Fidel Sánchez Hernández, al terminar su visita a "CODISUCO,"* published by CONASUPO (Carlos Hank González, Director General), January 24, 1968.

[21] This sequence is based on an official CONASUPO memorandum entitled *Qué es la CONASUPO?* distributed through official sources in 1968 (contains no other date).

very low prices and under a rationing system. On the basis of the present author's investigations it seems certain that many poor people in Mexico were benefited by this program and a part of their enduring respect for President López Mateos is rooted in the successes of CEISMA.

In 1961 CEIMSA was liquidated and replaced with CONASUPO S.A. (*Compañía Nacional de Subsistencias Populares Sociedad Anónima*). During June of that year the government announced a vastly expanded program of mobile units that would be managed under a subsidiary of CONASUPO called *Compañía Distribuidora de Subsistencias Populares S.A.* and would seek to extend services to all parts of the nation. Ultimately, in 1965, the S.A. was dropped and the organism became CONASUPO which differed from its predecessor in that it would be decentralized administratively with a headquarters in each state (prior to that time CONASUPO had functioned nationally out of a headquarters at the corner of Donceles and República de Argentina in the Federal District).

As it exists today CONASUPO has two basic functions: 1) protection of peasant and agrarian incomes generally via a system of price subsidies not unlike the North American parity system, at least in principle; 2) support for the purchasing power of the common people by means of a decentralized (and mobile) system for distribution of staple goods of high quality at the lowest feasible price. Price supports are in effect now for corn, wheat, beans, rice, sorgum, saffron, sesame, soy beans, and cotton seed. Official figures published by one of CONASUPO's dependencies called CIANO (*Centro de Investigaciones Agrícolas del Noroeste*) located in Ciudad Obregón indicate that a high level of productivity has been achieved throughout much of Mexico under the aegis of the protective price supports.[22] CONASUPO fixes the prices which may vary among regions for the individual commodities: for instance, the price fixed for wheat in regions of high productivity is 800 pesos per ton but in zones of low productivity the fixed price is 913 pesos per ton. This is done to provide an incentive to the farmer for increasing his productive capacity.

The effect of the price supports is to guarantee that the farmer will have an immediate market for his produce and a rapid financial return despite the various economic cycles through which Mexico,

[22] Ibid., p. 3.

like other countries, must pass. The agricultural producer, whether he be a small tract farmer, an *ejidatario* (one who has an *ejido* franchise), or a larger producer organized into associations or credit unions, takes his products to one of the 615 authorized CONASUPO receiving centers. There the grain is recorded and stored by the agency known as *Almacenes Nacionales de Depósito S.A.* which is also a part of CONASUPO, but with a limited separate autonomy from it.[23] When the agricultural product arrives at any of the authorized CONASUPO centers, a laboratory analysis is made of the quality of the grain to determine if it can be accepted for market within the program. If his grain passes, the farmer receives a form that is labelled CM-13 which he takes to one of the official banks (*Banco Agrícola, Banco Ejidal*) participating in the CONASUPO program where the total value of his harvest is determined and reconciled with any credits which may have been charged to his account. The difference is then paid to the farmer in cash or in a form of his choosing. The final record of each transaction is sent to CONASUPO headquarters in Mexico City.

There is no official limit to the amount of grain that a participant farmer may sell to CONASUPO but there are fixed dates that vary from year to year for the sale of various grains. It is intended that the guaranteed market approach will prevent the growth of black markets in staple crops. In addition to price supports and unlimited sale guarantees, CONASUPO provides a subsidized fertilizer program, irrigation development subsidies, and offers controlled credit to participant farmers via one of several participating government banks.

CONASUPO is governed by an Administrative Council that is composed of the federal secretaries of Treasury and Public Credit (Antonio Ortiz Mena), Agriculture (Juan Gil Preciado), Industry and Commerce (Octaviano Campos Salas). The secretariat for this Administrative Council is provided by the Bank of Mexico. This is a policy making body. The actual administration of CONASUPO is carried out by a permanent hierarchy of bureaucrats who staff a range of funtional departments about the nation.

The second basic goal of CONASUPO mentioned above, i.e. the distribution of high quality staple goods at low prices, is carried out

23 Ibid., p. 4.

via several dependencies. The *Compañia Distribuidora de Subsistencias* can be called the CODISUCO and operates sixty-two heavy trucks which are assigned to daily routes (except Thursdays) in nearly 300 working class neighborhoods throughout Mexico and serve an estimated population of over two million poor people. *Despite criticism of CONASUPO that will be cited presently, the mobile truck stores have done much to endear Mexicans to their government and are an evidence that someone in the PRI really "cares."* In addition the "distributor" operates a chain of 405 CONASUPO stores in poor neighborhoods where a system of rationing aids in guaranteeing a minimum diet to the poor. In rural areas there are 180 country stores providing the same function. The Mexican government projects significant increases in the numbers of such facilities during the coming years.

Another CONASUPO dependency has a special purpose function of critical import to the young. The agency known as *Compañia Rehidratadora de Leche "CONASUPO" S.A.* can be called an official milk service and distributes over 300,000 liters of powdered milk daily at a fixed price of about six cents per liter. This is done via nearly 200 special milk dispensaries throughout Mexico. A third CONASUPO subdivision, nicknamed MINSA (*Maíz Industrializado S.A.*), produces corn meal and flour. Official government ideology credits to MINSA the freeing of the Mexican woman from the slavery of producing flour for her family's bread. The flour is made available at a low fixed price and can be used for tortillas and pastries as well as bread. As with the other CONASUPO dependencies, it is intended that this subsidized service will go to benefit only the poor and will not be used in support of commercial establishments. There is a plan, however, whereby commercial food producers may obtain the flour at a rate that is not considered to be subsidization.

A fourth arm of CONASUPO is the *Comisión Promotora "CONASUPO" Para el Mejoramiento Rural,* a rural development commission that maintains direct contact with the *ejidatario* and the small farmer with programs of technical aid and self help. It could be said that this is Mexico's 4-H program. The Commission has a permanent cooperative relationship with the CONDISUCO distribution program and assists in the promotion of stable foods, clothing, and a variety of domestic items to the rural poor. In 1968 there were 225 rural centers of aid to the needy, and of technical aid to the small farmer operating under the direction of the commission throughout Mexico. These centers have been called popularly "the people's granaries."[24] They dispense more than food, however, and at times take on the function of a rural general store.

WHY CONASUPO FAILS TO BE WHAT IT SHOULD

Here I will translate relevant parts of an article appearing in the April 10, 1968 edition of *Por Qué* in the interest of presenting an indigenous criticism of CONASUPO.[25] The article offers valuable insight into the administrative problems involved in coordinating so large a program and tells of the political niche CONASUPO occupies in the power structure.

"There is no doubt that the original and founding motives of CONASUPO were generous, impartial, and represented a determined effort on the part of our government to reach the needy classes with staple goods at minimum prices. In actual practice, however, this intention has been frustrated by a series of facts to be elaborated herein. Multiplying the present budget of CONASUPO by one hundred could not make this program useful to the country. The principal reason for its impotence lies in the fact that its true motive is political, not economic, and rather than increase the production of foodstuffs it takes money from the people at large in order to lower prices for a small minority. The result is that CONASUPO is not producing wealth but suppressing it; and at the same time it acquires political power as a state-run monopoly."

"Two days following the eulogy which the President of El Salvador gave to CONASUPO on January 24, 1968 the evening paper *Ultimas Noticias* carried on its front page the story that in Matamoros, Tamaulipas, the local subsidiary of CONASUPO had been forced to burn as unfit for human consumption nearly three thousand tons of corn and over one thousand tons of sorgum because of humidity damage. The story did not say why CONASUPO with its 615 receiving centers about the country had not taken steps to avoid

24 Ibid., p. 15.

25 Manuel de la Isla, *Porque fracasa la CONASUPO!*, *Por Que*, 10 April 1968, pp. 32–34, translated by K. F. Johnson with permission.

such damage. This is merely one isolated even in a long history of administrative blunders."

"The text which CONASUPO distributes in explanation of its activities states that the farmer (*campesino*) suffers environmental hardships which make it necessary for the government to guarantee him a price for his harvest that will be just. Therefore, it is stated that CONASUPO is to have two basic areas of activity in behalf of alleviating misery, protection for peasant income and improving the purchasing power of the poor via a program of food subsidies. But that is not what really happens. Take the example of a farmer from Guanajuato who arrives at one of the CONASUPO receiving centers and 'seeks to get the laboratory specialist to give him a form CM-13 with which he can be paid for his crop.

The laboratory specialist finds that the corn in question is not of sufficient quality to be accepted by CONASUPO, at least that is until the farmer pays a bribe called *"un quinientón"* at which point the quality of the corn rapidly improves. The farmer then proceeds to the bank, the *Banco de Crédito Ejidal* (called BANJIDAL by the government and called BANDIDAL by those who wish to disparage it) where he must pay another bribe called a *"corta feriecita"* to put that administrative aparatus into motion. Then it is discovered that the farmer had a credit charged against his account and when this is added to the bribes he emerges with three thousand five hundred pesos as a final payment. This is less than three hundred dollars on which he must live and support his famly for much of the year."

"Aside from the specific administrative failures of the program what about its overall economic impact? Because the price of wheat is fixed substantially above the world market to protect the *ejidatarios* the cost of bread in Mexico is elevated correspondingly. And at this price the wheat surpluses of CONASUPO cannot be sold exclusively on the domestic market so it is necessary to export them. But here is the rub. On the international market there are no guaranteed prices and the ton of corn which CONASUPO purchased for 940 pesos must be sold at the market price which is 702 pesos, a loss of 238 pesos for each ton of corn that is exported. The same situation prevails with the other subsidized grains. Now look if you will at the Annual Report of Nacional Financiera (page 93) which says: 'the harvests of winter 1964–65 and the summer of 1965 achieved such a volume that after satisfying completely the internal necessities CONASUPO was able to export, principally to Poland and Switzerland, the unprecedented figure of 1,409,325 tons of corn which, despite the low price of 702 pesos for which the corn was sold, meant that for the first time in Mexican history corn became the country's second largest export.' *Caramba,* in large print."

"It would be great for us to aid Poland and Switzerland if our own necessities were truly satisfied and if we did not already have an enormous budgetary deficit. But this is not so. Even the Institute of Nutrition tells us that only around 35 to 40 percent of Mexican families enjoy even the basic minimum calorie intake daily, and that from 25 to 28 percent of the population suffers from anemia. And when we ask why CONASUPO does not sell its grain at a lower price within Mexico instead of sustaining this loss in favor of foreign countries the director of CONASUPO, Prof. Carlos Hank González, explains: 'When the price comes down internally the price supports will end and the local products will remain unprotected.' The logic, thus, is to keep the domestic price high so that the Swiss and the Poles can enjoy Mexican corn and wheat."

"It is noteworthy that the annual reports of CONASUPO have not been made public since 1964. There are many things which CONASUPO wishes to hide. When quizzed by a reporter from *La Prensa* the director Prof. Hank González said that the difference between the fixed price and the lower external price is a necessary cost of subsidy that all the people of Mexico must pay (*La Prensa* 11 March 1965, page 12). The price must be protected internally, even if it means the destruction of nearly three thousand tons of corn and over one thousand tons of sorgum at Matamoros. The impact throughout Mexico in terms of the price of bread and the nation's balance of payments deficit is ignored."

ON THE SIGNIFICANCE OF AUTOMEX AND CONASUPO

Probably it has not escaped the reader's attention that the name of the Secretary for Industry and Commerce figured at a high level of involvement in both the cases of Automex and CONASUPO. To catalogue all such multiple involvements would be an endless task. On the one hand, the government favors a given industrial complex; nationalism within the revolutionary mystique is the formal defense. On the other, the government creates a gigantic system of price fixing and foodstuff distribution that apparently results in an overall loss to Mexico; again, the justification is nationalism within the revolutionary mystique. The key is Mexicanization and this, or at best its appearance, is to be accomplished at national expense and via programs whose bureaucracies have instilled in themselves a moral purpose and justify what they must do in the name of good public policy, in the name of agrarian reform, and to the glorification of the Mexican peasant. An official CONASUPO document says that in 1963 the price of corn was raised from 800 pesos per ton to 940 pesos as "an act of social justice" which would benefit not only the farmer but the national industry as well.[26] Much of Mexico's governmental performance is deliberately enobled through such declarations of moral imperative.

What is important to recognize here is that paternalism is the predominant style of the process whereby government seeks to lend impulse to economic development. But in the very process new empires, and jealously guarded ones, are created. Old political cliques thus grow and subdivide into new ones. The ability to grant or withhold a blessing for economic development becomes at once a political sanction vis-à-vis a given individual or concern. The political cliques are instrumental, as we have seen in the case of Automex, in channeling such economic blessings outwardly from the upper reaches of policy making. Economic blessings used as political sanctions are nothing new in Mexico. In his study *Bankers as Revolutionaries* Charles W. Anderson recognizes the widespread acceptance of this practice in Mexico and he cites evidence of the abyss, both economic and political, which exists between the credit institutions of agrarian reform and the Mexican peasants.[27] Anderson's study which does not go beyond the era of CEIMSA (liquidated in 1961) leaves the rather general impression that Mexico's governmental performance has been effective in the economic development field in spite of the nation's experience of a highly inequitable distribution of total income.

Similar general conclusions result from the effort of William P. Glade Jr. which was published in collaboration with Anderson's work.[28] Glade contends that the Mexican Revolution unleashed forces

[26] *Qué es la CONASUPO?* op. cit., p. 7.

[27] William P. Glade, Jr. and Charles W. Anderson, *The Political Economy of Mexico* (Madison: University of Wisconsin, 1963), especially pp. 169–178.

[28] Ibid.

that have culminated in a "thoroughgoing restructuring of the whole economic environment and a corresponding radically new pattern of economic interaction."[29] This is probably true with respect to the before and after conditions of socioeconomic change as viewed across the sweep of a half century. He leaves also the definite impression that instability (in terms of the usually understood symptoms of coups, resignations of cabinet, anomic violence, etc.) is steadily on the decline in Mexico as a result of what the PRI is and does. Glade views the various suborganizations of the PRI as effective channels for communication whereby the interests of competing groups are articulated and/or satisfied. In total, he leaves the impression that the PRI is a capable agent for the promotion of Mexico's socioeconomic development.

The evidence presented in this chapter does not support the conclusions of Glade, and only partially supports those of Anderson. Considerable time has elapsed since their studies were conducted and I call the reader's attention to their efforts in the desire that he be exposed to a scholarly view which is essentially opposed to my own. I will return later to several key points from Glade and Anderson. Again, it is necessary to affirm that scholars who are sincere and honest may also disagree quite strongly, especially where Mexico's governmental performance is concerned.

The Governmental Style Alienates

Beginning in 1940 the Mexican government had a program of exempting special businesses and industries from the payment of

[29] Ibid., p. 98. Here it is worth the effort of quotation to allow one Mexican writer, Pablo González Casanova, who admittedly supports the revolutionary coalition, to reflect upon Mexico's politico-economic development in a style that is in contrast to Glade's. "Nuestros éxitos nos engañan a nosotros mismos y nos llenan de una satisfacción provinciana, que hace un tabú de toda crítica a fondo de la política nacional y del desarrollo de México, y convierte en herejes y delincuentes a quienes la enuncian o sostienen, precisamente para acelerar el desarrollo. Son éxitos relativos, importantes en el panorama de los países subdesarrollados; pero que no han acabado en términos globales con la estructura de la dependencia y la dinámica de la desigualdad, y que sólo nos permiten marchar lentamente con un enorme saldo de hombres miserables." (Pablo González Casanova, *La democracia en México*, México, ERA, 1965, pp. 137–38). He admits that gross figures on Mexico's economic growth may be made to look impressive but that the nation's wealth distribution continues to be inequitable and that Mexico remains an economic colony for United States investors.

certain taxes as a stimulus to economic development. The Bank of Mexico publishes a regular list of such favored industries that is called *Directorio de Empresas Industriales Beneficiadas Con Exenciones Fiscales*, a list that normally exceeds three hundred pages. This in itself is a huge index to the paternalism that characterizes Mexico's governmental style with respect to economic development. To delineate fully the perimeters of this paternalism would exhaust the patience of both author and reader and would, in all likelihood, be impossible. The most important issue here is the question of paternalism for whom? To the degree that economic paternalism is reserved for those whose ties place them in a favored position vis-à-vis any level of government it can be expected that "in-groups" and "out-groups" will be created. The case of Autómex is an extreme example but has a legion of miniature counterparts. And yet it cannot be denied that economic paternalism has pushed Mexico beyond the "take off" period. Economically, Mexico is the envy of many of her Latin American neighbors. But, as a later chapter will show, the distribution of the resulting wealth is poor and Mexico's rising population and burgeoning slums serve to discredit the plaudits given to many of the industrial achievements. Substantial political alienation does result among the multitudes who are poorly reached by these industrial blessings.

More severe are the cases of labor and agrarian policy in which the linkages between government and political monopoly are both obvious and odious. Especially in the latter area the Mexican government appears to have become a gigantic decentralized replacement for the landed estate system (much of which, ironically, continues to exist). The agrarian bureaucracy has taken on a life of its own, as bureaucracies do in any society. It has become infused with a moral purpose whose slogans are freely invoked to justify what is done and to obscure much that goes undone. The nexus between the government's agrarian performance and its approach to economic development is patent in the CONASUPO program. The relatively favorable views of Glade and Anderson notwithstanding, there is enough evidence even in their previously cited works alone to show that a grim and melancholy truth underlies the formalistic niceties that the government and its many information agencies make available to the outside world. When credit and blame are ultimately assigned, it is impossible to divorce governmental performance from the PRI. For that reason it is almost impossible for the PRI to construct a pluasible case for blaming opposition "reactionaries" of any ilk for the failures of the government. This is the crisis of Mexico's politico-governmental legitimacy. In his novel *La otra cara de México* Carlos Chavira has captured the spirit of this dilemma:

Si, por ejemplo, se preguntaba venenosamente desde los bancos de la oposición: "qué razón hay para que exista un partido oficial, que no es más que el Gobierno disfrazado de Partido, cuya sola presencia en el campo electoral no sólo corrompe y nulifica todo intento de autodeterminación del pueblo, sino que es la negación misma de la democracia?," la cumplida respuesta era "que Maximiliano había sido fusilado en Querétaro y que, cuantas veces fuera necesario, surgirían nuevos Cerros de las Campanas para ejecutar traidores.

If, for example, some one inquired bitterly from the opposition benches "why is it that we have an official party, which is no more than the Government disguised as a Party, whose single presence in the electoral field not only corrupts and nullifies every popular effort at self determination, but is in itself a negation of democracy?," the essence of the reply would be that Maximilian was shot in Querétaro and that no matter how many times it would be necessary there would be found new places like the Hill of Bells to execute other traitors.[30]

Here one approaches the nub of political alienation as a general phenomenon in Mexico. Government is expected to send out "streams of satisfactions" and if its failure to do so is widespread, those who are ill-affected will seek out channels through which to articulate their grievances. The story of the *ejido Cañón de la Madera* shows how such channels may actually stultify grievance articulation. Then they organize into "out-groups" whose pressures become an embarrassment to the regime and must, at times, be repressed. Since the electoral arena, and therefore the Congress, do not constitute effective mechanisms for criticism of governmental performance, there is no built-in system for correction of abuses when they occur, that is, until a scandal becomes sufficiently acute and public to involve the national press and anomic group protest behavior. As the PRI grows bigger and its brotherhood power structure becomes more complex,

---

[30] Chavira, op. cit., p. 20 (translated).

its internal watchdog capacity is weakened, thereby inviting anomic reactions to abuses which serve as trigger mechanisms in mobilizing popular alienation against the government.[31]

[31] Since this chapter was written, an excellent article has appeared which analyzes the use of extra-legal methods of political power in Mexico, especially those which can be justified under the controversial Article 145 of the Mexican penal code that is known as the *ley de disolución social*; cf. Evelyn P. Stevens, "Legality and Extra-Legality in Mexico," *Journal of Inter-American Studies*, January, 1970. This law was formally abolished in 1970 following the presidential election, but many Mexican observers feared that it would be replaced with an even more dangerously permissive statute vis-à-vis use of the police power to castigate subversion and political crimes. The author relates examples of suppression and liquidation of opponents in which the government employed extra-legal techniques including "cooptation of the leadership of such groups, generous subsidies, police repression, bribery, and corruption. When these methods fail to bring an organization fully under control . . . the principal preoccupation of the authorities is to liquidate the movement, in order to eliminate any possible threat to the government's omnipotence . . ." (p. 71). In the event that a challenge to officialdom is seen as a threat the Mexican government (i.e. the PRI) prefers extra-legal to legal means of dealing with the conflict, for to allow itself to be challenged in court would be a sign of weakness on the part of the official image. Early in 1970 the journalist Mario Menéndez Rodriguez was jailed for allegedly having blown up the offices of the party PAN and for organizing guerrillas in Chiapas. He was kept indefinitely in Lecumberri Prison without trial and was not charged formally with *delito de disolución social*, therefore being considered a common criminal. The government did not want him in court defending himself. His real "crime" had been exposes in the magazine *Por Qué* of electoral fraud the previous November in Yucatán, plus a series of stinging articles condemning the PRI and President Díaz Ordaz. PAN officials said the attack on their offices was done by the police, "after hours," and that Menéndez had defended PAN and other opposition parties against officialdom.

Menédez became a *cause célèbra* for the radical left, one championed by both the National Strike Committee and by several newly formed guerrilla organizations. Of the later probably the most important in terms of its threat potential was the ACNR (Acción Cívica Nacional Revolucionaria) under the leadership of Genaro Vazquez Rojas and José Bracho Campos. Mario Menéndez Rodríguez and eight other political prisoners were flown to Cuban exile November 28, 1971. Their freedom was granted in exchange for the life of Jaime Castrejón Díez, Rector of the University of Guerrero, and kidnapped November 19, 1971. Díez owned the Coca Cola concession in his state. This case placed the dependency of the PRI upon the commerical elite in bold relief as President Echeverría yielded to the ultimatum of a rural guerrilla band. Its leader Genero Vázquez was killed February 2 in what the government called a traffic accident. His second in command, Bracho Campos, was made a political prisoner and the guerrilla command passed to Lucio Cabañas who remains a threat to the regime and at large well into 1972.

5
Satellite and
Out-Group Politics

The Ideological Spectrum

One year following the violence of 1968 (see Chapter 6), President Díaz Ordaz looked backward to the massacre of Tlatelolco in his 1969 State of the Union Message. He said "for my part I assume entirely the responsibility—personal, ethical, social, legal and historical—for the decisions of the government in relation to the events of last year . . . a series of acts of terrorism made the intervention of the army indispensable."[1] Ostensibly there was no reason for him to bring up again this bitter threat to the revolutionary coalition, but the president continued to feel the weight of popular outrage. Also, he continued to see Tlatelolco as a terrorist conspiracy to be repressed. Díaz Ordaz remained unwilling to admit that the violence represented the critical imperative for socio-economic and political reform.

Disorders of the Tlatelolco variety have been rare in modern Mexico. Traditionally (at least since 1929) political grievances having violence potential have been channeled into the various mechanisms of the revolutionary coalition for resolution (and/or stultification).

[1] From the front page of the *Los Angeles Times*, September 2, 1969. On the same date *Excelsior*, the leading Mexico City daily, reported Díaz Ordaz as giving thanks to the Army for its role as guarantor of Mexican institutions. He also thanked the many workers and peasants "who would not listen to the sedition." Cf. *Excelsior*, 2 de septiembre, 1969, p. 23A. This left the distinct impression that one year later the President still blamed the students above all others.

Grievances that could not get a hearing via the esoteric system have found their way into a number of satellite movements and out groups, like those involved in the violence of 1968. I will not distinguish between satellites and out groups except to stipulate that the former tend to cluster in greater proximity to the periphery of officialdom, but the terms are relative and almost figures of speech. The essential point is that the future stability of Mexican politics depends greatly upon the mechanisms of esoteric democracy which must somehow forestall the rise of belligerence and violence among these satellites and out groups. In this chapter I will examine the spectrum of the Mexican opposition. There are, as yet, no impartial definitive works on the Mexican opposition. The present treatment is in the nature of an overview, bolstered in places by selected examples of ideological content and behavioral style.

THE MARXIST SECTOR

At the height of intellectual euphoria over the triumph of the Russian Revolution, the rise of constitutionalism in Mexico spawned a number of Marxian socialist movements. Among these was the Socialist Workers Party of Luis Morones which held a convention in 1919 to try to amalgamate the Marxist left. The heterogeneous membership of this assembly (it included foreigners like the North American socialist Frank Seaman) made it difficult to achieve a unified front, and as a result a number of party splinters emerged. Communications barriers impeded the rise of a closely knit proletarian consciousness and over the years the vicissitudes of the international communist movement did little to unify the Marxist sector of Mexico around a single voice. One of many recurring crises has been the impact of *"browderismo,"* the influence of the North American communist Earl Browder, whose name became synonymous in Mexico with elimination of the secret workers cells in factories and a soft line toward capitalism.[2] The PCM, Mexican Communist Party, is the parent organization of the Marxist-revolutionary sector and dates back to the Morones convention of 1919. However, its decidedly middle class and frankly bourgeois leadership orientation has resulted in a breaking away of radical and violence prone splinter groups. These

[2] Vicente Fuentes Díaz, *Los partidos políticos en México* (México: Editorial Altiplano, 2d ed, 1969), p. 382.

are frequently referred to as Trotskyite parties, so named for their radical and independent course.

Among such groups one finds the Mexican Workers and Peasants Party, POCM, which for all intents and purposes has been coopted into the Popular Socialist Party and today must be considered the "official left" of the revolutionary coalition. The same may be said for the formerly radical peasant movement UGOCM, General Union of Mexican Workers and Peasants, whose once firebrand leader Jacinto López has also been wooed into collaboration with the "official left." Radical groups unwilling to be coopted like the CCI, Independent Peasants Front, emerged during the 1960's in a broad and heterogeneous galaxie of satellite parties that constitute what has been labelled here the Marxist sector. In 1961 an effort was made to amalgamate this galaxie into something resembling a unified national movement, called the National Liberation Movement, MLN, under the leadership of Jorge Carrión and others. Almost immediately the MLN was denounced by socialist leader Vicente Lombardo Toledano who was by then the titular head of the "official (coopted PPS) left." Essentially, Lombardo insisted on the revisionist course in which socialists cooperate with and particpate in the bourgeois state. He also denounced efforts to hold up the Cuban Revolution as an appropriate model for Mexico. It is believed that Lombardo resented the influence of Lázaro Cárdenas within the MLN and was instrumental in keeping Jacinto López' UGOCM from integrating with the MLN.

The MLN embraced a Castro-communist symbolism in its challenge to the revolutionary coalition. Braulio Maldonado, the controversial former governor of Baja California, became an early leader in the movement and advocated converting the peasants into a militant political force (Rubén Jaramillo style). This was to be a counter force to the then more moderate appearance of the UGOCM. The MLN was responsible for the formation of the CCI, Independent Peasants Front, whose principal leaders Arturo Orona, Ramón Danzós Palomino, and Alfonso Garzón sought to institutionalize a true peasant counterrevolution. Although the CCI later broke away from the MLN, its genesis was clearly one of the movement's greatest affronts to officialdom (i.e. the PRI's agrarian sector in general and the CNC in particular).

In 1963 elements of the MLN sought to take advantage of Mexico's new electoral law which made it possible for opposition parties to win seats at large. It created the FEP or Popular Electoral Front which sought to acquire the 75,000 bona fide members necessary to qualify it as a legal party. When it failed to qualify, FEP entered the 1964 election campaign illegally behind the presidential candidacy of Danzós Palomino. Danzós and others, including the distinguished painter David Alfaro Siqueiros (who ran for the Senate while still in jail),[3] hurled scathing attacks on the PRI and preached violence to an extent that led to Danzós' arrest and imprisonment the year following the 1964 election. But the demise of the FEP was intimately related to the continuing fragmentation of the MLN, a division basically between those (following Lombardo) who sought to be an official opposition and those (following Danzós) who urged revolutionary opposition to the point of violence. In 1968 the death of Lombardo left the MLN congeries open to the possibility of a new effort at amalgamation. Danzós remained in prison and was unable to direct a regrouping of the radicals. A new charismatic presence was desperately needed if the Marxist sector was to achieve order.

It is rumored that early in 1968 a summit conference of the Marxist sector was held privately on the Michoacán ranch of Lázaro Cárdenas. One of its acts was *to attempt* to create a new unified front around the figure of the aging ex-president. This was to be called the FPI or Popular Front of the Left. Another result of this summit conference was the suppression of the publication *Política* which had been a voice for discordant factions of the MLN. The death of *Política* is important because it had been a source of extreme irritation to President Díaz Ordaz (for its uncomplimentary editorials and cartoons) and it is likely that Lázaro Cárdenas endorsed the suppression as a gesture in favor of coexistence with the revolutionary coalition. Cárdenas favored a sort of deceptive cooptation thus leaving the remaining elements of the far left without leadership. Carlos A. Madrazo was considered too bourgeois to fill this role which called for a refined Danzós or a sophisticated Rubén Jaramillo. Madrazo's death in 1969 ended speculation over his potential for unifying the revolutionary left (again it is well to note that political ideologues in Mexico follow men more vehemently than ideas).

[3] For a thorough discussion of the early tribulations of the Marxist sector, see David T. Garza, "Factionalism in the Mexican Left: The Frustration of the MLN," *The Western Political Quarterly*, September, 1964, pp. 447–460 *passim*.

Mexico's political left boasts a number of severely alienated out groups which are denied participation. Many of these cannot even be called satellites vis-à-vis the revolutionary coalition. Some of the groups fought the government during the series of events in 1968 leading up to Tlatelolco. The more radical among them are: 1) the POR, Revolutionary Workers Party, described as Trotskyite, anticlerical, guerrilla and violence-oriented, and contains several subgroups in the National University such as the *Grupo Miguel Hernández*, alleged to have committed acts of industrial sabotage during the summer of 1968; 2) the JCM, Mexican Communist Youth, a Moscow oriented youth arm of the Mexican Communist Party; 3) the MRP, Peoples Revolutionary Movement, formed largely by discontents and renegades from the MLN such as Raúl Ugalde and Víctor Rico Galán who have been imprisoned, charged with the derailing of trains and other acts of violence about the country, 4) the ONAR, National Organization for Revolutionary Action, a splinter from the "official left" PPS which has ties with guerrilla movements in Michoacán, Guerrero, Oaxaca, and Chihuahua; its leader is the former PPS deputy, Dr. Miguel Estrada Villa, who served as personal secretary to Lombardo Toledano and who masterminded plans to convert the Christian Democratic movement into a front for organized violence; 5) the MML or Marxist Leninist Movement which along with the Spartacan Communist League, LCE, operates in guerrilla fashion in the states of Guerrero and Michoacán and publishes the Red China oriented publication *China Nueva*; 6) the CNED, National Confederation of Democratic Students which will be discussed in the following chapter as a primary motivator of student radicalism and violence. There are other splinter movements whose number is legion. Unofficially, it is alleged that the extreme left wing of the CNC, the PRI's own agrarian sector, has a renegade clique whose leader is Cuauhtemoc Cárdenas, the son of ex-president Cárdenas. This group has allegedly fostered land invasion movements in derogation of official policy.

From the standpoint of dilemmas confronting Mexico's esoteric democratic system, the Marxist sector's greatest threat lies in the radical violence prone groups and renegade popular leaders who will not join the "official left" (the PPS) and whose alienation leads them to eschew the organs of legitimacy which have made the revolutionary coalition work. These are the groups most bitterly opposed to officialdom. Typical examples of their ideology are seen as follows. First, the Communist leader Gerardo Unzueta (imprisoned during the violence of 1968) who wrote from behind the walls of Lecumberri Prison:

The PRI and the government who turn their backs on all contemporary historical development in order to obscure the struggle among classes now accuse the student youth of unleashing a wicked theory of conflict between generations . . . the speech of Martínez Domínguez is, in no way, a political program; it offers no solutions, it condemns and renders all else anathema. He threatens in the name of the governmental team to let fall over all that moves the weight of the "supreme law." It is not a promise for the future, but a condemnation from the past.[4]

Those too radical for the relatively "bourgeois" Communist Party turn their criticism upon the PCM itself. One such group is the *Liga Leninista Espartaco* which is an outgrowth of the Spartacan Communist League mentioned earlier. The LLE states its case as follows:

The PCM criticizes the proletariat in an erroneous manner, i.e., it condemns anarchosyndicalism without taking into account the proletarian character of the class struggle that is involved; in this way it fails to provide the kind of internal self criticism which its role as vanguard demands. . . .[5]

Mexico's radicals in the Marxist sector have produced few enduring popular leaders. Indeed, the sort of leadership that has emerged has appeared frankly bourgeois and has often behaved treasonably. In the clandestine literature of protest there is probably no more damaging portrait of radical Marxist leadership as an agent of organizational atrophy than that contained in the book *Qué poca mad . . . era!* by Prudencio Godines Jr., released in 1968. The author, born in the state of Guanajuato, was educated in Russia and Cuba, fought with the FALN guerrillas in Venezuela, and the Camilo Torres movement in Colombia, and worked with the international Communist underground in Nicaragua and Guatemala. He was ordered home to Mexico in 1965. Godines' task was that of technical consultant to the top leadership of Mexico's insurgent Marxists who were planning

---

[4] Gerardo Unzueta, "Requiem para un sarcófago (nota sobre la ideología burguesa de la Revolución Mexicana," *Nueva Epoca*, Febrero, 1969, pp. 31–32.

[5] *Nueva Praxis*, abril–junio, 1969, pp. 22–23.

uprisings about the country. His first meeting was in June 1965 at the home of Víctor Rico Galán. Present were Ramón Danzós Palomino, Marcué Pardiñas, José Santos Valdés, Dr. Estrada Villa, J. Dolores López, Arnoldo Verdugo and Alfonso Aguilar, and other unnamed functionaries of the PCM and the MLN.[6] Santos Valdés, actually employed by the Ministry of Public Instruction as inspector for the Chihuahua and northeastern region, had presented to this group a list of persons in Chihuahua who had promised to sponsor and aid an armed attack on the military garrison located at Ciudad San Pedro Madera. Godines writes, "when I had in my hands the list of proposed collaborators I was disgusted to find they were all professors and only one peasant."[7] He shocked his superiors by asking why no more of the common people were pledged in mass to the uprising. The reply was to accuse Godines of being with the CIA. Victor Rico Galán had to guarantee Godines' identity.

September 15, 1965 had been picked for the assault on the garrison. Rifles and machine guns had been promised. José Santos Valdés pledged logistic support in the area of his specialty, incendiary bombs and gasoline. Victor Rico Galán, dynamite specialist, would provide a number of homemade bombs and would personally head a team of experts to launch these projectiles into the compound. It was understood that a gigantic peasant and proletarian uprising would shake the area and that Ciudad Madera would become the Sierra Maestra of Mexico. The plan had, according to the book, been approved earlier by Raúl Castro in Cuba. Godines then relates the tragic story of arms and supplies that never came, of popular apathy, of brave guerrillas who made crude gasoline bombs and trained with single shot 22 rifles and single barrel shotguns. He tells of a poignant last supper rite, followed by an advance on the military compound in the freezing early morning air. He writes of the horror of being wounded and miraculously escaping from a combat firefight in which almost all of his scarcely two dozen comrades were slaughtered. Then Godines tells what happened to his leadership cabal: "we were few against many, our help never arrived. Neither Victor Rico Galán nor José Santos Valdés were even in Chihuahua as they had promised. Instead they were conspicuously engaged in debate in the

6 Prudencio Godines Jr., *Que poca mad . . . era!* (México, 1968), p. 53.

7 Ibid., p. 55.

cafe *La Habana* in Mexico City, a place always under government surveillance, thus guaranteeing them an alibi."[8]

Godines relates how the FEP (Popular Electoral Front) offices in Chihuahua tried to make the disaster into an heroic event and sought to stir up the people's hatred by using the slaughter as an example of government cruelty. Such behavior, according to Godines, was easily in character for the FEP. He names José Santos Valdés, the man in whose derogation the book is principally written, as the mastermind of the famous 1964 attack upon Gustavo Díaz Ordaz in the Plaza of Chihuahua during the presidential campaign of that year. That event produced recriminations against Braulio Maldonado and other leaders of the MLN-FEP complex. But most of those sacrificed were students of preparatory schools. The same was true of the attack at Ciudad Madera in 1965: the humble people were sacrificed and José Santos Valdés (known in secret Communist parlance as "Jueves") remained innocent, aloof, and still on the payroll of the very government he was striving to destroy. Santos Valdéz is one among many who function as employees of the federal government (especially in educational roles) and exist on the small largesse they receive via the esoteric system while all the time conspiring to destroy it.

"He throws the stone and hides his hand" is a tactical norm especially well adapted to the behavioral style of extremists in the Marxist sector. This is apparently why the radical left does not win large popular followings, and why it was virtually unable to use even the traumatic experience of the events leading to Tlatelolco as a basis for forming an organic plan of political socialization and concrete action.

Godines notes that Mexico's radical Marxist left in reality seeks a revolution designed to serve the interests of a favored coterie. All others must be expendables and sacrificed freely to promote this cause. That was the essence of the lesson learned on September 15, 1965 outside the walls of the military compound at Ciudad Madera:

those who died were not invited to the "high level" reunion as the ringleaders' meetings are ridiculously termed. Very simply, Victor Rico Galán, Manuel Marcué, José Santos Valdés, and Jacinto López undertook to excite

[8] Ibid., p. 94. The title of the book is derived from the author's oft-repeated expression of contempt which I quote without translation as follows: "*Qué poca madre la de Santos Valdés! . . . Qué . . . poca . . . mad . . .!*"

and inflame their followers by appealing to love, valor, and vanity, to their spirit of self sacrifice and political discipline, thereby giving the order for attack against the garrison at San Pedro Madera. They gave their lives—or at least their blood—without knowing the murderous trap their leaders had led them to. Therefore, many of the few who survived the massacre are unwilling to give testimony against the leaders. But I will![9]

The PCM, which gave birth to the Marxist sector in 1919, has been unable to consolidate itself organizationally to confront the revolutionary coalition with anything other than ad hoc pressures or anomic violence. Too often the Marxist sector organizations have been content with momentary goals and have neglected long range programs of action. The National Strike Committee of 1968 was criticized for its failure to expand the student's six basic demands into a comprehensive plan for the "proletarianization" of all Mexico.[10] The students saw in the release of their 755 prisoner colleagues a triumph whose significance they greatly exaggerated. The PCM's political stance remains flexible. It will participate with the revolutionary coalition if it is allowed to do so, but is prepared to act clandestinely and violently if necessary. The Marxist left has not yet learned how to resolve the dilemma of divided group loyalty. It cannot handle the challenge of deviant charisma. It appears to be looking for a "caesaristic identification."[11] But an effective regrouping of the Marxist sector during the decade of the 1970's could force radical changes and/or

[9] Ibid., p. 135.

[10] *Tlatelolco,* op. cit., p. 107.

[11] Franz Neumann ties political alienation to persecutory anxiety which "is produced when a group is threatened in its prestige, income, or even its existence; i.e., when it declines and does not understand the historical process or is prevented from understanding it" (in Stein, Vidich, White, eds., *Identity and Anxiety* (Glencoe: Free Press, 1960), p. 286). Such persecutory anxiety may be manifest in political identifications with caesaristic movements or with what Shils calls "nativist leaders" (cf. Edward Shils, "Authoritarianism Right or Left," in Ulmer, ed., *Introductory Readings in Political Behavior* (Chicago: Rand McNally, 1961), pp. 27–33). Such formations often exhibit severe internal instability and low cohesion which drives them into zealous and chauvinistic actions and postures. Often they are impatient at a long wait for acquisition of power. Moreover, such groups will frequently embrace what Neumann terms the conspiracy theory of history. They take comfort in cryptic explanations and apocalyptic visions of social dilemmas, tending to blame public ills on a conspiring cabal, e.g., the Mexican extremists of both the far right and far left at the moment of this writing. Their political alienation becomes the overt manifestation of the conflict between inner aspects of the self and particular socio-economic-political forms perceived as threatening in the environment.

dislocations in Mexico's esoteric system. This will depend not only upon the Marxists' ability to compromise and organize internally. It will also require some pragmatic commitment to working with the exigencies of Mexico's socioeconomic ambient. Socioeconomic change is, after all, the greatest single challenge facing Mexico in the decade ahead.

THE RESTORATIONIST SECTOR

The PRI has its own "official right" in an amorphous group known as PARM, the Authentic Party of the Mexican Revolution, which is easily and intimately a part of the revolutionary coalition. There is little point in trying to distinguish this party ideologically. It consists of the older generation of revolutionaries who claim to be "purer" revolutionaries than anyone else. Along with its counterpart of the "official left" (the PPS) the PARM has a handful of seats in the Chamber of Deputies and none in the Senate. Also like the official left, the PARM supported the official candidacy of Díaz Ordaz in 1964 and Luis Echeverría in 1970.

To the right of PARM lies a party traditionally thought of as the only true opposition party in Mexico. This party PAN, the National Action Party, is certainly the only one recognized by the revolutionary coalition as a bona fide competitor. When I studied the presidential succession of 1964 I wrote an analysis concluding that PAN had been partially coopted into the single-party system. Following that election high officials of PAN made public noises which indicated they would like full membership in the revolutionary coalition. On one highly bizarre occasion reformist elements of the PRI actually teamed up with PAN in an effort to support Carlos Madrazo's crusade for democratizing the local political process. This took place on December 4, 1965, when a PRI senator challenged PAN's president Adolfo Christlieb Ibarrola to a duel in the stadium of Mexico's National University (UNAM). The proceeds of the duel were to be used to establish a specialized voting register throughout the nation to guarantee honest elections. Christlieb accepted the challenge, but of course it never took place. The parties involved merely wanted to dramatize an evil and prescribe a cure.

It is likely that the ouster of Madrazo a few weeks after this episode marked the turning point in the cooptation process if, indeed, there had ever been one. At any rate PAN seemed to steer an independent course thereafter and, as we shall presently see, mounted a critical threat to the PRI in a number of municipal elections in various states. My contentions about the cooptation of PAN based on the 1964 presidential succession have not been well supported by subsequent events.

I have chosen to classify the constellation of satellite parties and out groups to the right of PRI as *restorationists*. This merits a brief historical sketch of the development of right wing ideology in Mexico. One sees its genesis in the Queretaro Club of 1810 that produced Hidalgo and Allende and in the subsequent rebellions against the colonists. Reactionary ideology thrived during the regimes of Iturbide, Santa Anna, and burst forth in the clerical opposition to Lerdo, Juárez, Ocampo and to the Liberal Constitution of 1857. Ultra-conservative thought was rejuvenated for thirty-five years by the scientists during the *Pax Porfiriana* passing thereafter into the hands of those who fought Calles. Ultimately, it was crystallized in the organized popular reactions to Lázaro Cárdenas' reform era during the 1930's. The latter period is particularly important for it saw the rise of two principal groups that are central to the restorationist right. Cárdenas' sweeping nationalizations of industry accelerated distribution of agricultural lands via the usufructuary device of the state farm system and stricter enforcement of the anticlerical provisions of the Constitution of 1917 provoked a conservative reaction. Those who organized against Cárdenas and his political predecessors embraced a "world view" that I shall term "restorationism." Mexico's restorationists are those who would return to the Church its political and financial privileges; to the great families, the land; and to the unhampered forces of the marketplace, business and commerce. The most severe restorationists openly favor a theoretic basis for the socioeconomic and political system. Today, Mexico's restorationists have two principal organized forms, *Unión Nacional Sinarquista* (UNS) and *Partido Acción Nacional* (PAN).[12] The latter group is now undergoing a process of considerable liberalization without giving way to cooptation into the esoteric circle.

The term *sinarquismo* is a corruption of two words, *sin anarquía*, without anarchy or in better English, with order. Order, *orden* as the name of its official journal implies, is the hallmark of UNS. It is an order of Christian theocracy first under God, then under a God-fearing state. All UNS members are ardent Roman Catholics. They

---

12 Related groups are the *Acción Católica Mexicana* movement and the *Unión Nacional de Padres de Familia.*

are disciplined soldiers of a theocratic faith. The movement was born (according to official doctrine) amid an explosion of enthusiasm, faith, and courage.[13] The basic committee that proclaimed UNS from León, Guanajuato in 1937 consisted of José Antonio Urquiza, José Trueba Olivares, Manuel Zermeño. Juan Ignacio Padilla, Rubén and Guillermo Mendoza Heredia. So intense was the popular frenzy in response to their declarations that the Governor of Guanajuato, an appointee and puppet for President Cárdenas, drove the committee from his state, whereupon they established offices in Mexico City and began publication of a mimeographed *El Boletín* in an effort to develop a national organization.[14]

Although José Antonio Urquiza is most often called the Founder of UNS, its first national chief to hold working office was José Trueba Olivares of León. Soon after taking office, Trueba resigned for "economic reasons" and was followed by Manuel Zermeño.

The assassination of José Antonio Urquiza in 1938 was the first of many crises for UNS. Its stepped-up counter offensive against an alleged Communist design to liquidate UNS produced an ambiguous period of rioting and bloodshed that lasted throughout the war years in the 1940's and which the *sinarquistas* stubbornly blame on the political left.[15] The same disorders were blamed by the Cárdenas regime on fascist elements within *sinarquismo*.

It is fair to say that they did cause a great amount of trouble for Cárdenas and his successors. But since the early 1950's *sinarquismo* has tended to function as a pacific, although not passive, civic opposition.[16] As an ideology that is essentially restorationist, it finds little

---

[13] Juan Ignacio Padilla, *El sinarquismo* (México: Ediciones UNS, 2d ed., 1953), p. 25.

[14] *Ibid.*

[15] On July 11, 1939, in Celaya, Guanajuato, a woman *sinarquista* named Teresita Bustos was murdered (allegedly by police) while performing in a *sinarquista* rally. As a symbolic gesture of unity and martyrdom each outgoing national president of UNS delivers to his successor the blood stained flag which this woman carried to her death (*Orden*, 31 de mayo, 1964, p. 2).

[16] Here is a verbatim statement of *sinarquismo* vis-à-vis Cárdenas: "vivíamos la época cardenista . . . se ponían en peligro las libertades fundamentales de la persona . . . con el predominio del Estado, y en la educación se marchaba con descaro y con aceleramiento hacia el marxismo, pues esta tendencia había quedado hecha ley en el artículo tercero de la Carta General de la República . . . La Unión Nacional Sinarquista surgió como una defensa del pueblo contra esos peligros (*Orden*, 21 de junio, 1964, p. 4).

congruency between its own image of the ideal state and the phenomenal political realities of contemporary Mexico. UNS has, to say the least, a strong authoritarian bent.

The second major political group in Mexico that reflects a restorationist ideology is PAN. It was founded two years later than UNS, in 1939, as a part of the conservative reaction to Cárdenas. *Sinarquistas* are quick to point out that they antedate PAN which was formed out of splinter elements from their own group. Most scholars of Mexican politics have agreed that PAN is the only serious opposition to the official PRI.

PAN emerged as a political party in September, 1939, at a convention held in Mexico City and claims as its founder, Manuel Gómez Morín, an attorney who is still active in the party's national organization. Unlike UNS, PAN has always considered itself a political party and, with the exception of 1940 and 1946, has offered both congressional, state, and presidential candidates throughout Mexico. In its appeals, PAN carefully avoids direct attacks upon those institutions which are traditionally Mexican and are important symbols of nationhood. Thus the Constitution of 1917 (except for Article 3) is upheld as a basis for freedom and equality among Mexicans. PAN charges the PRI with "bastardization" of this great work through administrative abuses of liberty. Principal foci of the PAN attack are the anti-clerical provisions of the Constitution[17] and the extension of state capitalism into the traditionally private sector. Today's *panistas* include the old established families whose wealth and position has been reduced or threatened, certain of the *nouveau riche* who aspire to greater place, many of the upwardly mobile middle class who "never quite made it," and an uncertain base of peasants and artisans whose susceptibility to clerical propaganda has placed them within PAN ranks. Professor Philip B. Taylor observed quite accurately that PAN claims a heavy female membership.[18] Having never been able to claim more than 12 percent of the officially reported vote in a presidential election, PAN carries the image of a weak and ineffectual alternative to PRI. Many North Americans have been told that the PRI subsidizes PAN to maintain the facade of a two party

[17] This theme was developed in characteristic fashion by Gómez Morín in an interview published by *La Nación*, 26 de abril, 1964, p. 5.

[18] Philip B. Taylor, "The Mexican Elections of 1958: Affirmation of Authoritarianism?" *The Western Political Quarterly*, September, 1960, p. 729.

system to impress the outside world. My own investigations over the past decade totally reject this contention.

Several months prior to the presidential election on July 6, 1964, UNS entered into a coalition agreement with a nearly defunct splinter party, the *Partido Nacionalista de México*. The latter, PNM, enjoyed official recognition by the Secretary of the Interior and was to be placed on the official ballot as a registered opposition party. When word of the UNS-PNM alliance became widespread, the Secretary of the Interior cancelled the PNM registration, ostensibly on the ground that the party lacked the legally required membership of 75,000. Confidential sources in PAN, UNS, PNM, and even in PRI itself admitted to the present author that the cancellation was a reaction to the threat of a large *sinarquista* vote for PNM candidates for the Chamber of Deputies. UNS claimed it could muster a popular vote somewhat in excess of one million. Under Mexico's new electoral law, this could place up to twenty *sinarquistas* or their sympathizers in the Congress.[19] Moreover, the author learned that the original demand for the cancellation came from the national committee of *Acción Nacional* which feared loss of its own "privileged" status as the only legal opposition party."[20]

Examples of PAN ideology are easily secured via its official publication *La Nación* that is allowed to circulate freely about the republic and cannot usually be considered a part of the clandestine literature of protest. But *La Nación* does protest and occasionally its editions are seized in a given locality for an especially penetrating expose against public officials. In general PAN faces a dilemma that is difficult to overcome in terms of the party's desire to be considered a bona fide opposition to the revolutionary coalition. It is an ideological and programmatic dilemma. Whereas the PRI cannot con-

---

[19] The reformed electoral law, still in force, provided a "mixed system" of proportional representation. In addition to winning electoral districts for the *Cámara de Diputados*, a political party could (for the first time) win as many as twenty deputies at large (called *diputados de partido*). This required, first of all, that a party get at least 2.5 percent of the total national vote for deputies which would automatically win five seats. Then one seat would be awarded for each one-half percent of the national total up to a limit of twenty seats (PRI, *Primera Reunión nacional de Programación* (México: 1963), pp. 292-293).

[20] The testimony given at that time was that PAN had agreed not to charge fraud when Gustavo Díaz Ordaz won the election and in return PAN would be guaranteed twenty deputies at large in the *Cámara de Diputados*. The cancellation of the PNM registration was only one part of the larger bargain.

vincingly blame its opposition for the failure of governmental performance (in which the opposition scarcely participates) neither can the opposition take credit for the positive accomplishments (or the facade thereof) that the esoteric system can claim. The PRI has many good things to its credit and claims many more. PAN may never have done bad things to Mexico, but neither has it distinguished itself with good ones. A reading of most of PAN's official programs during the past decade reflects the party's preoccupation with carrying out various goals of the Mexican Revolution with which not even the PRI could disagree. The only issue, really, is who should be entrusted to undertake these important works: the PAN with no experience, or the PRI which claims fifty years of it. Thus PAN is usually forced into the negative role of attacking officialdom for its abuses and failures, a role not unlike that of the Marxist left.

A brief glance at the presidential succession of 1964 illustrates this point. PAN's candidate, José González Torres, carried out an attack upon officialdom that was, in many ways, analogous to some of the campaign pronouncements of Senator Barry Goldwater in the United States. González Torres, in a speech in Ixtlahuacán, Colima, stressed the problem of bureaucratic waste in government "cooperatives" (e.g. SCOP, Secretariat of Communications and Public Works) and that of tax assessments for these enterprises in excess of operating costs. He admitted that Mexico's Federal government had performed certain valuable public works but insisted that much more could have been accomplished with available capital.[21] The PAN candidate called for administrative decentralization, branded as unconstitutional the concentration of power in the hands of the president, and generally decried the corruption and weakness of state and local governments.[22] In his native state, Michoacán, González Torres attacked socialism in Mexico as a creeping disease leading eventually to Communism.[23]

PAN demanded an end to the system of state supported collective farms and condemned the *Banco Ejidal* for corrupt lending and foreclosure practices. These agrarian charges brought a prompt rejoinder from peasant leader and PRI stalwart, Jesús Yurén, who was quoted as saying "González Torres is worse than Goldwater," a

[21] *Novedades*, 12 de junio, 1964, p. 37.

[22] *Novedades*, 13 de junio, 1964, p. 25.

[23] *Novedades*, 15 de junio, 1964, p. 3.

gratuitous testament to the similarity between the concurrent Mexican and American campaigns.[24] Another major point for PAN's campaign attack was the program of free textbooks for the public schools (initiated during the López Mateos regime) that was promised continued support by all candidates of the PRI. González Torres argued, "free textbooks and liberty of education are not incompatible, they complement each other and we should have both."[25] In private conversations with PAN members I learned that their basis for resentment of the textbook program is that the books are compulsory and make no mention of God or of religion. This is seen as a deliberate program of "dechristianization" of Mexico which, according to PAN, is 96 percent Catholic.[26] All in all, PAN launched a vigorous, well-financed campaign that was characterized by moderate (in this writer's estimation) promises and pronouncements and with a relative minimum of vindictive and bitterness.[27]

The official platform of *Acción Nacional* for the period 1967–1970 departed little from the above. It favored most of the things the PRI has traditionally offered and that PAN would like to offer but can't. Significantly, PAN's 1970 program stressed the problem of municipal autonomy in much the same terms as Carlos Madrazo had done five years earlier. PAN also called for abolition of the appointive local governmental arrangement in the Federal District and its replacement with an elective process. In addition PAN stressed the need for electoral reform and criticized a range of abuses of human liberties which were laid (appropriately) at the door of the PRI.

Approaching the reactionary extreme of the restorationist sector, the UNS, one finds a somewhat greater difficulty in securing examples of political ideology. The UNS is admittedly a secret and clandestine organization. I have visited its inconspicuous national headquarters in Mexico City several times, but always with an officially signed note

[24] *Novedades*, 17 de junio, 1964, p. 1.

[25] *Novedades*, 2 de julio, 1964, p. 20.

[26] PAN handbills and those of the *Unión Nacional de Padres de Familia* called attention to the "atheistic" free text.

[27] González' Torres pronouncements were mild in comparison with those of his predecessor six years earlier. In the 1958 campaign Luis H. Álvarez blamed all the ills of the world on the PRI which contributed to a tense atmosphere in which violence did take place. One of Álvarez' campaign workers was killed and several were wounded. I interviewed Álvarez and did not find him to be the demagogue that Taylor pictured him, op. cit., p. 741.

of request for admission. The same level of secrecy prevails in the regional branches about the country. Its literature is highly emotive, often poetic, and carrys an ominous tone of doomsday. It has given León, Guanajuato, the city where it was founded, the menacing epithet *Sinarcópolis* where every three years a major pilgrimage is held to witness the installation of a new national president. On could almost say that the UNS is a giant political clique and that its president is a fixed term boss.

At the moment it is difficult to list precisely all that it favors but one can specify certain key things it opposes. It opposes the PRI, and the United States; it denies the frequently made charge that it is a fascist organization; it opposes all Jews, Masons, Communists, and exhibits a general xenophobia. Its official statutes contain a *pentálogo sinarquista* which condemns political tyranny and human misery, opposes collectivization as tantamount to communism, and champions a fiercely proud Mexican nationalism. What should the government do? The *sinarquistas* have a curious reply: "The UNS has no finished program that can solve on paper all of the troubles of Mexico; rather than written words, *sinarquismo* is spirit and action."[28]

The politics of the UNS are now largely restricted to civic protest movements in the states and localities, like the Union for Civic Defense of the Peoples Interests of Tepic, Nayarit formed in the early 1960's to protest abuses in the assessment of fees for public water.

Sinarquismo is a conspiratorial interpretation of political life. The conspiracy began with Cárdenas and he is excoriated in rituallike fashion for having launched Mexico on the path to ruin.[29] Somehow the UNS has instilled in its membership (claimed at around five million) the belief in an apocalyptic vision of revealed truth. Each member is fervently confident that the vaguely defined apocalypse will come to fruition during his lifetime.

Beyond the UNS lie a number of well-financed but lesser known movements. Most powerful among these is the OPUS DEI organiza-

[28] Unión Nacional Sinarquista, *Estatutos*, 1960, p. 36 (my translation).

[29] I have in my possession a secret unpublished manuscript of the UNS that will be treated in a forthcoming study; this document develops fully the *sinarquista* points of attack against Cárdenas et al. Another representative treatment of the same theme is found in Juan Ignacio Padilla, "El verdadero peligro," *Orden*, Mayo, 1961, p. 7.

tion, which is not a unique Mexican movement since it is directed from Spain by reactionary clerics. OPUS DEI operates through numerous organizations including USEM, Social Union of Mexican Businessmen, which opposses the "Monterrey Group" cited earlier. OPUS DEI works through another of the cliques, the AUTOMEX group also cited earlier. It contributes financial support to the publication *La Hoja de Combate* whose director, Salvador Abascal, is also a major figure in the *sinarquista* movement. The principal publication of OPUS DEI, however, is *Gente* which frequently lends its support to causes embraced by the PAN and carries on a vigorous anti-communist propaganda barrage. To the right of OPUS DEI, and allegedly apart from it, is the clandestine student movement MURO, which contributed to the disorders of 1968 by its storm troop actions against the National Strike Committee. MURO has strong roots in the University of Puebla and is allegedly financed by extremists within the "Monterrey Group." It is structured into secret cells and is known to overlap with the small university youth sector of the UNS.

The restorationist right has other lesser movements including ACM, Mexican Catholic Action; UNPF, National Union of Parents; and CPRM, Property Owners Confederation of the Mexican Republic. None of these groups has relevant political power apart from linkages with one or more of the major groupings cited above.

Barriers to Integration of Satellites and Out Groups

Here we reach the crux of the many dilemmas of Mexico's esoteric democracy. The political system performs to maintain an esoteric democracy. To embrace the terminology of a recent and penetrating analysis by Charles W. Anderson, it is a question of which power contenders can be admitted without threatening established vested interests.[30] Most of the groups listed in the foregoing survey, in either the Marxist or restorationist sectors, cannot be admitted to competition in the electoral arena because the PRI feels threatened and is unwilling. None of the above mentioned groups has ever been ad-

[30] Charles W. Anderson, *Politics and Economic Change in Latin America* (Princeton: Van Nostrand, 1967), p. 108.

mitted to more than token participation in the governmental process. The technique of allowing PPS, PARM, and PAN to win seats at large in the Chamber of Deputies is little more than a facade by which PRI tells the outside world that Mexico has a competitive democratic system. Because legitimacy is denied to would be power aspirants, many of them have tried to force their way into the governmental system via electoral confrontations with the PRI in the states and localities. Here are some illustrative examples of what has happened.

SAN LUIS POTOSÍ 1961

This state, an historical birthplace of Revolutionary thought, was a cradle of political reaction in the late 1950's and early 1960's. The UNS, the PAN, and an amorphous public spirited citizenry joined forces to combat the repressive tactics of Gonzalo N. Santos, the governor who sought to perpetuate his influence via a Calles-like system of puppets. The regime was especially odious for its use of torture and assassination in repressing its opposition. From the protest movements rose the figure of Dr. Salvador Nava whose name has become synonymous with restorationist civic protest in Mexico. The book *La grieta en el yugo* (the crack in the yoke) tells of the tribulations of Dr. Nava and his followers.[31] The first edition appeared in 1963 but most of the copies were destroyed that February when state police broke into the printing press and demolished it. By the end of that year a second edition had appeared clandestinely.

La grieta en el yugo is a collection of memoirs of the civic protesters in San Luis Potosí. It is loosely organized and liberally sprinkled with poetry and poetic diction, traditional hallmark of *sinarquista writings*. On the basis of the adjectives alone, one knows that its author was deeply embittered from the wounds he received in the service of Dr. Nava and his cause. For this reason also, the scholar must examine carefully the factual character of much of the contents. What is clear is that in 1961 Dr. Nava and his Civic Union lost the gubernatorial contest to Professor Manuel López Dávila in San Luis Potosí. They made the following petition of complaint about the election to the Supreme Court of the Nation asking that the results be declared null and void.

[31] Antonio Estrada M., *La grieta en el yugo*, 2d ed. (Mexico, 1963).

1. No regular offices were established by the government for voting registration. Voting registers were drawn up arbitrarily and in most localities there were none.

2. Only representatives of the PRI were allowed in the voting places to supervise the voting.

3. Ballot boxes were picked up without an open count to guarantee the contents.

4. The state congress took note of the robbing of certain ballot boxes but declared null and void only those votes that went to the PAN and the *Unión Cívica*.

5. In defiance of the law the PRI candidate Professor López Dávila was not a legal resident of San Luis Potosí having spent the last twenty years in Chihuahua and Mexico City.

6. The following violations of individual guarantees were committed by the state government: the assassination of Lic. Jesús Acosta, a campaign worker for Dr. Nava, the use of troops to disrupt political rallies, the jailing of various Nava campaign workers, and the military take over of Nava campaign headquarters at Avenida Carranza 700 in San Luis Potosí.[32]

These well documented charges could be easily verified or disproven. That the Supreme Court of the Nation refused, for all intents and purposes, to even hear the case supports subsequent testimony it received in support of Dr. Nava's case. The insight given into the practices of voter registration coincided exactly with the Chihuahua experience cited in an earlier chapter from the book *La otra cara de México*. The use by the PRI of a candidate not legally a resident of the district in which he ran for office was a precedent which, ironically, PRI would invoke in its own defense nearly a decade later.

NUEVO LEÓN 1965

A totally different experience from that of San Luis Potosí occurred in the northern state of Nuevo León. On the outskirts of the large Monterrey urban complex the municipality of Garza García fell from the revolutionary coalition and came under a PAN administration in 1965. Garza García is a predominantly upper middle and wealthy class community having many influential residents within

---

[32] Ibid., pp. 239–243.

the powerful "Monterrey Group." An overwhelming public turnout on behalf of the PAN in the municipal elections plus these strong group ties of the PAN organization made it impossible for the state's PRI dominated officialdom to intervene. Garza García's first PAN mayor, Humberto Junco, said that he found the municipal government in financial and moral ruin. He alleged that the outgoing administration had an average monthly income of only 30,000 pesos and that during his first year in office this was raised to 160,000 without raising taxes. Junco claims that he accomplished this by eliminating existing dishonest practices in the local administration. Special reform attention was given to the police department where there were many personnel changes. In 1968 another PAN mayor, Mrs. Norma Villarreal de Zambrano, took office promising vast improvements in social services, public works, and education. It is well to note that this apparent coup took place in an area that must be considered a PAN (if not restorationist generally) stronghold. The persons who were instrumental had powerful wealth-based ties, a situation totally unlike that of the Nava campaign earlier in San Luis Potosí. The marked socioeconomic differential seen here between PAN and UNS tends to typify the two organizations throughout Mexico.

In the municipal elections of 1969 Garza Garcia's government fell into PRI control by a tiny vote margin as the revolutionary coalition began again to rebuild itself in areas of ostensible defeat. Although that election's honesty was challenged by PAN, Garza García seemed lost.

SONORA 1967

As is customary in state politics the local PRI organization designates, with the blessing of the national CEN, its candidate for governor. Such designation is normally tantamount to election. The PRI designated Félix Faustino Serna as its candidate for governor of Sonora in 1967. Serna was not a popular figure and in March a group of PRI renegades reinforced by a random selection of "out group" supporters confronted the PRI's state party headquarters in Hermosillo with a demand that it rescind Serna's candidacy. This resulted in violence and bloodshed. The following month students of the state university attacked Serna's campaign entourage and staged a pitched gun battle with the police which resulted in several deaths. Federal troops were called and the violence was repeated. By the end of June the death toll had reached 15. The election took place in a tense atmosphere on July 2 and the next day the PAN candidate, Gilberto Suárez Arvizu, claimed victory. The PAN won (or was allowed to win) the mayorality election in Hermosillo, the state capital. This was just one of 15 PAN victories in municipal elections during 1967 throughout Mexico. Winning a state capital was an important victory, especially following the triumph of Garza García. It is apparent that the overwhelming public resentment at the PRI's designation of the unpopular Serna, coupled with police brutality against the students, made Sonora ripe for the PAN victory. One additional barrier to out-group participation in the governmental process had been lowered. Again, Carlos Madrazo's vision of a democratized local politics was being honored, but through violence.

BAJA CALIFORNIA 1968: A SPECIAL CASE STUDY

Mexico's newest and one of her fastest economically growing states has had more than its share of traumata, both social and political. This northwestern state which shares the international border with California-USA grew with fantastic speed as a consequence of the booming American tourist trade in the 1950's. It received a major population stimulus with the coming of contract labor migration in the early 1960's. Baja California has had its troubles. It has been cursed with prostitution, gang warfare, political kidnappings and murders, enforcement rackets, reprisals against the press, stolen ballot boxes, and exaggerated campaign promises that were never honored. To many *bajacalifornianos*, however, their new state was something of a little homeland to be nurtured, developed, and respected.

It is generally agreed that the first governor of Baja California Norte, Braulio Maldonado Sández, left much to be desired from the standpoint both of opposition groups and his own PRI organization. In 1958 the graft-ridden regime of Maldonado was forced by constitutional stricture to yield in favor of a popularly chosen successor. His regime had been marred by numerous scandals including the intervention of the Federal Government which voiced embarrassed indignation over the existence of *"Los Kilómetros,"* "an enormous zone of prostitution established in Tijuana where more than eight thousand whores were exploited for the profit of the governor and his friends, and which helped to pay for a front organization called the Committee for Destitute Children that was headed by the governor's own wife."[33] When that scandal alone (plus numerous others) reached national and international proportions the *Procuraduría General de la República* ordered the gigantic brothel closed. It has been alleged that when the journalist Manuel Acosta Meza publicly demanded that the governor and his cohorts be punished for their complicity (and punishment never occurred), Acosta Meza was assassinated by order of Maldonado adding one more name to a long list of unsolved political deaths in Baja California Norte. An ignominious climax came to the Maldonado regime with the violent displacement of some five thousand persons from the Tijuana River bed as part of a public works project in which the governor and certain North American counterparts had financial interests.

No lawyer would defend the interests of the displaced squatters. No one dared to force a showdown with Braulio Maldonado over the political assassinations, nor over his dope traffic or gambling interests. At this point there were concrete signs of internal disaffection within the local PRI. The opposition party PAN began to be looked upon with favor by many who had formerly seen it as representing the oligarchs and the old porfirian syndrome.

At this point a PAN leader became known as "the people's attorney." Lic. Salvador Rosas Magallón had helped to found *Acción Nacional* in Baja California in the late 1950's and ran unsuccessfully for governor in 1959. Rosas Magallón had attempted, fruitlessly, to take the Baja California government to court for its abuses. His efforts barely dramatized the evil due to lack of public news dissemination on behalf of his cause. At various times Rosas Magallón and José León Toscano of Ensenada were arrested, harassed by the police, and forced to take up brief exile for the safety of their families in neighboring San Ysidro, California. Nevertheless, the efforts of Magallón on behalf of the distressed Tijuana colonists did win him and PAN an extended public confidence. Many *bajacalifornianos* came to see in PAN a viable instrument for articulating wrath and outrage against the corrupt single-party regime.

In 1959 the PRI nominated Elegio Esquivel Méndez as its candidate for governor. Given the popular mood at the time in the wake of the Maldonado scandals, his selection was perhaps poorly timed.[34]

---

[33] *Por Qué*, 2 de julio, 1968, p. 37.

[34] Cf. Braulio Maldonado, *Baja California: Comentarios Políticos* (Mexico: Costa-Amic, 1960), *passim*.

Esquivel had been known as an intimate member of the outgoing regime who had enriched himself generously through control of water for irrigation purposes in the Mexicali Valley. From the standpoint of opposition politics the regime of Eligio Esquivel Méndez was an effort to fulfill the undelivered promise of erradicating the PAN from Baja California. Key PAN leaders again claimed that government boycotts were levied against their establishments and that momentary exiles in the United States were necessary. The PRI leaders apparently felt sufficiently threatened to justify a greater attentiveness to the public and responded with numerous declared programs of social welfare, all of which enjoyed much publicity in the government-influenced "free press." Then major defections from PRI began to occur. In March of 1968 Luis Enrique Enciso Clark took the oath of candidate for the office of Mayor in Tijuana on behalf of PAN. His gesture was a brave one. In effect, it scrapped a lifetime of active service in the PRI. Such a gesture is usually seen as treasonable in Mexican circles and is not to be smoothed over easily. Enciso Clark took with him many PRI leaders and members who were well known in Baja California. The desertion was bitterly condemned by PRI stalwarts. Pejorative epithets ranging from extreme right to left were widely employed against the PRI defectors. Enciso Clark and his followers bolted PRI knowing full well that it would most likely be political suicide.

Enciso Clark contended that his opposition candidacy was not necessarily due to a suddenly enduring or spontaneous love for the PAN but rather because the PRI had ceased to represent a level of moral decency that he could accept. It was no longer a viable electoral alternative for him and his followers. Had he founded a new party, the electoral system would have required that each voter write in the complete list of names of Enciso Clark's slate should they have chosen to run independently. The PAN candidacy had practical advantages as *Acción Nacional* was the only other registered political party in the state that could appear on the ballot.

PRI countered the Enciso Clark desertion by naming its own favored candidate, Dr. Luis Mario Santana Cobián, a veteran PRI bureaucrat and a former deputy to the national Chamber of Deputies. This was intended as a direct blow at PAN for Dr. Santana Cobián represented, and was sympathetic only to interests that sought to appropriate to themselves a large part of the real estate of the city of

Tijuana. Highly *panista* versions of the situation urged that the entire PRI municipal electoral slate was, in one way or another, tied to the former Maldonado regime, its dope traffic, and a legion of illicit deals that served conveniently to discredit the PRI.

However, the main target for the opposition attack in the 1967–68 period was an organization known on paper as ICSA, *Inmuebles Californianos S.A.* PAN candidate Enciso Clark and his supporters challenged that this organization, which sought to become the major proprietor of the city of Tijuana, and the PRI candidate, Santana Cobián, were one and the same. The case reveals how the intricacies of Mexico's Roman law structure could be manipulated in the service of special interests and pressure groups within the PRI.

Except for public buildings, streets, and sidewalks, the ICSA laid claim to the entire city of Tijuana. The claim of ownership was based upon a complicated history which I will only sketch here. In the middle of the nineteenth century the settlement of Tía Juana known for the women who produced clothing and textiles there, was converted into the more easily pronounced verbal combination "Tijuana." In 1864 President Benito Juárez donated land to Santiago Arguello, a resident of the area, who had aided the cause of Juárez' liberal reform. The area then became known as Rancho de Tijuana. During the *porfiriato* the land was ceded to the descendants of Santiago Arguello with special provision made to respect the legal autonomy and identity of the actual village of Tijuana. On November 7, 1929, the Mexico City government decreed that the remaining Arguello titles were to be nullified. Later, in 1938, the Supreme Court granted a partial relief action to the Arguello descendants which, unfortunately, did not make clear exactly which lands were to be returned to their legal possession.

In 1943 public pressures forced the Arguello heirs to abandon their claims to property with the exception of the Bull Ring and several entertainment attraction sites in Tijuana proper. But one of the Arguello descendents, Alejandro Arguello, did not go through the legal procedure of renunciation even though the general public impression was that he had indeed done so. This fact remained hidden away in the national archives of the Supreme Court in Mexico City. It was discovered however by entrepreneurial interests in the new state of Baja California Norte who sought to avail themselves of a legal technicality that would give them control of one of the most valuable pieces of real estate in all Mexico. In 1967 a federal court ruled that these territories legally belonged to the Arguello heirs in the person of Alejandro Arguello and via the ICSA that had now acquired his rights to ownership.

A wave of outrage swept the property owners of the city, and a Committee for the Defense of the Community of Tijuana was organized. Its leaders were disgruntled PRI renegades including Luis Enciso Clark who were outraged and financially threatened. The group of entrepreneurs who had purchased the property rights of Alejandro Arguello and formed ICSA were inseparably tied to the financial entourage of ex-president Miguel Alemán. This tie is one of the most critical facts of the case. ICSA had maintained an impressive legal staff with offices both in Tijuana and in Mexico City. Their game was deadly serious. The payoff was to be millions and a future that would be difficult to estimate except in very broad financial terms.

The opposition of Luis Enciso Clark and his civic committee to ICSA required him to abrogate the possibility of a PRI nomination for the office of Tijuana mayor. Had the ICSA controversy not occurred it was believed that Enciso Clark would have easily won the PRI nomination (and undoubtedly the election as well). But the PRI instead selected Dr. Santana Cobián who was linked with ICSA. Curiously, immediately following the nomination of Santana Cobián, ICSA began to operate with ostentatiously increased confidence, even to the point of beginning evictions of property owners in selected places.

Adding to the tension of the opposition politics in Tijuana, an equally bitter contest was underway in Mexicali, the capital of Baja California. There the mayoralty race featured Norberto Corella as the PAN candidate opposing Gilberto Rodríguez of the PRI. Here the ostensible issue of debate was an end to administrative and moral corruption, dope traffic and prostitution.[35] But the real issue was a groundswell of poular support for a break with the past, as well as an end to the moral legacies of governors Maldonado and Esquivel and to the empires of vice presided over by Governor Raul Sánchez

[35] Although the frontier city Tijuana receives (perhaps) more attention in the North American press for its vice activities it is nonetheless true that Mexicali, the capital of Baja California, serves as the "administrative center" for vice in Mexico's northwest.

Díaz and his brother-in-law Mario Medina. As in the case of Tijuana, Corella's movement did not mean a great switch of popular attachment for PAN per se but rather an enormous rank and file desertion from the PRI. The prospects of a PAN upset-victory were especially menacing for Baja California's PRI senator, José Ricardi Tirado, and at the national level for CEN president Alfonso Martínez Domínguez, both of whom had invested considerable time in campaigning for the PRI candidates (including Pedro Luis Bartilotti, Martínez Domínguez protegé) throughout Baja California.

When the votes were counted following the June 2nd election it appeared that PAN had won the race for mayor in Tijuana and possibly also in Mexicali.[36] The PRI was unprepared to accept this. Defeat at the polls brought the crisis of legitimacy to a head. Everyone knew the PRI had been corrupt and had been denied a popular mandate. Governor Sánchez Díaz, Senator Ricardi Tirado, and CEN president Martínez Domínguez had been challenged in a way so grave that it could not be allowed to stand as a precedent either locally or nationally; and so reprisals were taken. On June 20, the Secretary of the Interior, Luis Echeverría, declared that "irregularities" had occurred in Baja California's June 2 elections and the state legislature had been directed by Mexico City to nullify the results and to plan for new elections. There were a legion of machinations and charges involved in justifying this action but the essential points could be reduced to two: in Tijuana ballot boxes had been stolen (since witnesses saw this being done by government and police officials it required a most curious set of mental gymnastics to argue that PAN had committed the illegal acts), and in Mexicali the Mexican citizenship of the PAN candidate, Norberto Corella, was challenged (the United States-born Corella had become a Mexican citizen at age 18 and had served in Mexico's armed forces). Few persons believed these charges, especially the latter when it was rumored that the then incumbent mayor of Tijuana, Francisco López Gutiérrez, had been born in El Paso, Texas and had never achieved full citizenship as had Corella. Clearly, a double standard had been invoked. Besides the journals, *Por Qué* (of the Marxist sector) and *Gente* (of the restora-

---

[36] Most reports agreed that the PAN had won in Tijuana. The journal *Por Qué* (July 27, 1968 p. 30) reported that Corella had won also in Mexicali. The *Los Angeles Times* (June 15, 1968, p. 14) had shown Corella the loser with nearly 30,000 ballots in dispute.

tionist sector) both published exposés of the fraud including photos of ballot boxes being taken.[37] Alfonso Martínez Domínguez, newly installed as president of the PRI's CEN, had been shaken. Ironically, it was once again in the very arena, the municipality, whose politics former CEN president Carlos A. Madrazo had sought to democratize. Had Madrazo's will prevailed party primaries in both Mexicali and Tijuana could very well have selected candidates within the revolutionary coalition who would have been pledged to satisfy popular indignation over abuses such as the vice activities and the ICSA affair. Baja California 1968 became a bitter reflection on the roots of PRI power, a critical one for understanding the frailties of the revolutionary coalition.

YUCATAN 1969

There is a growing body of evidence to suggest that political independence from Mexico City increases with geographic distance from the capital. This is true both with respect to the fortunes of opposition groups and reform elements within the PRI as the case of Nuevo León, Sonora, and Baja California have shown. Mexico's southernmost state, Yucatán, can now be added to the list. The PRI has never had a particularly strong state machine in Yucatán, since much of its direction actually comes from Mexico City without a strong local boss. The people from Yucatán may be *priistas* but their staunch regionalism makes them *yucatecos* first and foremost. They believe that the federal government has exploited their natural resources, drained their wealth off to Mexico City, and done very little to help them secure the material accoutrements of the good life. Public disconfidence in Yucatán's PRI organization grew throughout the 1960's in the light of numerous public scandals (like the waste of an Inter-American Development Bank loan for public water systems and the resultant water shortage and high costs which militated against the poor).[38]

In Yucatán, and especially the capital city Mérida, the PAN assumed an active role of protest. In November 1967 a slate of PAN candidates captured the municipal government of Mérida. They were

---

[37] Op. cit.

[38] Cf. Mario Menéndez Rodríguez, "El escandaloso fraude del agua potable," *Por Qué*, 13 de marzo, 1968, pp. 26–29.

backed by enormous public sentiment that saw PRI-PPS renegades and social reformers of the moderate left cast ballots for the traditionally rightist opposition party. The reasons for PRI's loss to PAN in Mérida were as follows. The incumbent municipal administration of Agustín Martínez de Arredondo was flagrantly and openly corrupt in nearly every aspect of local public service. The state government had also been discredited for the water scandal mentioned briefly above. PAN became the beneficiary of the resulting popular indignation. Even the federally-owned rope making monopoly CORDEMEX had come to symbolize governmental oppression of labor and it is known that the PRI's labor sector suffered membership loses to PAN as a result.[39] Finally the PRI was seen as responsible for numerous abuses of state farmers and for corruption in the Department of Agrarian Affairs and Colonization which affected Yucatán directly. One discussion of this latter problem went as follows:

It is known that in Yucatán there are 58,000 *ejidatarios* which cost the federal government three million pesos monthly. The DAAC has ordered an investigation of the current census for the 500 existing *ejidos*, but you can be sure that there is a great quantity of false registrations, *aviadores* who collect illegally. Many *ejidatarios* have died but agrarian leaders continue to collect their checks from the DAAC. The *ejidatarios* live a pauper's life as mere employees of the government, paying cynical hommage to their lord as it were, but at the same time casting their support for the PAN in condemnation of the system that feeds them. Nor does this prevent the *ejidatarios* from asking that their subsidies be increased.[40]

These failures of the PRI and ensuing citizen outrage contributed to PAN's 1967 victory in Mérida. All of this would suggest a rather jaundiced view of PAN's appeal in that its Mérida campaign seemed to thrive out of PRI's shortcomings. But that was not so. Throughout Yucatán PAN is known for the distinguished and charismatic leadership of Victor Manuel Correa Rachó who led the victorious municipal slate in 1967. His strengths as organizer and popular leader are impressive evidence of the ability of PAN (and potentially other opposition parties) to assert itself far from the capital city.

Before the end of PAN's first year in Mérida a battle had shaped up featuring state vs. municipality, Governor Luis Torres Mesias

[39] Cf. Mario Menéndez Rodríguez, "Yucatán separatista?" *Por Qué*, 28 de febrero, 1968, pp. 24–27.

[40] *Gente*, 16 de julio, 1969, p. 30.

against Mayor Correa Rachó. The PRI-controlled state government campaigned vigorously to produce crisis after crisis that would induce the resignation of Correa Rachó. This included strikes of taxi and bus drivers, the withholding of the state's financial subventions to the city of Mérida, and the inducement of several defections of prominent *panistas* in favor of the PRI. These tactics seem to have generated popular sympathy for Correa Rachó more than against him. The breach between mayor and governor was opened, perhaps irreparably, when on June 9, 1969, the head of the state police, Andrés Toledo Alvarez, arrived at the municipal offices with armed soldiers and took possession of the local police department.[41] Federal power had been enlisted on behalf of PRI's weakened state organization in Yucatán.

But Correa Rachó refused to capitulate and he contested the state's gubernatorial office in 1969. The elections of November of that year resulted in what was almost universally denounced in Mexico as a gigantic fraud against a popular reform oriented regional leader. Ballot boxes were seized by armed force under high PRI orders, and the PAN "lost." Nevertheless, Correa Rachó had won in two distinct ways when compared with the experiences of his predecessors in the other states we have treated. First, his organization had been able to penetrate the PRI's membership sectors effectively. Second, Correa Rachó won and held on to a major jurisdiction of far greater prestige than had been involved in the PAN wins of 1967 in Sonora and elsewhere, and certainly more important than in Nuevo León. Between the defeat of Dr. Nava in San Luis Potosí (1961) and the Yucatán campaigns of 1967 and 1969 a popular opposition psychology had grown in Mexico and along with it PAN was trying to shed its former image of rightism, racism, and *sinarquismo*. People who might otherwise have favored the PRI increasingly saw in PAN a viable opposition alternative, perhaps leaving much to be desired, but the best available.

Prognosis on the Mexican Opposition

It is significant that the PRI seems to have become more desperate in its raising of barriers to the political integration of competing

---

[41] Ibid., p. 28.

power groups. Surely the story of events leading to the massacre of Taltelolco tells much of PRI's defensive posture vis-à-vis the militant left. As noted in Chapter 6, at the height of the aroused tempers over the student riots, the PRI's leadership accused the students of being led by a communist cabal. Paradoxically, in the confrontation with Correa Rachó in Yucatán the PRI accused PAN of being in league with the communists. When I first began to study the out-groups of Mexico in 1962 it would have been unthinkable to suggest that one day PRI would be accusing PAN of collusion with communism for then it was, habitually, the other way around.[42]

Developments during the last years of the 1960's seem to indicate that PAN is trying to remove itself from what I have labelled the restorationist sector. PAN demands that it be granted legitimacy but refuses to become (or to continue as) an "official opposition." It has been able to produce regional leaders capable of winning public respect and inspiring the desertion of both leadership and membership from the PRI. Nuevo León, Sonora, and Yucatán are examples of the ability of PAN to force the PRI to accept an honest vote count as an operating norm by which the legitimacy of one's claim to public office is judged. A curious, and perhaps significant, development in the PAN's behavioral style is its increasing use of women as candidates and as party spokesmen and organizers. PAN has long been known as a "ladies party," an image which PRI stalwarts have encouraged in its most pejorative sense. Earlier, of course, it was clerical propaganda which did in fact swell the ranks of PAN with female participants. In addition to the lady mayor of Garza Garcia, the Yucatán campaign featured Mrs. Carmen Robleda de Solis Aznar who is said to be a brilliant speaker and organizer. It will be argued by more traditional scholars that "feminization" of a Mexican political party would be the kiss of death, especially in view of the traditionally assumed political role of "machismo."[43] Yet given *machismo* as an

[42] At least up until the González Torres campaign in 1964 it was standard operating procedure for PAN to accuse the PRI of being communist oriented. Significantly, since PAN has given up this right wing posture (or at least since many of its principal spokesmen have become more moderate and progressive) it has had greater success in opposing the PRI as the municipal victories of 1967 indicate. To the degree that PRI's principal opposition sheds its rightist spectre so does the PRI come to look less and less "revolutionary." As the decade of the 1970s begins the PRI looms as a conservative force resisting major socioeconomic-political change.

[43] See the article by Evelyn Stevens, op. cit.

intimate component of Mexical political life, it would certainly be in better taste for an angry PRI officialdom to displace the aggressive mayor of Mérida than to try the same thing with a lady. It remains to be seen whether PAN will employ increasing numbers of women in the future as a tactical device.

At the moment of this writing it is clear that Mexico's political left continues in disarray. It is unable to produce popular leaders with both sufficient charisma and sufficient skill in the art of compromise to enable a unified opposition on the left. Most of the promising charismatics of the Marxist sector are either in prison at the start of the 1970's or are under intense scrutiny by security forces. But this in no way means that PAN is the key to Mexico's salvation nor even that it will continue to be an effective opposition to PRI. Much remains to be seen and the results of the presidential succession of 1970 will be critical. As Luis Echeverría's term as president (1970–76) begins, there is a burgeoning protest literature coming out of Mexico to indicate that the performance of her esoteric democratic system is breaking down, and that it is becoming less and less effective as a reconciliation system. Either the PRI will be reformed from within, or outside pressures will force such reforms, or the PRI will be displaced. That eventuality could be a bloody one. Perhaps one foreshadowing of this was the withdrawl of PAN from the federal electoral tribunal following the presidential elections of 1970. PAN charged that its presence there only lent legitimacy to the PRI's post-electoral effort to veil the fraud which had occurred.

Evidence that unrest is imminent continues to fill the literature of protest. Scandals abound in the aftermath of the Torres Landa regime in Guanajuato, and following the police state visited upon the people of Veracruz by Governor López Arias. Additional controversies surround the campaign of Prof. Carlos Hank González (former director of CONASUPO) for the governor's chair in the state of Mexico. There is no heuristic or otherwise redeeming purpose in compiling here an endless list of PRI failures. Indeed, because of the regrettably pejorative quality of what has appeared already in this book, the author feels obliged in the concluding chapter to present his own defense of the PRI lest this work be taken erroneously as the author's personal vendetta against an institution which has much that is laudatory to its credit.

The cardinal fact of contemporary satellite and out-group politics in Mexico is this: where breakdowns have occurred in the esoteric system it is PAN that has been best prepared to take advantage of them. PAN has been able to consolidate itself as none of the other groups originating in the restorationist sector have done. Regional leadership roles have been central to this growth of strength. Neglect of the municipalities and of the socioeconomic demands of increasing urbanization has given PAN a viable basis for turning itself into a progressive opposition party, and this in turn has tended to strengthen the regional leadership roles. Distance from the federal capital seems to complicate the efforts of the PRI aimed at stultification of its opposition. The heterogeneous Marxist sector suffers from such intense ideological cleavage and inept leadership that a catalytic event like that described in the following chapter must take place to bring about even a short lived unity.[44] Equally ineffective is the far reactionary right which continues to see its role in apocalyptic terms, the *sinarquistas* waiting for their day of theocratic revolution, the MURO hoping to precipitate it with violence and terror. Unlike other countries (Guatemala, Panama, Colombia, Venezuela, Peru, and Chile) this mosaic of political nuances has not fostered the rise of a progressive Christian Democratic movement in Mexico although one is now in its embryonic stages. The decade of the 1970's will be one of critical political change in Mexico.

Finally, two additional principles may be adduced from this discussion that will merit testing by field researchers who explore Mexico's opposition politics. The first is that the PRI, the custodian of the revolutionary coalition, seems most prone to attack publicly, and in the political arena, its "rightist" opposition, PAN. This is because PRI is not the "revolutionary" institution that is claimed but has, in fact, become a conservative bastion for defense of the status quo. Second, when the PRI does attack the Marxist left it will not be in the open political arena but most likely, will be militarily and

[44] Deep ideological divisions within the Marxist sector stem from a number of abortive insurrectionary efforts during the 1950's and later as described in the Godines book. In one of the earlier fiascos, Jacinto López and Danzós Palomino led an assault on a radio station in Cananea and "announced their intention to invade lands from the 400,000 hectares of Cananea Cattle Company in the area." (Gerrit Huizer, *Peasant Organization in the Process of Agrarian Reform in Mexico* (St. Louis: Washington University, 1969), p. 139).

under the guise of internal security. It represses the violent left not only for purposes of public order but because it is the radical left which most effectively reveals through its literature the truth that the PRI is a mid-century replacement for the *porfiriato*. Such criticism is devastating to the preferred image of *"revolucionario."* And the implications of the political death toll resulting from this struggle between PRI and its militant left are well understood in the watching ranks of *Acción Nacional*. If PRI sees PAN as its greatest threat, then PAN may be well indeed on the road to public political legitimacy.[45]*

[45] In viewing the spectrum of political out-groups in Mexico the scholar must consider that for constitutional reasons, and because of PRI cooptation, a true Christian Democratic left has never emerged as has occurred in so many other Latin American countries. One Mexican author sought to cast the entire congeries of the Christian Democratic left (incipient) as a communist conspiracy accusing the PAN, CIDOC, and Bishop Méndez Arceo as conspirators along with numerous others (cf. Manuel Magaña C., *Poder laico*, Mexico, Ediciones Foro Político, 1970). See also José Guerra Utrilla, *Los partidos políticos nacionales*, Mexico, Editorial América, 1970, for an officialist (i.e. PRI) view of the spectrum of Mexican political parties.

*On June 10, 1971 (*Jueves de Corpus*) the regime suffered a loss of legitimacy in the public eye that was politically more significant than the massacre of Tlatelolco described in Chapter 6 to follow. On that day, a government sponsored paramilitary group known as *Los Halcones* attacked students who were marching to protest political prisoners (like Mario Menéndez Rodríguez) and to dramatize a number of youth complaints. The *Halcones* also attacked members of the press corps who presented graphic evidence of the aggression to President Echeverría days later. The proof of official complicity was so overwhelming that high officials were forced to resign, including Alfonso Martínez Domínguez who was then serving as Mayor of Mexico City. On the 1972 anniversary of the event the students were confronted in advance with armed troops and cavalry. Echeverría promised to make public results of an investigation of the affair but well into 1972 no such disclosure had been made, further calling into question the integrity of the president and his entourage.

SPECTROGRAM OF THE MEXICAN POLITICAL SYSTEM

Official Revolutionary Coalition **PRI**

Centralist Opposition **PAN**

Official left **PPS**   *Official right* **PARM**

Electoral groups

Non-electoral groups

RESTORATIONIST SECTOR (tinted area)

MARXIST REVOLUTIONARY SECTOR

Extreme left—pro-violence

CNH (National Strike Committee)
CNED (National Committee of Democratic Students)
PCM (Mexican Communist Party)
JCM (Mexican Communist Youth)
POR (Revolutionary Workers Party) (Trotskyite)
LCE (Spartacan Communist League)
UGOCM (Union of Mexican Workers and Peasants)

Extreme left—nonviolent

CCI (Independent Peasant Confederation)
DC (Christian Democratic Party)
FAT (Authentic Workers Front) (this is a Christian Democratic group tied to the international union CLASC)

ECCLESIASTICAL BLOC

Marxist left

Third World Jesuit Priests
The University Iberoamericana
EMAUS (rebel group of Benedictine monks at Cuernavaca led by Gregorio Lemercier)
CIDOC (Inter-cultural center for documentation at Cuernavaca, directed by Iván Illich and associated with Bishop Sergio Méndez Arceo)
CENCOS (National Center for Social Communication directed by Alejandro Avilés, former editor of the PAN journal *La Nación*)

Moderate right

Traditional bishops
OPUS DEI (principal outlet the magazine *Gente*)
"Hoja de Combate" group (led by Salvador Abascal, formerly of the *sinarquistas*)
UNS (National Union of Sinarquistas) (anti-anarchists)

Extreme right

MURO (University Organization of Renovationist Orientation) (sponsored informally by Octaviano Márquez y Toriz, Archbishop of Puebla and centered in the University of Puebla)
Institute for Social and Economic Investigations (publishes the magazine *Espejo*)

ANTI-COMMUNIST BLOC

USEM (Social Union of Mexican Entrepreneurs)
AUTOMEX (discussed in Chapter 4)
COMPAREX (freely translated as the Protective Employers Association of Mexico)
UNPF (National Parents Union)
ACM (Mexican Catholic Action)
MFC (Family Christian Movement)

6

The Saliency of Alienation: Mire + Muro + Sph = Tlatelolco

In the month of September, 1968, a North American magazine cheerfully announced to its readers that "half the population of Mexico are under 17 years of age. Sixty-five percent are under 25."[1] This was, in the eyes of the magazine's editors, evidence that Mexico was blessed with a "young revolution." Testimony was presented from such as the son of the former president Alemán to show the confidence of youth in themselves and their environment. Alemán was quoted, "the youth of Mexico are moving. We have original ideas and are making it on our own."[2] While a Los Angeles press ground out this accolade thousands of Mexican students were pouring down the fashionably shaded walks of the *Paseo de la Reforma*, attacking police, burning busses, and demanding the death of President Díaz Ordaz. They were indeed "making it" on their own. The students reflected the grim intensity of ideological cleavage that marked a point of culmination in the ongoing "march" of Mexico's "revolution." A subsequent account of the crisis, written by a communist leader from behind the walls of the Lecumberri Prison, detailed some of the principal human ingredients in the cleavage and recent contributory events. Witness: "in August of 1966 the MURO, a fascist organization, assaulted preparatory school Prepa No. 7 in gangster style," "in 1967 the students of the National School of Economics protested the appoinment of the new director, Mrs. Ifigenia M. de

[1] *Pace*, September, 1968, p. 13.

[2] Ibid., p. 10.

Navarrete, who is the wife of the director of *Nacional Financiera* and linked to the financial and bureaucratic bourgeoisie of the nation; the new director has organized groups of hoodlums who act as strike breakers against the students." Another group MIRE (*Movimiento de Izquierda Revolucionaria Estudiantil*) saw a "MacCarthyist" cabal of the far reactionary right posed ominously above them.[3]

MIRE is the Leftist Revolutionary Student Movement, one of many devoted to a Marxist pattern of class conflict with the commercial-industrial complex and against the PRI dominated government which they see as a gigantic privileged clique. MURO (*Movimiento Universitario de Reformadora Orientación*) may be called the Reform Oriented University Movement which seeks a totalitarian solution to the problem of Mexico's crisis of political legitimacy and socioeconomic injustice, an approach with strong fascist overtones. The equation MIRE + MURO + SPH (*sistema político hueco* or "hollow political system" as quoted in the preceding chapter) = TLATELOLCO is a convenient symbolic representation of a process that led to disaster on October 2, 1968. At a place in the capital city known as Tlatelolco, the cleavage between officialdom and the people, especially the young people, erupted in a violence that commanded world headlines for months. It was anomic violence to be sure; but it carried profound implications for the direction of change in Mexico's esoteric democratic system.

Development of the Violence

Of the worst sociopolitical conflict to occur in Mexico since the great Revolution of 1910–17, the Jesuit priest Arnaldo Zenteño was later to comment: "two years ago President Díaz warned Mexican industrialists that there might be disturbances. In March of this year (1968) Hoover of the FBI also said that there was going to be an outbreak of violence in Mexico. The press denied this, yet talks between the United States and South Vietnam were not held in Mexico for fear that they would become a pretext for conflict."[4]

[3] Gilberto Balam, *Tlatelolco: reflexiones de un testigo* (México: (no publisher given), 1969), pp. 24–26.

[4] *Christus*, February 1969, p. 171.

And looking back on what had happened nearly a year later the dean of a prominent university in Mexico City wrote "the preoccupation is with national issues. Established institutions are considered corrupt, be they inspired by leftist or rightist ideologies . . . in the eyes of the students, and other participants counted by the hundreds of thousands, the national situation has become explosive to the extent that action is required."[5]

Mexico had often witnessed violence in the countryside and in its labor-management relations as the foregoing chapters have shown. But never had there been violence on so large a scale and in the streets of the capital city. According to the impression disseminated throughout Mexico by the officialist press and throughout North America by the news services, Mexico had arrived at its place in the world through its hosting of the summer 1968 Olympic Games. The photo of Paco Rubio, a 25-year-old engineer in charge of building Mexico City's Sports Palace, was proffered about as evidence that Mexico was a nation in which talent and dedication received their just rewards. Said Paco "it's the chance of a lifetime. I have to prove they didn't make a mistake in choosing someone so young."[6] But a menacingly large figure was needed to describe the ranks of those without such opportunities on which to erect so towering an optimism. These ranks were the overwhelming majorities of university and secondary students without sufficient ties to let them share in the social deference and financial largesse. In short, the majority of students saw the Sports Palace as a gigantic and arabesque symbol of the ingredient SPH. They saw the regime pursuing its own self-aggrandizement via international image-building while the masses did without. Many could see the Sports Palace, few could purchase a ticket to enter it, and none could fill their stomachs with the prestige it would earn.

The PRI needed the Olympic Games and had sought tirelessly to convince the populace that they also shared this need. The mayor of the Federal District, General Alfonso Corona del Rosal, had been forced to take action in July which he considered necessary in order to maintain a peaceful atmosphere in which work on the Sports Palace and other facilities could proceed. On July 22 the principal

[5] Karl Lankersdorf, "The Philosophy of the 1968 Mexican Student Movement," *Specialia*, No. 1, Summer 1969, p. 36.

[6] *Pace*, op. cit., p. 18.

of a privately operated high school called for police help in handling a fight between her students and those of the nearby Vocational
School No. 2. This is where a disaster of major national proportions
began.[7] Fights turned into small riots are not unusual given the traditional rivalries between the vocational and preparatory schools, the
latter often jealously seen as stepping stones to a college education.
The request for police assistance was no more than routine, yet,
Corona del Rosal sent 200 grenadiers to handle the students. At that
point their fight could have been over games or girls. What followed
strongly indicates that the grenadiers overreacted and visited brutality
upon the students. A political element was injected into the incident
where none had existed before and the police brutality quickly
inspired an atmosphere of "students vs. the state." The officialist
newspaper chain of Colonel García Valseca (e.g. *El Sol de México*)
tried to blame the students and lauded the police,[8] but most other
reports condemned the military for the reprisals taken. A psychological catharsis was beginning as the *cause célèbre* grew more real.

On July 25 the National Federation of Technical Students
(FNET), a dependency of the PRI, sought a permit to hold a public
march, at the end of which the resignation of General Luis Cueto
Ramírez, chief of the Federal District's police force, would be demanded. Here was open conflict between powerful pressure groups
within the PRI. Coincidently, the march was planned for the following day, July 26, which is generally known as Fidel Castro Day to the
youth of Latin America. Not unexpectedly, the same day had been
picked by the principal youth group of the Mexican Communist Party
for its celebration. This group, CNED, National Confederation of
Democratic Students, merged at Mexico City's famous central square
the Zócalo with around three thousand other students who had been
invited by the FNET. Hostile acts occurred and police units were
summoned to disperse the students. Immediate recriminations were
taken against the Mexican Communist Party and seven employees of
La Voz de México including Gerardo Unzueta, a member of the
PCM's central committee, were jailed. Charges were traded in the press

---

[7] Balam, op. cit., p. 32. In the narrative of events to follow the author employs
a considerable amount of testimony from persons wishing to remain anonymous.
The author is grateful to Mr. David Bellis whose work as a research assistant is
reflected in parts of the narrative.

[8] *El Sol de México*, August 19, Sec. B, p. 2.

as to who was to blame, with most of the venom directed against the students. The next day, July 27, student bands appeared once again at the Zócalo and demanded release of the previous day's prisoners. They repeated their demand that Cueto Ramírez be fired and added his principal assistants to the list. By Monday July 29 the students were claiming that hundreds of their numbers were incarcerated and that scores were missing and dead. The students began addressing their demands to the President of the Republic. It was believed that the crisis was already of national proportions and that Díaz Ordaz was personally responsible. The chain of command was Díaz Ordaz, to Luis Echeverría (Secretary of Interior) to Corona del Rosal, to the police and army commanders. By July 30 the Zócalo had been cleared of students and secured under military command.

At this point a critical ideological marriage began to show itself, featuring the union of a number of groups and *camarillas* both within the revolutionary coalition and outside of it. Student radicals retreated into the National University (UNAM) and the National Polytechnic Institute (IPN) to begin the work of creating a youth coalition against the state (it is well to keep in mind the approximate student figures for UNAM, 90,000 and for IPN, 70,000 as a crude index to the human resource potential on which the organizers could draw). It is important to note that Interior Secretary Echeverría, who was widely rumored to have presidential aspirations for 1970, came to be a principal target for student wrath as the new coalition was being formed. The ideological marriage came to fruition with the declaration of the National Strike Committee *(Consejo Nacional de Huelga)*. It handed Echeverría a list of six basic demands: 1) the firing of the police chief and his assistants, 2) public admission of the government's responsibility for atrocities and violence, 3) freedom for all jailed students and for a loosely defined spectrum of other "political" prisoners, 4) dissolution of the grenadiers, 5) payments to families of the victims of police brutality, 6) and the abolition of Articles 145 and 145 b of the Penal Code which define the Mexican version of sedition and which has been a traditional legal backstop for jailing opposition critics of the PRI. These demands were deliberately framed in language which would have made the government's accession to any one of them a major confession of guilt. It is doubtful that any of the student leaders expected the government to give in. Indeed, they wanted further confrontations to dramatize the ideological gulf between them and officialdom. Demand number three was especially explosive as its refusal by the government opened the way to student oratory in favor of imprisoned labor leaders Demetrio Vallejo and Valentín Campa. The National Strike Committee was gaining symbols of unity and attachment.

Amid reports of supportive student uprisings at other universities about the country, the law student-faculty contingent of the UNAM took temporary control of the National Strike Committee on July 31 and sent out brigades of five to ten students to circulate throughout the city carrying handbills and placards to the public. They went to factories, office buildings, and slums such as Cuidad Netzahuacoyotl on the edge of Mexico City.[9] Their psychology stressed the dichotomy of people and state. The blame assigned went to the doorstep of the government and the political cabal which surrounded it. One handbill urged citizens not to be "taken in by those who through the press, radio, and televison try to hide the truth about what is happening in Mexico. They never mention the hunger, the lack of freedom and the corruption in the unions, and how the government uses your *pesos* to line the pockets of a select few."[10]

On Thursday August 1 the Rector of the UNAM, Javier Barros Sierra, led an estimated 50,000 faculty and students in a demonstration against the police tactics of the government. Subsequently, all classes at UNAM were suspended. The National Strike Committee began to assemble students from other schools and nonstudent sympathizers within the walls of UNAM; at times it was estimated that as many as 40,000 persons congregated there to hear antigovernmental oratory. Many of them were women and children whose presence, it was hoped, would discourage police invasion of the campus. Demands continued for capitulation by the government and these were met with silence until August 8 when the mayor Corona del Rosal offered to set up a commission to investigate the charges of atrocities. But he continued to trumpet the conspiracy theory, telling a gathering of sanitation department employees assembled in the Lázaro Cárdenas Park that the student behavior was part of an international communist plot.[11] The National Strike Committee won encouraging

9 Cf. *Por Qué?*, September, 1968, passim.

10 Handbill, *Comité de Lucha*, UNAM.

11 *Por Qué?*, September, 1968, p. 43.

support when on August 13 the Teachers Coalition for Democratic Liberties was formed and placed itself to a common cause by endorsing the six basic student demands. This is significant, for many of these teachers were also members of the officialist CNOP via a number of subgroups.

On August 22 Minister of the Interior Echeverría made what he considered to be a concession, by agreeing to a private dialogue with the student leaders. The National Strike committee countered that any such discussions would have to be broadcast publicly with government officials, including Echeverría, submitting to questioning. Surely, none of the student leaders expected the government to accept this challenge. Another march of protest followed on August 27 in which the National Strike Committee succeeded in assembling parents, workers, and a number of small businessmen, farm laborers, and medical students who stood out in their white uniforms. The government learned of this march and assembled its own "counter-demonstration" in the Zócalo by giving all employees the day off with encouragement to participate on behalf of the government. Here the government was hoping to draw upon a membership reserve which is an important power base for the PRI, namely, the CNOP, or popular sector, in general and its bureaucrats union, FSTSE in particular. There is impressive testimony to indicate that this was where the PRI showed serious evidence of frailty: many of its popular sector personnel, released from government jobs to support the status quo counter demonstration, actually cast their lot with the National Strike Committee. By noon August 27 nearly half a million people jammed the Zócalo. The counter-demonstration had failed and the students claimed an impressive victory. The oratory on that day stressed the "oneness" of the Mexican people against the government. One speaker, a laborer, said that if a peasant asked for better wages or tried to join an effective non-PRI union, his employer spoke to police and the man would be jailed.[12]

It is worth stressing that, at least during the past decade, such open attacks on the government were customarily issued at opposition rallies sponsored by the PAN, the *Sinarquistas*, or the MLN, and were almost never made in front of the National Palace. Now they were

[12] See G. M. Bergman, "Flags, Tanks, and Students," *The Nation*, September 30, 1968, pp. 298–300; and John Womack, "Unfreedom in Mexico," *The New Republic*, October 12, 1968, *passim*.

emanating from heterogeneous congeries of disaffected groups from both within and without the revolutionary coalition, directly in front of the National Palace. To climax the demonstration, students invaded the main Cathedral and set off the fireworks stored there for the planned Independence Day celebration on September 16. The invasion of the Cathedral brought an angry reaction from the establishment press which said "Communist guerrillas . . . took control of the Cathedral converting the sacred temple into a center of agitation."[13] Students also hoisted a flag of North Vietnam on the national flagpole. Late that evening (August 27) the Zócalo was still occupied by multitudes sympathetic to the National Strike Committee. Then, between 1:00 and 2:00 A.M. on August 28th the troops moved onto the Zócalo under protection of tanks and armored cars (largely of United States manufacture). By dawn Wednesday the students had fled and only the troops remained. During the night it was alleged that army elements disguised as hoodlums of the reactionary right carried out attacks on student hiding places. One of these, at Vocational School No. 7 in the housing complex Tlatelolco, gave an ominous foreshadowing of a tragedy yet to come.[14]

Mexico City waited nervously for Díaz Ordaz' State of the Union Message on Sunday, September 1. Traditionally these messages are routine affairs but this time it was a special occasion. A Mexican president had been confronted with the most serious public challenge since, perhaps, the Cristeros rose against Calles in the 1920's. Díaz Ordaz held his audience in uncomfortable suspense for two and a half hours. Then he touched the theme everyone was waiting for: "the situation has reached the point where methods of expression have been grossly abused."[15] He told the nation that he could not permit the "juridical order to deteriorate" and that any force necessary would be used to keep antisocial elements from disrupting the Olympic Games. Despite student disclaimers that they wanted to interfere with the Games, Díaz Ordaz stated that foreigners whom he implied to be Cuban agents were hoping to destroy the Olympics. He said that for the first time the Games were to be held "in a country that speaks Spanish, for the first time in a Latin American nation, and for the

[13] *El Sol de México*, August 28, 1968, p. 1, and *Excelsior*, August 29, 1968, editorial page.

[14] Balam, op. cit., p. 77.

[15] *Visión*, September 1, 1968, p. 16.

first time in a developing nation. This accomplishment should be a legitimate satisfaction for the Mexican people."[16]

In the light of the more than 150 million dollars invested by the Mexican government to promote the Games, the president's concern was to be expected. He ended his address with what he considered to be concessions, one of them a promise for legislation granting more "autonomy" to the Polytechnic Institute and the high schools; the other, a congressional investigation of charges that the sedition laws had been in abuse. But the second concession was followed by a caveat. Díaz Ordaz asked "should it not be considered a crime to affect our national sovereignty, endangering the territorial integrity of the republic in compliance with the dictates of a foreign government?" "If it (the subversion law) is abolished, no crime will have a political character. Is that what is desired?"[17] Díaz Ordaz seemed to be forewarning his congress to disregard the second concession in order to protect its own immunity from political attack; at least, that is how the students understood it. Students, professors, and a multitude of sympathizers answered Díaz Ordaz' message on September 13 with another large demonstration. Thousands paraded in silence carrying placards of Ho Chi Minh, Fidel Castro, and Che Guevara. Public orators reiterated the demand for a dialogue with the government that would be broadcast by radio and television. Interior Minister Echeverría ignored the demand and the government maintained a determined but fragile calm.

Although the government controlled the streets of the capital city, the students and the National Strike Committee controlled the schools. Before September 18, no tanks or soldiers had entered the university or the Polytechnic Institute, but it was clear that some sort of confrontation was in the making. On September 17 Echeverría spoke. He repeated the government's determination to safeguard the Olympic Games within constitutional means and at any cost. The officialist García Valseca newspaper chain stressed repeatedly that the National University—was being used as a staging ground for direct attacks on the Sports Palace. An impressive effort had been made to convince the public that the UNAM was a center of subversion that must be stifled. On September 18 this occurred. An estimated 10,000 troops in battle dress occupied the campus. Federal district attorney,

---

[16] Ibid.

[17] *Los Angeles Times*, September 29, 1968, p. 18.

Gilberto Súarez Torres, said that some 145 persons had been arrested. An American newsweekly put the figure at close to 1,000.[18] Interior Minister Echeverría defended the action saying that the UNAM was public property being used illegally by persons who intended to perpetrate antisocial and criminal acts.[19] At this point the breach between the government and the National Strike Committee became complete, the latter having been branded as criminals. The action also helped to mend the traditional animosity between students of UNAM and the Polytechnic Institute, the latter bearing a stigma of social inferiority. With UNAM occupied, its students were welcomed into the IPN which remained the National Strike Committee's last operational bastion. Both politically and tactically this was a union of no small importance.

On Sunday, September 22, UNAM Rector, Javier Barros Sierra, submitted his resignation in protest against the military occupation of his campus. The UNAM's governing council unanimously rejected his resignation under the threat that if accepted, the university's 7,000 professors would also resign. It was rumored that Sierra's action was taken as a disguise for his real complicity with the government in the campus takeover, but this has not yet been substantiated. What is clear is that the government had taken its toll of students, and the well organized cadres of the National Strike Committee were falling into atrophy. Bands of disillusioned anarchists began roaming the city pillaging and looting wantonly without the "legitimizing" pretense of an ideological commitment. Busses were commandeered and set afire and streets were barracaded. Such events lasted until the end of September, giving Mexico City the terrifying spectre of anarchosyndicalism gone rampant. It was clearly the worst outbreak of anomic violence and political alienation since the great Revolution. By the end of September a lull had fallen over Mexico City. The violence subsided, and a Mothers March was staged from Insurgentes Avenue to the Chamber of Deputies in protest of the deaths of youth. On October 1st, Javier Barros Sierra returned to his office at UNAM as the last contingent of troops left the campus. The Olympic Games were only a few days away and all officialdom prayed that the insurgency had ended; in truth, the end had just begun.

[18] *Time*, September 27, 1968, p. 33. *The Los Angeles Times* reported the same figure of arrests since September 18 (Sept. 21, 1968, p. 11).

[19] *Visión*, October 11, 1968, p. 13.

The climax to this episode came with an agony from which much can be gleaned that should be relevant to the interests of social science scholars. An analogy from game theory comes to mind of the shepherd who relentlessly pursued a wolf into a corner where the animal was forced to fight and succeeded in destroying the shepherd in what amounted to an unnecessary defeat. Looking back on the Mexico City violence it appears that on October 1, 1968 the point of no return was crossed. The government failed to take advantage of the temporarily improved atmosphere to seek a negotiated peace with the National Strike Committee. Instead, a decision was made to pursue the students like wolves and drive them into a corner from which there was no escape. The name of that corner was Tlatelolco, a major apartment complex, housing an estimated 75,000 persons of middle class status. It is popularly alleged that most of the residents of Tlatelolco are permitted to live there because they are loyal supporters of the revolutionary coalition; if this were true it was little in evidence in the early days of October.

The National Strike Committee had resolved to make a final public effort to regroup its ranks and to mobilize additional public support behind its challenge of the government. A well circulated public rumor carried news of a gigantic rally to be held at the Plaza of the Three Cultures near Tlatelolco. In the early morning hours of October 1st, police agents had discovered the hiding place of two Guatemalan terroritsts in one of the giant bulidings that adjoins the Tlatelolco complex. Anachronistically, the name of this building was Miguel Alemán, the former president and financial boss, whose son had been busy during the summer telling the press optimistic tales about Mexico's progressive youth.[20] The terrorists were said by police to have been well stocked with weapons. Their names were given as Carlos Ruelas and Leopoldo Ernesto Zepeda who, along with a Mexican accomplice named Luis Sánchez Cordero, were taken into custody and offered as evidence that Mexico was the victim of an international plot. From interrogations the police claimed to have

---

[20] *Pace,* op. cit. There is really no point in blaming Miguel Alemán nor the top echelon of his *camarilla* as discrete individuals. It is the collectivity of the Mexican political system, or to repeat the aphorism of Carlos Fuentes *el sistema político hueco,* that is responsible. If the bizarre truth could ever be ascertained it just might be that the Mexican power elite is so removed from "pedestrian realities" as to be genuinely uninformed as to the true dilemmas of youth in their quest for upward mobility.

learned that other violence prone student groups had rented apartments in the area which were being used as bases for planned insurgency (at this point one could seriously doubt the strength of the government's control over the Tlatelolco project). Their strategy appeared to be provocation of conflict in zones of great population density where riot police would be least effective and where it was hoped that a great amount of public support (or at least sympathy) for the students would be found. Rumors spread of police invasions of the Tlatelolco apartments, but it is not known to what extent these stories were well founded. They were, however, believed and widely communicated.

In order to protest these police actions and to reiterate earlier demands, the National Strike Committee announced that it would hold a demonstration march to begin at Tlatelolco and to end at the Casco de Santo Tomas that had recently been occupied by troops.[21] At the last minute, according to the account given by Gilberto Balam, the National Strike Commitee called off the march thinking it would provoke troop reprisals.[22] If this is correct, then a slim possibility for dialogue still remained. Instead of the march the Committee called for a public meeting to be held in the Tlatelolco plaza and in the neighboring Plaza of the Three Cultures. The purpose was ostensibly to articulate grievances. Around four thousand persons gathered (not a huge group compared with previous meetings) and a large number of these were women and children. Speakers cajoled the audience that the government had shut off all discourse on the six demands and urged the throng to "unite and take the city." This occurred at approximately 6:30 on the afternoon of Wednesday, October 2, 1968.[23]

At that moment the army and police appeared and surrounded much of the area with tanks and armored cars. The speakers on the platform tried to calm the people: *"no se muevan compañeros! Permanezcan tranquilos ante las provocaciones de la tropa y la policía!"*[24] Using a bullhorn, an officer ordered the people to abandon the area and when they did not obey, white-gloved riot police moved into the

[21] Balam, op. cit., p. 96.

[22] Ibid.

[23] Again, I am relying upon eyewitness testimony by persons who prefer to remain anonymous.

[24] Balam, op. cit., p. 97.

crowd swinging clubs and chains against the people. This was the signal that converted the spectator-participant crowd into a mob.[25] The police were attacked furiously by the citizens. When police opened fire they were greeted by rifle shot from the upper floors of the building, Chihuahua, that had also served as a frequent meeting place for leaders of the National Strike Committee. It was clear now that elements were present that either wanted a violent confrontation or at least had become convinced, however reluctantly, of its necessity. The police retired and called for troops. The Army then responded with mortars and armored cars, and a helicopter began dropping green flares about the area and into the crowd.[26] General José Hernández Toledo, Commander of the First Batallion of Paratroopers attempted to speak to the crowd via a portable loudspeaker. As he did so snipers opened fire from the building Chihuahua and the general fell seriously wounded to the pavement. This was approximately at 7:00 P.M. on the night of October 2.

A firefight then ensued with incredible vehemence until nearly 4:00 A.M. the next morning. Thousands of Mexicans were caught in the murderous crossfire. Mob behavior was mixed with crowd panic. People ran in terror from the nearby Tlatelolco Movie Theater, and many of them were slugged and wounded without provocation. Backed up by armored vehicles firing tracer bullets from high calibre machineguns the soldiers are said to have fired at nearly anyone who moved. Automatic weapons swept building ledges where some youngsters had climbed to safety. Many innocent people were killed and many more

[25] Were it possible to gain access to unbiased information on both sides of the strategy it would be possible for the scholar to make several interesting applications of game theory to the student-government conflict. Consider, for instance, the following description as applied to what happened at Tlatelolco: ". . . people require some signal for their coordination, a signal so unmistakably comprehensible and so potent in its suggestion for action that everyone can be sure that everyone else reads the same signal with enough confidence to act on it, thus providing one another with the immunity that goes with action in large numbers." ". . . the mob's problem is to act in unison without overt leadership, to find some common signal that makes everyone confident that if he acts on it, he will not be acting alone. The role of 'incidents' can thus be seen as a coordinating role; it is a substitute for overt leadership and communication." From Thomas C. Shelling, *The Strategy of Conflict*, New York: Oxford, 1963, 74, 90.

[26] Balam, op. cit., pp. 97–98. See also *Newsweek*, October 14, 1968, p. 64, and *America*, October 19, 1968, p. 340.

injured. The Italian woman journalist, Oriana Falaci, herself a veteran of Vietnam reporting, was seriously injured.[27] When the holocaust was over, the Army was in command of Tlatelolco and the Plaza of the Three Cultures. Sniper nests were discovered in the buildings Chihuahua, Molino del Rey, General Anaya, Xicoténcatl, and also (ironically) in a nearby building which houses the service organization of the CNOP's favored bureaucrats union (FSTSE) known as the Institute of Social Services for Workers of the State (ISSSTE). Several dead snipers were identified as of Cuban and Guatemalan origin. The death toll at Tlatelolco will never be known. Gilberto Balam places it in the upper hundreds, and official estimates claimed around two hundred. Defense Minister General Marcelino García Barragán said that his orders were to crush the uprising at any cost,[28] even (apparently) at the cost of first having to create conflict.

It would be inaccurate to blame the government for the entire disaster, for it is clear that the students were armed and had brought in experienced guerrillas to help them. This came, however, after it appeared certain that a dialogue with the government would never be allowed. The students had also been encouraged by various sectors of the press and clergy. Alejandro Avilés (a former PAN militant) wrote sympathetic articles in *Excelsior*. Thirty priests of the diocese of Cuernavaca signed a document sympathetic to the student cause and support came from Enrique Maza and Ramón de Ertze Garamendi, priests who lauded the students for their bravery. There is at least one other melancholy truth underlying the holocaust: Many of the students who (with and without arms) attacked police had first inebriated themselves into a hideous pitch of revelry by consuming a mixture of tequila, rum, and a drug known as "cyclopal" whose effect is to make one reckless and impervious in the face of certain death. Many students "liberated" themselves in this suicidal fashion.

[27] Oriana Falaci, a 40-year-old Italian newspaperwoman, was shot three times. Two men standing near her were killed outright. She said "I have covered the Vietnam war but I have never seen anything similar to what happened at Tlatelolco . . . I lay on the ground with blood pouring out of my body. Every time I tried to raise my head and call for help a policeman was pointing his gun at me. It was a terrible, unbelievable thing." *The Los Angeles Times*, October 4, 1968, p. 4.

[28] *Los Angeles Times*, October 3, 1968, p. 1.

Prognosis and Vignettes

The rampaging students and their sympathizers had broken several cardinal norms of Mexico's esoteric democracy. First and foremost they had abandoned the traditional reconcilation system, condemning it (i.e. the PRI) as corrupt and took their cause directly to the street in a confrontation with the state. Second, they attacked the person of the president while he was in office. Third, the National Strike Committee won away impressive numbers of the cadres normally supportive of the revolutionary coalition. Here it is worth repeating the rumor (but apparently well founded on the basis of this author's interviews) that many federal bureaucrats of the FSTSE either joined the student movement or else withheld support from the government to the extent possible. This is believed to have contributed to the government's decision to authorize that the march and rally of October 2 be crushed at all costs. Fourth, the students gave up their condition of "solitude," as Octavio Paz has described it, and sought to create a true mass consciousness that was free from doctrinaire attachments.

Finally, the students' principal leadership group, the National Strike Committee, did not blame the United States for what had happened. North Americans will react, "of course! how could they." But it must be remembered that the United States is a traditional whipping boy throughout the hemisphere, especially in Mexico. There were individual charges against the United States: Marcellino Perello, a 23-year-old student of physics at UNAM said that the shooting was started by "either Mexican police agents or members of the CIA."[29] Notice how he equivocated: "either/or." He went on to say that the CIA's purpose in getting involved was to create a pretext under which Mexico would have to break relations with Cuba in that CIA agents, allegedly, had posed as representatives of Fidel Castro. This, said Perello, would please Mexican oligarchs in the employ of North American companies. Balam's account also says, "of course the CIA was involved" but goes on to cite the fact that it was Mexican officialdom which made the charge and not the National Strike Committee.[30]

[29] Los Angeles Times, October 10, 1968, p. 7.
[30] Balam, op. cit., p. 99.

The significance of the final point is simply this: when the bodies and blood were removed from the sidewalks of Tlatelolco everyone knew that this had been a Mexican affair. The blame stayed at home, where it belonged. Individually sponsored charges against the United States, Guatemala, and Cuba were not accepted as true by the majority of the students. It was painfully like PRI attempting to blame PAN for the failures of any of the government programs (such as CONASUPO) in which PAN is conspicuously not involved. Most reasonable humans simply will not believe that the moon is made of green cheese. And no one other than Mexico's SPH factor was to blame for the events of 1968 which culminated at Tlatelolco on October 2nd. The system was not well adapted to resolution of conflict which originated in an attack upon the very legitimacy of the system itself.

The events which ended at Tlatelolco are symtomatic of what is probably Mexico's most acute socioeconomic determinant of political alienation. I refer to the generation gap and its attendant causal factors such as urbanization and rural displacement, limited sources of employment, stultified wage and salary structures, overpopulation and values that inhibit family planning. Mexican youth are indeed on the move, but for most of them it is not an upward socioeconomic mobility. They emerge from the high schools and universities filled with visions of what could be (and of what *is* in the more developed countries) and are thwarted with stark recognition of what Mexico is. Of the some 90,000 students at UNAM it is estimated that only 20 percent will receive degrees and only one percent or less of them will secure jobs with anything above a subsistence income. Yet the university has taught them to articulate their grievances, to form cliques and movements, and to take their case to the street against the government. If sixty-five percent of Mexico's population is truly under twenty five years of age, then the imperative for bridging the generation gap is frighteningly acute. Something other than a "hollow political system" will be needed to meet this challenge. What is especially threatening about the student behavior during 1968 is the relative ease with which a singularity of purpose could be operationalized among the normally discordant factions of the UNAM and the IPN. It has been difficult for a Mexican youth to act the role of a responsible first class citizen when in his eyes the socioeconomic-political system is deliberately rigged against him. Awareness of this sparked a mass consciousness among the students, and led to the violence of 1968.

A conservative estimate places property damage and commercial losses in the whole affair at around eight million dollars, but an exact figure will never be known. While no one won the conflict, surely the PRI had lost. Its image had been badly smeared. In his own wry fashion Carlos Madrazo capsulized the dilemma in an earlier press interview when he said: "Do you know what one of Díaz Ordaz' ministers told me the other day? He said the people didn't count. What does count is the impression we create with our newspapers."[31] Madrazo could have hardly been surprised when the government paraded before the press witnesses who accused him and others of having financed the student rioters.[32]

[31] Manuel de la Isla, "Habla Madrazo," *Por Qué?*, August 15, 1968, p. 16.

[32] Of the several witnesses only one was permitted to speak openly with reporters immediately after the crisis of Tlatelolco. He was Sócrates Amado Campos Lemus, a member of the National Strike Committee, who charged ("confessed") that the students were financed by Madrazo, Humberto Romero Pérez (formerly private secretary to President López Mateos), the writer Elena Garro, the director of the Colegio de México Eduardo Gorostiza, and the former governor of Baja California (and controversial leader in the MLN) Braulio Maldonado Sández. No official action was taken against the accused persons. As a concessionary act the government published a list of 755 names of students which it said were to be released. This, officially, ended the student violence of 1968. Cf. *Excelsior*, October 6, 1968, passim. Substantially after this chapter was written the author discovered the clandestine book *El móndrigo*, México: Editorial Alba Roja, 1969, no author cited except Bitácora del Consejo Nacional de Huelga, that has been cited variously throughout this book. See also *Mexico '68: The Students Speak* published by the United States Committee for Justice to Latin American Political Prisoners, New York, no date. It is significant to note the comments of one critic of this chapter, Kenneth M. Coleman, who objected to my use of the term "anarchists" "because it conveys the impression that *only* leftists were involved when, in fact, there is substantial evidence that governmental supporters engaged in some such activities with a conscious goal of having their activities blamed on the students . . . the evidence is incontrovertible that off-duty police and military personnel also engaged in the destruction of property." See also Edmundo, Jardón A., *De la Ciudadela a Tlatelolco*, México: Fondo de Cultura Popular, 1969.

7
On the Psychology of Mexico's Political Impasse

In Defense of the Revolutionary Coalition

The foregoing chapters may have convinced the reader that my intention in this book has been to excoriate the PRI for its failure to bring about social justice and economic plenty to millions of Mexicans and to paint in the darkest of colors its widespread financial and political corruption. This is not so. While it is true that I do not view the esoteric political system in the comparatively laudatory terms that have appeared in the writings of most other North American scholars it is, nonetheless, my desire to treat fairly a political system that is often characterized by its lack of social justice toward a burgeoning population.

The opening sentence above contains, ironically, the key to an otherwise bizarre argument which I will now advance in defense of the revolutionary coalition. The phrase is "widespread financial and political corruption." I suspect that the decade of the seventies will reveal the political corruption of the PRI to have been its Achilles Heel. But I also suspect that, at least during the two previous decades, this financial corruption served a functional purpose of distributing and redistributing wealth simply because the corruption was widespread, so widespread in fact that money and other forms of material largesse reached the hands of thousands who otherwise would not have maintained attitudes supportive of the state. This may be like saying "where all men are rogues no one is a rogue," but the financial sharing of the PRI has been intimately involved in Mexico's political stability. I do not refer to compulsory profit-sharing schemes, but rather to the dispensation of largesse via political channels that has quieted much potentially violent opposition. It is, of course, a central theme of this book that Mexico's esoteric democratic system cannot maintain a "democratic" image through buying off its opposition permanently. Nor can it expect to continue to purchase the acquiescence of thousands of marginal members of the body politic when the real substance of socioeconomic change goes untouched. But the gigantic and overwhelming fact of Mexican political life during this century is that of stability, political socialization, and socioeconomic development at levels that are the envy of most Latin American nations.

One of the developmental requirements that is central to W. W. Rostow's *Stages of Economic Growth* is that when capital is generated or imported it must be shared and redistributed via supplies of loanable funds for entrepreneurship. Such funds must be kept out of the hands of those who would "sterilize" them. Wealth must be ploughed back into the economy via entrepreneurial schemes that create employment, itself a basic social function. Much capital has been ploughed back into the Mexican economy, a quantity that can never be known but which is believed to be considerable in comparison with the experiences of other Latin American nations. In the process, Mexico's national wealth distribution has been *relatively* equitable (in the same comparative terms). Moreover, by means of development agencies like *Nacional Financiera*, agriculture and industry have moved beyond the stage of economic "take off" and have entered the stage of mass production and consumption. This, of course, must be considered as a *formalistic* aspect of the PRI's success as a wealth redistribution system. Its *informal* counterpart is the "trickle up and down" system of largesse which North Americans (and, by the way, most Mexicans) lump under the rubric of corruption. Nevertheless, the wealth has been shared in a way that has made political stability possible.

The revolutionary coalition began with a reformist image of the socialist left, although its original leaders were *decidedly* not socialists. The presidency of Lázaro Cárdenas accentuated this image, but it has not grown into a gulf of alienation between labor and industry. Indeed, the PRI has, in recent years, enjoyed much success in courting the wealthy industrial and propertied classes (see epilogue to follow). A recent example is that of the linkages between AUTOMEX (discussed in Chapter 4) and the Secretariat of Commerce and Industry. This is nothing new. Ten years ago an excellent study by Merle Kling pointed up the ease with which right wing causes (in this case *laizzez faire* economic champions) could establish a rapprochement with an officialdom ostensibly dedicated to "liberating the masses."[1] But at the same time, the PRI has skillfully integrated the laboring poor and rural peasants under its aegis (or at least it has won their acquiescent participation). Unquestionably failures have occurred and abuses have been perpetrated but a system for wealth redistribution has been created, and via its ubiquitous reaches enough largesse has been shared so that the overwhelming majority of the Mexican population has been able to accept their governing institutions with confidence, and at times pride, for the better part of fifty years. Considering the obstacles that lay in the path of Mexico's development (not the least of which was the loss of the most valuable half of her national territory to the United States in 1848) during her "Fifty Years of Revolution" one must conclude that something close to miraculous was achieved. A large part of this credit belongs to the PRI. It has given Mexico symbols of group attachment by means of which many share a common and ongoing historical experience.

Ultimately, if one must press for distinct indices of relative effectiveness of achievement, one might select the success of Mexican esoteric democracy vis-à-vis the competition of International Communism in the hemisphere. Between 1929 (when Calles formed the PRN) and 1968 (Tlatelolco) the revolutionary coalition was able to supplant and/or coopt the communist left to a degree sufficient to prevent eruptions of anomic alienated behavior from that sector that could severely threaten the upper echelons of the power hierarchy. This is to say that the cases of Demetrio Vallejo, Rubén Jaramillo,

[1] Merle Kling, *A Mexican Interest Group in Action* (Englewood Cliffs: Prentice-Hall, 1961). Especially relevant is this contention by Kling: "this study yields the hypothesis that ideological marginality does not correlate with economic marginality or marginality in the area of governmental decision-making. The doctrines of the *Instituto* are not within the mainstream of Mexican revolutionary ideology; but members of the *Instituto* represent some of the most powerful business interests of postwar Mexico and, as individuals, enjoy ready access to key government officials." (The *Instituto* refers to the *Instituto de Investigaciones Sociales y Económicas A.C.*, p. 66.)

and others of this ilk were blemishes on the PRI that did not shake its foundations. During the first fifty years of the Mexican revolutionary experience, the PRI displaced the communist left and sublimated its disruptive potential. The PRI served as a gigantic political sponge that could absorb a considerable amount of threat without destroying its own organic functions. Manuel Velázquez, an intellectual who defends the PRI, has put the case as follows (my translation):

The PRI is not a party of class, but of classes, which permits the participation of the most diverse groups within its midst. In this circumstance the Marxist argument does not stand up, for the working class has no cause to fight for power since it is already within the power system. . . .[2]

This utopian sounding vision contains, nevertheless, much truth. Mexico simply has not, during fifty years of revolutionary experience, been torn by the ravages of communist upheaval that have plagued other Latin American nations. Few other political systems in Latin America can make a claim of this magnitude. And the reader should be reminded once again that for this author to argue in the present instance that the PRI could be vastly improved upon is in no way tantamount to suggesting that it be destroyed or abolished. All of Latin America can learn much that is positive from the revolutionary tradition of the PRI.

Into the 1970's: The Challenge of Socioeconomic Change

The decade of the 1970's promises to be critical in that the esoteric system is faced with the imperative of reestablishing its political legitimacy and of extending its sphere of allegiance into new sectors and toward those that have been alienated. As the epilogue to follow argues, the PRI has ceased to be a popularly based movement. Instead, it has come to depend heavily upon the wealthy industrial and propertied classes for support. It has not coopted the alienated left but only repressed it. Nor has the PRI coopted its only substantive

[2] Manuel Velázquez, *Revolución en la constitución* (México: Costa-Amic, 1969), p. 208 (my translation).

opposition the *Partido Acción Nacional*. The PAN, as the foregoing chapters reveal, mounted a severe threat to the PRI in state and municipal elections during the three year period 1967–69 and this proved too much for the PRI to accept. The regime of Gustavo Díaz Ordaz repeatedly denied the opposition PAN access to the political arena at the state and local grass roots where such abuses of single party democracy were most painfully visible to the Mexican public. Ultimately, the leadership of *Acción Nacional* seriously considered removing its candidate, Efraín González Morfín, from the presidential campaign of 1970 and even discussed plans to abolish the party. Looking forward to another six-year period of hardline suppression under Díaz Ordaz' hand picked successor, Luis Echeverría Alvarez, the leadership of *Acción Nacional* saw little hope of gaining political fortune by licit competitive means. Clearly, the governance of Mexico during the balance of the 1970's would be left to the esoteric system, i.e. the PRI. Having clearly demonstrated its aversion to political change, the PRI would have to confront the necessity for socioeconomic change in a fashion that would be sufficiently concrete to forestall new expressions of alienation against the government.

The imperative for socioeconomic change can be seen in the following table which contains wealth distribution figures for the Federal District alone (where the situation is probably better than in most parts of the nation). The figures show that, independently of worker occupation, a third (35.78 percent) of all workers in the Federal District received monthly incomes of between 300 and 749 pesos which is roughly 25 to 64 dollars. Approximately a fifth of the workers in the Federal District earned between 1,000 and 1,500 pesos or an average of 120 dollars per month. Less than 2 percent of the working population earned more than 800 dollars per month and this percentage consisted almost entirely of the professional and managerial classes.

Although one must always be cautious of official statistics in Mexico, the above figures tell a grim story as it prevailed toward the end of the 1960's. An inspection tour of worker quarters around Mexico City would easily lead one to expect such a niggardly distribution of wealth. Most of the worker families are large with many mouths consuming and few hands earning produce. The women seldom practice "family planning" because it is financially out of their reach, because it is condemned by the Church, and because many of

WORKER OCCUPATION BY SEX AND MONTHLY INCOME[3] (IN PESOS) Federal District

Occupation	Total	Men	Women	earnings to $299	$300 to $749	$750 to 999	$1,000 to 1,500	$1,501 to 2,000	$2,001 to 3,000	$3,001 to 5,000	$5,001 to 10,000	$10,000 or more
Professional, technical and related occupations	161,040	121,512	39,528	---	4,873	5,830	45,186	10,204	28,213	31,578	22,537	13,119
Managers, administrators, and supervisorial positions not including agriculture	167,112	123,904	43,208	7,086	22,677	12,233	35,929	17,008	8,909	21,530	27,044	14,696
Office workers in general	467,016	276,696	190,320	7,313	187,492	96,537	143,342	40,955	31,183	7,189	3,005	---
Salesmen and agents	117,120	92,232	24,888	7,292	46,761	13,151	16,074	7,321	14,849	7,165	4,507	---
Farm, ranch and lumber workers, fishermen, hunters and other similar occupations	11,748	11,748	---	2,998	5,914	---	2,836	---	---	---	---	---
Gas and petroleum workers, quarry and salt miners and miners in general	8,673	8,673	---	---	4,336	2,892	1,445	---	---	---	---	---
Skilled factory workers, truck and bus drivers, and similar occupations	462,627	404,064	58,563	23,563	204,848	86,888	111,924	10,308	20,790	4,806	---	---
Unskilled workers and laborers	99,552	86,376	13,176	10,248	61,488	2,928	19,032	5,856	---	---	---	---
Domestic servants and related workers	453,696	95,160	358,536	210,910	209,340	16,111	8,004	6,431	---	1,435	---	1,465
Total	1,948,584	1,220,365	728,219	269,410	697,229	236,570	383,772	98,083	103,944	73,203	57,093	29,280
Percentage	100.00%	62.62%	37.38%	13.82%	35.78%	12.14%	19.69%	5.03%	5.33%	3.75%	2.93%	1.53%

[3] Source: Banco de México, *Estudio de la economía de México* (México: 1966).

them simply do not know about it. Incomes are thus dissipated and most Mexicans live only slightly above the subsistence level. Here is great socioeconomic potential for generating expressions of political alienation from the custodians of the state. This is the challenge that Mexico's esoteric democratic system must confront during the decade of the 1970's It is doubtful whether programs like CONA-SUPO (which do little to enhance individual self respect and degenerate into spurious subsidies for other nations) will be able to meet the demand.

Political outrage can erupt violently at any time in Mexico and the provocations can vary, but socioeconomic wretchedness is in the background of most such expressions. It is doubtful whether the massacre of Tlatelolco would have taken on the political proportions it did without the broad underpinning of socioeconomic despair that predisposed the National Strike Committee to organize against the government. (A similar observation might be made with respect to the massacre of Acapulco on August 20, 1967, in which some thirty copra workers died and over one hundred were seriously injured, but the PRI has been successful, by and large, in sweeping this bizarre affair under esoteric democracy's "ubiquitous rug.") When socioeconomic despair leads to violence, the losers are usually the wretched poor and their bondage to poverty normally goes untouched.

There have been leaders in Mexico who favored making democracy "exoteric" and allowing the people to choose their representatives from the localities on up. The late Carlos A. Madrazo, to whom I have alluded throughout this book, sought to confront the imperative for socioeconomic change by strengthening the municipalities where the principal *de facto* responsibility lies. He saw political change and socioeconomic change as a marriage of necessity, and once alleged that 65 percent of the Mexican people were, for all intents and purposes, living outside the national economy as well as beyond the political system[4] (one of Madrazo's favorite expressions was "you cannot govern by killing hope"). President Díaz Ordaz ended Madrazo's campaign to democratize the PRI and a tragic accident thereafter cut short his attempt at regrouping the dissident left into a new and unified opposition movement. There are many political veterans in

[4] Carlos A. Madrazo, *El drama del campesino en México*, handbill, 1967; and *La revolución mexicana está en peligro*, handbill, 1967; and *Seis temas de México*, México, La Comisión Editorial del Frente Nacional Progresista, 1968 passim.

Mexico today who believe that Madrazo could have forced reform upon the PRI via his preoccupation with both political and socioeconomic problems at the grass roots. Madrazo was a child of the PRI, knew its folkways, and was not unfamiliar with skeletons hidden away in many closets of men in high places. It is also for that reason that many Mexicans believe that Madrazo was murdered.[5] And his basic query still goes unanswered: "what good does it do to have a gigantic political party in which all can pretend to participate when only a handful of persons control both it and the national wealth?"

Mexico is now reaching the 50 million population mark. Her urban areas (population clusters of 10,000 or more) account for between sixty and seventy percent of the population total. These figures are educated estimates, but it is clear that Mexico today is predominantly urban, whereas during the 1950's it was predominantly rural The burgeoning of urban areas has made more people acutely aware of their socioeconomic plight, and their proximity to one another has facilitated the articulation and communication of demands for reform that are directed to the political system. When such demands are ignored, the urban milieu lends itself to gestures of protest and challenge as well. In earlier writings I suggested that increased urbanization in Mexico might promote intensified political party competition, an hypothesis that has since been challenged (and with good cause) by a number of scholars. But the clustering of people together into such mammoth aggregations as the Federal District does, I submit, contribute directly to an atmosphere in which alienated behavior of anomic violence is likely to occur. One study of urbanization in Mexico (which was based, unfortunately, on highly superficial and unrealistic survey data) seems to overlook the violence potential of rural to urban migration and the subsequent clustering of the urban poor.[6] Events leading to the disaster of Tlatelolco point to this poten-

[5] Although the official investigation of the plane crash that killed Madrazo concluded that it was an accident attributable to pilot error plus bad weather, there are credible rumors that indicate the presence of evil intent. The truth may never be known.

[6] Cf. Wayne A. Cornelius, Jr., "Urbanization as an Agent in Latin American Political Instability: The Case of Mexico," *The American Political Science Review*, September 1969, pp. 833–57. This author writes "in any event, we find little empirical evidence to support the standard conception of the city as essentially a radicalizing environment. Nor does there appear to be an empirical basis for frequent perceptions of imminent threat to existing authority structures stemming from the rapid influx of migrants to cities." (p. 855). This does not square with the *empirical* data presented in this book. Indeed, it is doubtful whether the above

tial. My own extensive interviews in the Federal District reveal an enormously alienated capacity for anomic violence that can readily be directed against the state. Officialdom does not, of course, like to admit this, but it is there nonetheless. As Mexico continues to become an urban nation the problem of political alienation will surely grow unless concrete socioeconomic change occurs in such a way as to produce a more equitable distribution of the nation's wealth. Rhetoric about "revolutionary" symbolism will not take the place of full stomachs, and it will be to the everlasting benefit of Mexico if this simple truth is thoroughly understood in the upper echelons of the *Partido Revolucionario Institucional.*

Psychological Keys

Those who would revolutionize Mexican politics, indeed her entire socioeconomic system, have characteristically confused tactics with

---

quoted author actually had access to what we would term relevant empirical data. His information came from Almond and Verba's *Civic Culture* which neglected the overwhelming majority of politically relevant satellite parties and out groups. In addition, "the modal respondent in our *Civic Culture* sample is over 35 years of age and has resided in a city of over 100,000 population for ten or more years" (p. 837). The age of the modal respondent does not necessarily prove that the sample was biased but, in fact, over sixty-five percent of the Mexican population is under 25 years of age. These were by and large the people who rioted during the summer of 1968. We do not know their rural to urban migratory characteristics. The modal respondent cited above was decidedly not a new urban arrival. It is also worth noting that the Almond and Verba data were gathered on a contractual second person basis and totally ignored such groups as the *Unión Nacional Sinarquista* and the *Movimiento de Liberación Nacional.* The survey did not isolate alienated political nuclei and contains a number of truly incredible statements from the standpoint of those of us who have taken the trouble to study Mexico's political culture *empirically* and in the field, by means of direct sensory-linguistic techniques. One such statement is: "the low percentage (of refusal by respondents to tell an interviewer how he voted in recent elections) in Mexico is due no doubt to the fact that the overwhelming majority of Mexicans vote for the Revolutionary party, which is the dominant party in the country. *In other words, Mexicans, unlike Italians of the extreme left, have nothing to conceal* [italics added]." (in Almond and Verba, *Civic Culture* (Princeton: 1963), p. 117). If nothing else, this conclusion dramatizes the imperative for attitudinal surveys that have a sound cultural anchoring, especially vis-à-vis the expertise of the principal investigators. The fact is, nonvoting is unconstitutional in Mexico and to admit to strangers under the circumstances of a survey poll that one had voted for any group other than the PRI would be a most rare happening. Following this criticism of Almond and Verba it is only just to stress the important theoretic contribution contained in their work despite some of the cultural incongruities reflected therein.

strategy and in so doing have failed to mount a unified opposition force. This is one of the psychological keys to understanding the growth and tenure of esoteric democracy in Mexico. The clandestine monograph *El móndrigo* that was cited in Chapter 6 offers a behavioral portrait of the labor leader, Demetrio Vallejo, whose struggle with officialdom made him an everlasting *cause célèbre* (see Chapter 4): he, Vallejo, engaged in combat without once considering the probable immediate consequences; his initial successes inflated his vanity which clouded his reason; he did little to nurture permanent grass roots for what remained a transitory movement of conflict; he did not know how to withdraw so as to fight again another day.[7] Vallejo was an easy victim for the suave cunning of President López Mateos as was his peasant counterpart Rubén Jaramillo. It was with similar ease that Agustín de Iturbide had seduced Vicente Guerrero over a century earlier. Many Mexicans have a capacity for gullibility that contributes to the maintenance of the esoteric democratic system; if they are told convincingly that all is well, they are likely to believe it. If they can convince themselves that all is going well via token successes they easily forget the imperative for putting a long range drive for change into motion.

At the time of the Spanish conquest Cortes failed to metamorphose the Indian mentality he confronted. There is something unique in the peculiar mixture of races which produced the ethnic strain now called *mestizo* that characterizes Mexico today and underlies her operative systems of value. Mexico has undergone the many ravages of traumatic change and each has helped to nurture a unique Mexican character: witness the military conquests, Latin America's longest dictatorship, the foreign interventions, and a major social revolution. The unique psychological syndrome belonging to the *mestizo* has been changed little during fifty years of "revolution." The typical Mexican today is a conformist. He will tolerate incredible waste of his public resources. He will seldom rise up in rebellion unless the corruption touches his personal honor. Whenever he has tried to intervene against political officialdom he has been thwarted and frustrated and this has forced upon him a stoical withdrawl that is so well documented in the writings of Octavio Paz and Carlos Fuentes (see Chapter 2). Such frustrations have been visited upon Mexican

[7] *El móndrigo*, México, Editorial Alba Roja, 1969 (Bitácora del Consejo Nacional de Huelga), p. 140.

intellectuals as well as upon the common man. Successive regimes have placed roadblocks in the way of intellectuals who seek to inspire change. The greatest of these roadblocks is the giant family of political cliques that monopolizes control of the state via perpetuation of the myth that theirs is the only authentic claim to the succession of principles and ideological symbols that stem from the Revolution of 1910–17.

The concept of government as a private business, the concomitant death of civic spirit in Mexico today, the conformist response of her people, the suppression of competitive political groups, the desertion of her intellectuals, and the glaring material disparity between those who enjoy the blessing of being revolutionaries and the rest who must live outside the "public budget," all of this has fused itself into a new and explosive mood that will prevail throughout the decade of the 1970's. The urban localities and metropolitan areas will be foci of demands for revolutionary change.

The imperative for Mexicans to be revolutionaries is losing its popular grasp. This truth was envisioned by the playwright, Rodolfo Usigli, in 1937 at the height of the great Cárdenas "revolutionary upsweep." In his play *El gesticulador*, the rogue Navarro conspires to murder César Rubio, father of Miguel, and political aspirant around whose abortive career the story is built. Miguel tells Navarro that he will tell the world who has assassinated his father. Navarro replies:

When you get hold of yourself, boy, you will understand your true obligations. I was, of course, a political enemy of your father. But he who spills his blood for his country is a hero. *And Mexico needs its heroes in order to live.* Your father is a martyr of the Revolution.[8]

There is a kind of apostolic succession in the way revolutionary symbols are transmitted and shared among generations of Mexicans. It is essential to the esoteric system that the intrinsic "purity" of this succession be maintained. This will be a key psychological element in the political impasse that Mexico must confront during the decade now beginning.[9]

[8] Rodolfo Usigli, *El gesticulador*, Mexico, 1937 (Appleton-Century-Crofts version, 1963), p. 101.

[9] For a thorough analysis of the direction of urbanization and demographic change in Mexico, see Luis Unikel, "El proceso de urbanizacion en México: Distribucion y crecimiento de la poblacion urbana," *Demografía y Economía*, Vol. II, No. 2, 1968, pp. 139–182.

Epilogue

by Lic. Manuel de la Isla Paulín
(translated by Kenneth F. Johnson)

Note: The opinions expressed herein do not necessarily represent the views of the publisher, the consulting editors, nor those of of Kenneth F. Johnson. They are included to expose the North American reader directly to a set of attitudes that typify many in the Mexican middle class.

One measure of a nation's well-being is seen in the rise of a commonly shared national consciousness. My country boasts an enormous population mass that has been denied this common historical experience. Mexico passed from a primitive (indigenous) life into direct contact with a superior culture. Following that encounter the yet unborn nation was thrown into a maelstrom of cultural adaptation and miscegenation between tribal and modern values and thereafter it entered a process of transformation that has not yet ended. Here, I will attempt to describe that process and in so doing I shall hope to offer my North American readers a brief portrait of the Mexican people.

Many authors, in an impulsive desire to draw psychological caricatures of the Mexican, have gotten carried away by their own linguistic charms. Usually such efforts have strayed from reality. For instance, the Mexican writer César Garizurieta (diplomat and often political official) has written an essay entitled "Mexican Catharsis" which offers the comedian Cantinflas as a prototype of the Mexican psychology. He says that Cantinflas never combs his hair and therefore has no need to take off his hat; his mustache is cultivated like a mask whose purpose is to lend the appearance of dignity where none is really present. Physically he is weak due to malnutrition. He has little desire to live in a place that is better than the one he has and accepts his low station in life like a confirmed stoic. Garizurieta is not the only author, to be sure, who has painted the Mexican in such jaundiced colors. I know of various studies by North American and European scholars that have treated the Mexican with equal disdain. We must, however, take into account that there is no single definitive type, morally, psychologically, racially, or socially, that can be said to represent the "Mexican." Permit me to offer an exemplification of the diversity of the Mexican by constructing a useful, albeit simplistic, conceptual dichotomy of our race.

The Pre-Mexican and the Modern Mexican

The diversity of our problems is born, as I have already suggested, of an inadequate national consciousness and from the accompanying scarcity of responsible people who might impose a progressive influence upon the entire nation. From our uncertain and weak condition as a young country emerge numerous conflicts, those of economic development, agriculture, commerce, housing, and many others. But I venture to repeat that the cause of this comes from within ourselves more so than from our external environment. Let me sketch my basic notion in the form of two hypotheses that I shall state as follows:

1. There is a racially indigenous leadership nucleus in Mexico that is conscious of its own being and of its responsibility toward other Mexicans, but it is not self-sufficient and often acts in a manner that creates disunity. This nucleus will be termed here the *Modern Mexican*. He knows that he belongs to the twentieth century, but is uncertain of his future.

2. By way of contrast we have a mass of people who as yet lack dynamic aspirations, who live more as vegetables than as humans; they are beings destined to be molded for good or for bad, but whose psychological and social configuration is changing and diffuse. This enormous cross-section of the Mexican population will be termed here the *Pre-Mexican*.

The difficulty inherent in defining the Mexican in generic terms is reduced somewhat if one takes into account the evidence that there exists a minority which has a national consciousness and a majority which as yet is without a national consciousness. The former is the Modern Mexican (the minority); the latter is the *Pre-Mexican* (the majority). Habitually, both have been grouped under the generic rubric of *"mexicano"* which is, in truth, an enormous oversimplification and serves to obscure the fact that there are two distinct social nuclei that must be accounted for.

Symbolism and Characteristics of the Pre-Mexican Nucleus

The fundamental characteristics of the Pre-Mexican nucleus are the following: on the positive side, his stoicism acts as an immunizing agent which allows him to suffer inhuman deprivations in silence; on the negative side are his personal irresponsibility, his lack of conscious restraints toward himself and those who surround him; he is a nomadic creature without a steady job who is perpetually bitter about his bad luck and eternally jealous of the accomplishments of others. We might say that the Pre-Mexican lives to vegetate, thereby absorbed in his ritual of self-preoccupation and a captive of his own individual limitations. His thoughts and emotions never rise to the point of fusing themselves into a spiritual collectivity which could be the essence of a nation. Frankly, his thoughts and emotions are mutual strangers.

An important fundamental characteristic of the Pre-Mexican is his altering world-view. Today's thoughts and pronouncements are likely to be diametrically opposed to those of tomorrow, or at least *opposed by the implications* of tomorrow's actions. The Pre-Mexican is hypersensitive and often takes offense at the slightest act or word that was intended in the most innocuous of ways. Also, he runs the span of his life like a pilotless ship, searching desperately for a point of fixation toward which to sail. Here let me paraphrase the words of Salvador Borrego in saying that the Pre-Mexican is caught up in a cultural whirlpool that impedes his identification with his Indian heritage and, at once, keeps him from gaining a sense of identification with the broad and ongoing quest for a national consciousness. He waivers anomalously between the fear of a phenomenal reality (which is, by chance, his life) and the instilled indifference to the ever-menacing spectre of death. In the captive midst of this vile existence the Pre-Mexican is humbled and thwarted before the entrepreneurial skills of the Modern Mexican. He becomes a helpless and self-perpetuating victim of continuing abuse. His life progresses more by accident than by design.

Economically speaking, the Pre-Mexican is a disaster. Not only must he suffer poverty and misery, but he lives a pauper's life of sickness, filth, and hardship as well. This point is of particular importance because a number of social scientists have argued (in an attempt to justify the existence of poverty and misery in Mexico) something like: "we are inferior because we are poor, but not because we are Mexicans." This says nothing really. If it pleases the ear by chance it is nonetheless a chauvinistic and false argument. In truth, the Pre-Mexican is poor because of what he is, because of his behavioral psyche. The lands of any country produce only if someone makes them productive. The Pre-Mexican lacks this initiative; he is not an entrepreneur nor does his misery, which he tolerates willingly and stoically, move him to demand a better life. No social assistance program could make an entrepreneur out of the Pre-Mexican, for all he really wants is charity and paternalism. The woman of the Pre-Mexican genre shares these traits with her husband. The slovenliness of her person, her uninspired acquiescence in fate, do little to inspire her husband and children to improve their lot. The transitory pleasures of the moment take precedence over the longer range goals. The North American student must have a clear picture of the Pre-Mexican for he represents one of the basic psychological problems that confront schemes for socioeconomic development in Mexico today. His acquiescent existence also has implications for the direction of political change in my country.

Symbolism and Characteristics of the Modern Mexican

In contrast with the Pre-Mexican nucleus, the Modern Mexican represents the triumph of miscegenation, the blending of cultural heritages into a single human type. The Modern Mexican has acquired a national consciousness. He feels that he is part of an ongoing and dynamic experience of socioeconomic change. The Modern

Mexican is not a social class but is scattered throughout various classes; nor is he a single political or economic group. The Modern Mexican may be a consciencious worker whose frugality surmounts the demagogery which surrounds him; he can be a dedicated peasant who makes the land yield food despite the lowness he is accorded socially; he can be a bureaucrat who performs honestly while surrounded by administrative corruption; the Modern Mexican is any Mexican who deliberately strives to better himself and, at once, to improve Mexico. This is a new and incipient class in Mexico today, but its members are fragmented and without a technique or structure for unification. Certain groups of practicing politicans have all the trappings of the Modern Mexican except his concern for honor, frugality, and self-disciplined industry. These individuals are characteristically found in the key positions of officialdom, i.e. the single-party structure which governs Mexico. It is they who are most prone to talk loudly about freeing the Pre-Mexican from his wretchedness while, all the time, making a huge profit by exploiting that very condition. Such individuals may be distinguished by the coined term "Modern Mexican-*revolucionarios.*"

We have in Mexico great deficiencies in human and natural resources. But the nub of the problem continues to be the general absence of a truly national consciousness, the lack of true social cohesion; and I would dare to add, although it sounds distinctly radical, the absence of a true Mexican nationality. Mexico is not an organic whole of values and elements that are integrated into a single national will. Rather, Mexico is like a prism that casts a rainbow of cultural nuances, ideological and spiritual shades, that as yet have not merged into a national consciousness.

Mexico will achieve her greatness as a nation when the mass of Pre-Mexicans have been incorporated into the national consciousness, when they have become Modern Mexicans. But this process will not evolve automatically. An enlightened government is requisite, but with Mexico dominated by a single political "family" this is still an enigma. Mexico's dominant governing institution, the PRI, seeks to make itself into the object of popular affection and attachment rather than to promote a national consciousness. The inability of Mexico to solve many of its problems via the governmental apparatus which we have can be traced directly to the fact that a single political organization has appropriated to itself exclusive rights to the symbolic accoutrements of nationalism. What is often termed nationalism in Mexico is more accurately to be called *"priísmo,"* the officially prescribed image of the PRI.

Two Key Problems That Mexico Must Solve

THE RURAL-AGRARIAN PROBLEM

Mexico is potentially capable of feeding 200 million people but at the moment of this writing it is barely able to feed its population of 50 million. Unfortunately, the backward state of abandon and waste which characterizes Mexican agriculture is well known, as is the dilemma of bureaucratic and political corruption that permits this situation to continue. This is why agriculture cannot become the major factor in our economy that it should be. According to the Mexican Society for Nutrition and Diet there are fifteen million Mexicans who have never tasted milk, eleven million who are unable to eat bread regularly, and six million who consume only a tiny portion of meat each week. If industry and agriculture could combine to produce greater employment opportunities, these conditions would be erased. But here are some shocking figures: only 32.7 percent of the Mexican population can be considered economically active (according to the Bank of Mexico's annual bulletin for 1969). Of these, 52 percent are devoted to primary activities such as agricultural labor, cattle raising, hunting and fishing, and miscellaneous unskilled jobs. This is to say that 52 percent of Mexico's *economically active* population is tied to those activities which generate the poorest salaries in the nation. The other 48 percent of the economically active population contributed (in 1967) 83 percent of the total internal gross national product. This means that there is an enormous mass of largely agricultural-rural labor in Mexico that is virtually outside the national economy. These individuals figure within the Pre-Mexican nucleus.

Aside from the fact of rural unemployment, the land itself offers little hope as it stands. Less than 15 percent of Mexico's land is arable and of this percentage only 20 percent enjoys irrigation. Moreover, despite some fifty years of slogans about Mexico's agrarian reform, it is a fact that the great landholders of the Porfirian era were *displaced and replaced* with an official *latifundismo* via the politicians and bureaucrats who run the *ejido* system. Today, there are very few Mexicans who can claim ownership to any land, much less productive land.

THE PROBLEM OF EDUCATION

Mexico's national growth depends intimately upon the solution of the educational problem. This, of course, underlies our inability to solve the agrarian and rural problem mentioned above. In concrete terms the educational problem may be summarized as follows: a high rate of population growth presses increasingly on the existing shortage of classrooms and teachers, leading to abandonment of the classroom by both students and teachers; the country's financial deficit adds to this pressure; governmental subventions are too small to meet the challenge. The entire Mexican educational system needs a new, honest, and professional administrative revamping. Obviously the state must be prepared to pay the cost of this service. Reduction of pupils via birth control devices (often promoted by obscure international interests) is prejudicial to our nation and should be prohibited.

Our educational dilemma is intimately linked to that of economic development, and here again reducing the birth rate is not the answer. Rather we must achieve a vast restructuring of our educational system from the ground up so that the 27 million children who need to attend school in 1970 will be able to do so, and with the expectation of economic opportunity thereafter. Education is probably Mexico's number one problem, but it will go unsolved unless the federal government provides new support and relinquishes its authoritarian control over the system. In the latter respect it is urgent that local school administrators be given more freedom to adapt their curricula to local needs. A short time ago the Secretariat of Public Education sent out a circular to all private schools telling them that a new regulation now allows the federal government to select directors of private schools and control their salaries. Thus, Mexico City has sought to wipe out private education entirely. In doing this the government will find itself with the exclusive responsibility for the failures of our educational process, and only one political organization, the PRI, can ever be blamed for the consequences.

On the New Tactics of the PRI

During the decade of the 1970's the PRI will have the exclusive responsibility for solving the two key problems (and all the others they imply) mentioned above, if economic development is to offer

Mexicans a more equitable distribution of the national wealth. We are a poor people, but we will not tolerate this forever. Eventually, the Modern Mexican will lead his Pre-Mexican brother out of the wilderness of servitude and the method chosen will be violence if that is the only way. In the light of the massacres which occurred here during 1968 let us pray that additional violence will not be needed. The direction of socioeconomic change in Mexico depends upon the political arena. And here the campaign for the presidential period 1970–76 offers what may be a critical foreshadowing of what may lie ahead. Let me review the campaign and several of its antecedents as a prelude to the 1970's.

The regime of Lic. Gustavo Díaz Ordaz (1964–70) has been characterized by tyranny and noncommunication between the government and the people. During the last two years of the Díaz Ordaz presidency there developed an open breach between the working class and the various elements commonly referred to as the "middle class." There was severe conflict between the intelligentsia and officialdom. In large part, this was due to the inflexibility and intolerance of President Díaz Ordaz who refused to allow opposition groups the freedom of speech and press which our Constitution guarantees them. In this respect it is important to note that Mexico's clandestine press organs of *both* the far right and far left have made it possible for some minimal level of intellectual freedom to exist in Mexico, and on a more or less public basis.

More important however, the "esoteric" governmental family was afflicted by a crisis that originated in an opposition sector. This occurred when several pressure groups (*camarillas*) within the PRI sought to win acceptance by the PRI's National Assembly of their own preferred presidential candidate. One of these groups, that may be called the "Jalisco Group," and was led by the incumbent Secretary of Education and noted author Agustín Yáñez (an intellectual known as a one-time opponent of officialdom during the *Cristero* revolts of 1928–29). This group supported the incumbent Secretary of Agriculture and former governor of the state of Jalisco, Prof. Juan Gil Preciado. Additional support went to the candidacy of Dr. Emilio Martínez Manatou, the Secretary of the Presidency (a new ministerial position that had been created by President López Mateos). Those supporting Martínez Manatou were by and large young professionals and intellectuals; in addition, he enjoyed support among opposition groups. Many thought that he would be a viable alternative to the hard line of Díaz Ordaz. His career had been distinguished by unusual honesty in terms of the normal PRI standards. Another group supported the incumbent governor of the Federal District, Gen. Alfonso Corona del Rosal, but he had no popular base upon which to erect a campaign. Finally, a group of old line politicians (called in Mexico *señores de horca y cuchillo* and referred to more simply as *caciques*) took an early stand in favor of the candidacy of Lic. Luis Echeverría Alvarez, then Secretary of Interior (*Gobernación*), the same position which President Díaz Ordaz had occupied during the López Mateos years. Ultimately, Echeverría won the PRI candidacy, hence, the first presidency of the 1970's. Echeverría belongs to the old regime of Mexican revolutionary tradition; he is the son-in-law of a powerful old political boss from Jalisco, Guadelupe Zuno Heŕnández, and comes from a family that is deeply entrenched in Mexican politics. Echeverría had long been favored by the old line *camarilla* that formed around former president Lázaro Cárdenas del Río. Echeverría is widely seen (as explained earlier in Professor Johnson's analysis) as the principal governmental figure responsible for the student oppressions of 1968 and the unpardonable massacre that occurred at Tlatelolco on the night of October 2, 1968. For these and related reasons, Luis Echeverría is probably one of the most unpopular men ever to assume the presidency of our nation. This, I am sorry to say, is a well recognized truth.

In the face of popular and opposition group pressures stemming from such semiofficial opposition groups as the CNC/CCI peasant-worker complex, the PRI has only two courses of action from which to choose its immediate path. The first would be to reach an accord with opposition groups of both right and left and to steer Mexico into a tripartite political system. This would be a popular democratic solution. The other course is to retain all power within the PRI dominated government and to repress with economic blackmail and physical violence all opposition groups that should threaten. The PRI appears to have opted for the second course of action during the first part of the 1970's. Its behavior in the recent cases of Baja California and Yucatán demonstrates that fact well.

Early in 1970 there was uncertainty as to whether the PAN candidate Efraín González Morfín would ultimately remain in the presidential race, and the national directorate of the PAN actually discussed plans to disincorporate the party in the face of mounting repression from the PRI controlled government. For all intents and purposes there is only one candidate in the 1970 presidential campaign, the PRI candidate, Luis Echeverría Alvarez. In order to show to the world a facade of popular support for Echeverría the government brought unbelievable economic pressure upon top businessmen and industrialists to force them to identify in public with the PRI campaign. Well known bankers like Agustín Legorreta and Ladislao López Negrete (both of the National Bank of Mexico) were victims of the PRI's economic blackmail. Another financier, Carlos Trouyet, saw himself "obliged" to concur in symbolic acts of hommage for the PRI candidate rather than accept economic reprisals. The appearance of such figures was in marked contrast to earlier PRI campaigns. Then, orators, labor and peasant leaders (called in Mexico *charros* for their affinity for English cashmere and Swiss bank accounts) habitually attacked with outrage the Yankee capitalists who allegedly exploited Mexico. All of the press and radio media carried their denunciations of imperialism. But in the 1970 campaign the labor and peasant leaders were silent for the most part. In their place we saw the great bankers, the landed gentry and powerful industrials, who found themselves "caught up" in the overpowering political thrust of Mexico's ongoing "revolution."

On Mexico's Immediate Future

The present author, during a conference given before students and faculty at the University of Southern California in the spring of 1968, had occasion to quote a well-known axiom that goes to the very heart of Mexico's esoteric political system: "to live outside the public budget is to live in error." In Mexico those who live outside the public budget desperately seek access to it; those who are already within the budget refuse to abandon their sinecures and are bitterly jealous of those in quest of entry. The public budget is the PRI. In the event that a brilliant young challenger distinguishes himself as an opponent of the government, he is summoned to the seat of power, first to chat and to "break the ice," and later to offer him a public position *within the budget* and thereby to eliminate him as an enemy This is a risky but often sure way of gaining entry into the esoteric democratic system. Here is one very concrete example: the late president of my country, Adolfo López Mateos, was a well known opponent of the government of Calles and fought not only on the side of the *cristeros* but in support of the candidacy of José Vasconcelos in 1929. López Mateos was a brilliant young challenger. Suddenly, he renounced all of his "reactionary" trappings. The official regime of Lázaro Cárdenas "discovered" him and called him to participate in carrying out the destiny of the Revolution. This is how Mexico's esoteric democratic system works.

The job of governing Mexico during the 1970's will not be an easy one, especially for an intolerant man like Echeverría. His creed is that of dogmatic inflexibility and he can be expected to castigate all those who did not join his entourage from the start. Echeverría, very possibly, is the reverse of the coin from López Mateos. It is true that López Mateos left the country (and the public budget) poor and exploited, but he was widely respected for his political tolerance and for his support of the electoral reform law at the end of his term which gave new hope to opposition groups (principal beneficiary of this reform was the PAN which, anachronistically, the Díaz Ordaz regime elected to suppress in Baja California, Yucatán, and in numerous municipal contests about the country). López Mateos was well liked personally for his sense of humor, his passion for adoration from both friends and enemies. A surprisingly large number of his political opponents liked him personally. For that reason he seldom vented fury upon opposition groups (although he felt compelled to suppress individuals at times) and he loosened the reins of government to an extent that made some opposition appear viable. In contradistinction, Luis Echeverría is a faithful mirror of the incumbent Díaz Ordaz, intolerant and unyielding. He is a Mexican politician of the 1930's wearing clothing of 1970.

Echeverría will not change Mexico's esoteric democratic system nor will he solve the problems of agrarian need and urban overcrowding. The PRI will continue indefinitely as the political steward of Mexico. Challenging political newcomers will have two choices, to become part of the official team or *carro completo,* or they can join clandestine subversive groups of either right or left. At the moment the attitude of the official regime leaves no other lawful alternative that is feasible. Paradoxically, Mexico will continue to press forward step by step and somehow limited socioeconomic progress will occur. Whether or not Mexicans will always tolerate this rate of change is the key question for our near future.

Index